DOES A POSIT[...] TWO-BID GUARAN[...] IN THE SUIT BID?

(Don't bet on it. The answer is in Argument 51 and it might surprise you!)

HOW DO YOU RESPOND TO BLACKWOOD WITH A VOID?

(When responding to Blackwood, never count a void as an ace. The master explains in Argument 115.)

WHEN SHOULD THE RESPONDER PREFER A DOUBLE RAISE TO A BID IN A NEW SUIT?

(This one can destroy lifelong friendships, so check the answer in Argument 37.)

GOREN SETTLES THE BRIDGE ARGUMENTS

Don't play without it!

GOREN
Settles the Bridge Arguments

Authoritative answers to knotty problems that are the cause of frequent misunderstandings at the bridge table.

Charles H. Goren

BALLANTINE BOOKS • NEW YORK

Library of Congress Catalog Card Number: 72-86458

ISBN 0-345-29391-6

This edition published by arrangement with Hart Publishing Company, Inc.

Manufactured in the United States of America

First Ballantine Books Edition: July 1977
Sixth Printing: August 1983

Contents

v

CHAPTER 4

Opening Bids of One Notrump

CHAPTER 5

Opening Bids of Two Notrump

CHAPTER 6

Opening Bids of Three Notrump

CHAPTER 7

Responses to Opening Suit Bids of One

CHAPTER 8

Responses to Opening Suit Bids of Two

CHAPTER 9

Responses to Opening Suit Bids of Three, Four, or Five

CHAPTER 10

Responses to an Opening Bid of One Notrump

CHAPTER 11

Responses to an Opening Bid of Two Notrump

CHAPTER 12

Responses to an Opening Bid of Three Notrump

CHAPTER 13

Opener's Rebids

CHAPTER 14

Secondary Responses

CHAPTER 15

Competitive Bidding

CHAPTER 16

Slam Bidding

CHAPTER 17

Doubles

CHAPTER 18

Responding to Doubles

CHAPTER 19

Proprieties

Foreword

I believe this book is unique. It is primarily a reference book, enabling the reader to find the answer to most of the bridge arguments likely to occur at the bridge table.

In addition to being a reference book, this volume presents over 150 bridge situations which you will enjoy analyzing. You yourself can take sides in the argument. You can decide for yourself who is right and who is wrong. You can determine how you would rule if the argument were submitted to you for decision.

Then you can read my verdict, and the reasons for it. You can even disagree, if you like, and appeal to some other court.

I am reminded of the story of the missing duplicate board. At the conclusion of a game, when the tournament director went to collect the trays in which the hands are kept so that they can be passed from table to table and played again by others, Board Four was found to be missing. Eventually, out near the elevator, the director found a forlorn bridge player with the missing board in his hand, shaking his head dolefully and asking, "Won't *anybody* bid two hearts?"

Admittedly, the game of contract bridge creates more arguments than any other card game in history. I believe this is part of the game's fascination. I vehemently deny the charge that these arguments break up families and friendships. In fact, they rarely break up the immediate game in which they occur.

Oh yes, I recall the story of an argument where one player left the table in a huff over an argument about something that never even happened. It was the first hand of the game. After three passes, the fourth player studied his hand a while, reluctantly said "Pass" and showed his cards, announcing, "I nearly opened the bidding with one club."

"If you had," said his partner, "I'd have jumped to three notrump." And he tabled his hand, a maximum pass.

"What?" was fourth hand's incredulous response. "Deal me out! I'm not going to play with an idiot who'd make such a bid." And he got up and left the table.

However, this happened in a club where all that irate player had to do was cut into another game, and where there were plenty of other players to take his place. I doubt that he'd have taken this action if it was the only game available. The worst that ever happens in such a situation (the Bennett murder case to the contrary notwithstanding) is that somebody issues a challenge: "Get yourself a partner and I'll play against you until your money runs out." Or more frequently, to judge by the size of my incoming mail, "Let's make a bet and leave it to Goren."

Hopefully, this book will resolve such arguments. And even if you never argue at the table, you might enjoy getting in on the arguments presented herein. Join the court. You can be defendant, plaintiff, or juryman, as you wish.

CHARLES H. GOREN

CHAPTER 1

Opening Suit Bids of One

ARGUMENT 1

Should you ever pass a 14-point hand?

THE HAND

                    NORTH
                    ♠ A 10 9 2
                    ♡ 10 5 4
                    ◇ 10 6
                    ♣ A Q 10 2

WEST   EAST
♠ 63   ♠ J 8 7
♡ A 8 3   ♡ K 9 7 6
◇ K 9 8 4 3   ◇ A J 2
♣ 8 7 6   ♣ 9 5 4

                    SOUTH
                    ♠ K Q 5 4
                    ♡ Q J 2
                    ◇ Q 7 5
                    ♣ K J 3

THE AUCTION

SOUTH	WEST	NORTH	EAST
1 ♠	Pass	3 ♠	Pass
3 NT	Pass	4 ♠	Pass
Pass	Pass		

THE RESULT

The defenders cashed the ace and king of each red suit.

The declarer was down one.

1

THE ARGUMENT

To the accompaniment of some caustic observations that South obviously didn't know the rudiments of bidding, North claimed that South should not have opened his collection of garbage.

South insisted that his hand was worth a full 14 points in high cards and therefore was a mandatory opening bid. "Besides," he added indignantly, "why didn't you pass three notrump? I could have made that."

For the sake of decorum, let us skip North's withering retort, and get to the problem. Which player was to blame?

GOREN SETTLES THE ARGUMENT

First of all, let's dispose of South's fantasy. There is simply no way that three notrump could have been made against a diamond lead. East wins the ace of diamonds and returns the jack. The defenders can take five diamond tricks plus the ace-king of hearts before South even gets under way.

But let's get back to the crux of the matter.

All 14-point hands are not equal, and some 14-point hands should not be opened.

Some hands contain an inherent flaw. Allowance should be made for such weaknesses in deciding whether or not to open the bidding. South's hand was such a hand. For one thing, South's hand is aceless. I have always recommended that an opening bidder deduct one point if he doesn't hold an ace. Thus, strictly speaking, South's hand is worth only 13 points.

In addition, perfectly balanced hands—those of a 4-3-3-3 pattern—should be regarded with great wariness.

Thirteen points constitute an *optional* opening bid. The determining factor of whether to open or not to open a 13-point hand lies in the defensive potential of the hand.

Hands of 13 points should be opened only if they contain at least two quick tricks.*

South's hand was short of this requirement and should have been passed.

The point count is merely a mathematical method of evaluating a hand. One should not permit the point count system to become his master.

The 4-3-2-1 point count, though extremely useful, has a weakness: It tends to undervalue aces and kings, which are worth fractionally more than the 4 and 3 points respectively awarded them, and to overrate queens and jacks. In most hands, these discrepancies will offset each other. But in this case, South's hand has a surfeit of secondary honors, and a paucity of prime honors. The effect is that the point count inflates the value of this hand.

To illustrate this point, let us take away from South's hand the 2-point queen of diamonds and the 1-point jack of clubs, and replace these cards with the 3-point king of hearts, making the hand:

> ♠ K Q 5 4
> ♡ K Q J
> ◊ 8 7 5
> ♣ K 8 2

We have now elevated South's holding to the status of a full opening bid, for we have added a quick trick, even though the point value of the hand has not been changed. Yet with the hand constituted in this way, four spades would have been made.

Even so, if I had held the South hand, I would have chosen to launch the auction with one club.

Also see: Arguments 2, 3, 7.

---

* Quick tricks are: Ace; king-queen of the same suit. The ace-king of the same suit are equal to two quick tricks. A king guarded equals ½ quick trick. Ace-queen of the same suit equals 1½ quick tricks.

ARGUMENT 2

Can a 12-point hand be strong enough to be opened?

THE HAND

```
                NORTH
                ♠ A J 5
                ♡ 8 7
                ◇ K Q J 4
                ♣ 9 8 5 2
WEST                              EAST
♠ 6 2                             ♠ 7 4
♡ 6 4 2                           ♡ K Q J 3
◇ A 9 7 6                         ◇ 10 5 3
♣ A J 10 3                        ♣ K Q 6 4
                SOUTH
                ♠ K Q 10 9 8 3
                ♡ A 10 9 5
                ◇ 8 2
                ♣ 7
```

THE AUCTION

NORTH	EAST	SOUTH	WEST
Pass	Pass	Pass	Pass

THE RESULT

Both sides were vulnerable. The players faced their cards and it was apparent to all that North-South could have made 10 tricks in a breeze.

THE ARGUMENT

South pointed out that he didn't have an opening bid for, he was at pains to explain, he held but 9 points in

4

high cards, and but 12 points altogether. The table listened sympathetically, and held him blameless.

"Just a bit of tough luck!" consoled West. "After all, the book says 12 points are insufficient for an opening bid."

"It seems wrong," chirped East, "that a hand that is a spread for game should be passed out. Either you are wrong or Goren is."

That's when the fur began to fly—eventually soaring in my direction.

GOREN SETTLES THE ARGUMENT

I most certainly agree. South never should have passed.

A distributional 12-point hand may be worth an opening bid if the high cards are located in the long suits.

There is no doubt that in most cases a 12-point hand should be passed. However, high cards work better when they are located in long suits, and gain additional value *when they are in the right location.*

To illustrate this point, let us change South's hand somewhat:

♠ 10 9 6 5 4 3
♡ 10 9 4 2
♢ A Q
♣ K

Now South has exactly the same high cards as before; but this time, his high cards are located in his short suits. Even a novice can see that this hand has nowhere near the trick-taking potential of the hand actually held by South.

When the high cards are located in the long suits, as little as one honor in your partner's hand can sometimes allow the complete suit to be brought in. For instance, if you hold A J 10 9 5 2 and your partner holds Q 7 4, a successful finesse will enable you to take six tricks in the suit.

Also, 10s and 9s, though assigned no value in the point count, help to give a hand "body"; and these "strong intermediates" should be taken into consideration when valuing a hand as an opening bid.

Consider this holding:

NORTH
Q 7 2

SOUTH
J 8 3

If South has to break this suit, he might not make a single trick in it. Now for the 7 substitute the 10. Though the point count has not been increased, this holding will yield a sure trick!

A prime factor, too, is what is the suit that is held. Whenever you hold spades, you should strive to open the bidding, for the spade suit has pre-emptive advantages. If you open a hand with one spade, the opponents have to come in at the two-level. Had South's suit been a minor, it might have been wise to pass and await developments.

Also see: Arguments 1, 3, 7.

ARGUMENT 3

Is an 11-point hand ever good enough to be opened?

THE HAND

```
                    NORTH
                    ♠ Q 6 3
                    ♡ K Q 7
                    ◇ 5 4 3
                    ♣ A 9 4 3
    WEST                            EAST
    ♠ 4 2                           ♠ K 7
    ♡ 8 4 3 2                       ♡ J 6 5
    ◇ K Q 10                        ◇ A J 9 2
    ♣ K Q 6 5                       ♣ J 10 8 7
                    SOUTH
                    ♠ A J 10 9 8 5
                    ♡ A 10 9
                    ◇ 8 7 6
                    ♣ 2
```

THE AUCTION

SOUTH	WEST	NORTH	EAST
Pass	Pass	Pass	Pass

THE RESULT

When the players faced their cards after the auction, North-South realized that four spades depended only on the trump finesse.

THE ARGUMENT

South bitterly criticized North for failing to open a "protection" bid in the third position.

7

North briefly recounted the libel case brought by a wrestler named Zbysko because his picture had been placed in the newspapers alongside that of a gorilla. "The judge's verdict," reported North, "was that the gorilla had a better case."

East and West were amused, but South observed with considerable vehemence that if third hand couldn't open with 11 points, certainly the dealer couldn't.

An argument over a passed hand? Well, bridge is like that. And so the case was referred to me.

GOREN SETTLES THE ARGUMENT

It is South—not North—who was to blame. Though South's hand adds up to only 11 points, I would open the bidding with one spade.

An 11-point hand that is well constructed and provides an easy rebid constitutes a good opening bid.

Just a smattering of key honor cards in his partner's hand could produce a game for South's side. Though I don't mean to insist that North-South should necessarily end in game in this hand, even if North is broke, South cannot come to much harm with a bid of one. The key point is that he held an irreducible five playing tricks against any distribution.

There are secondary advantages, too. By opening, South consumes much of the opponents' bidding room should the hand belong to them. And if the opponents do buy the hand and his partner doubles, South holds two quick defensive tricks plus other defensive potential.

Lastly, should the opponents buy the hand and North is on lead, probably the best lead would be a spade; any other lead might prove costly. Indeed, against an opposing notrump contract, a spade lead might be the only chance to beat the hand.

There is little danger of getting too high if your partner has a good hand. With such a hand, South would make minimum rebids in spades on his next two turns. That should convey to his partner that he started with a weak opening bid, with almost all his strength in the spade suit.

Also see: Arguments 1, 2, 7.

ARGUMENT 4

May one ever open the bidding with a two-card suit?

THE HAND

```
                    NORTH
                    ♠ A 5
                    ♡ 8 6
                    ◇ A K J 9
                    ♣ Q 10 9 8 5
  WEST                                EAST
  ♠ J 9 7 4                          ♠ 8 6 2
  ♡ K Q 7 3                          ♡ A J 4 2
  ◇ 10 6 3                           ◇ 7 2
  ♣ 7 6                              ♣ J 4 3 2
                    SOUTH
                    ♠ K Q 10 3
                    ♡ 10 9 5
                    ◇ Q 8 5 4
                    ♣ A K
```

THE AUCTION

SOUTH	WEST	NORTH	EAST
1 ♣	Pass	3 ♣	Pass
3 ♠	Pass	4 ♣	Pass
Pass	Pass		

THE RESULT

The declarer lost two heart tricks and a club.
He just made his contract.

THE ARGUMENT

Since North-South were playing five-card majors,

South's choice of an opening bid lay between a diamond and a club. "Of course," said South, "I chose clubs since my strength in that suit was so markedly superior."

South remarked upon the fine judgment he displayed in passing four clubs, only to find himself under violent attack from North.

"Magnificent judgment, my foot!" North disdainfully exclaimed. "Five diamonds is a laydown. What on earth made you open the bidding with a two-card suit? How was I to know that even five in your suit would prove to be inadequate trump support?"

"We play the 'short club'," replied South coolly, "and that's exactly what I held—short clubs!"

"All you are short of is—sense," muttered an unmollified North.

GOREN SETTLES THE ARGUMENT

Never open a two-card suit.

When you bid a suit, your partner generally expects you to hold at least four cards of the suit. However, where the partners have agreed among themselves to open a major suit with no less than a five-card holding, such an agreement implies that either minor can be opened with a three-card holding.

I have never recommended opening with a so-called "short club," though on occasion I do open the bidding with a "convenient" bid of a club. This means that I do not open one club *because* I am short in clubs: I do so *in spite of* being short in clubs.

Consider this hand:

♠ Q 8 3 2
♥ K 9 7 6
♦ K 10
♣ A Q 9

I would like to open with either one spade or one heart. But neither suit is biddable as an opening bid. A biddable suit should contain at least 4 points in high cards. Accordingly, I misrepresent my hand slightly by opening with a *convenient* bid of one club. The minimum suit requirement for this bid is three cards, headed by at least the queen.

Exchange the clubs and diamonds in the above hand, and I would open the bidding with one diamond.

I might open with a convenient club, *even though I have a biddable four-card major suit.* I will do so, if opening the major will leave me at a disadvantage when I have to rebid. For example, let's say I hold:

♠ A Q 9 5
♡ 9 8 2
♢ A J 3
♣ Q J 7

If I open the bidding with one spade, a response of two hearts from my partner would embarrass me. The hand is neither good enough to rebid two notrump, nor to raise to three hearts. Obviously a rebid of two spades would indicate I held a five-card suit. Accordingly, I suggest that on this type of hand, you open with a convenient bid of one club. You will find you have an easy rebid, no matter what your partner responds.

When you open the bidding, if your partner responds in a new suit, you guarantee a rebid. It is essential that you prepare your opening bid, so you have a convenient rebid available.

If you can't find a convenient rebid, my sincere advice is that you pass the hand. In such a situation, you'll find that silence is golden.

ARGUMENT 5

*Holding two four-card suits, which suit
do you bid first?*

THE HAND

```
                    NORTH
                    ♠ 10 4
                    ♡ A J 6
                    ◇ Q 8 7
                    ♣ A J 10 8 2
     WEST                              EAST
     ♠ J 9 5 2                         ♠ A 8 6
     ♡ Q 7 3                           ♡ K 8 5 4
     ◇ 10 9 6 3                        ◇ 5 2
     ♣ Q 6                             ♣ K 7 4 3
                    SOUTH
                    ♠ K Q 7 3
                    ♡ 10 9 2
                    ◇ A K J 4
                    ♣ 9 5
```

THE AUCTION

SOUTH	WEST	NORTH	EAST
1 ◇	Pass	2 ♣	Pass
2 ◇	Pass	3 ◇	Pass
Pass	Pass		

THE RESULT

South made ten tricks, losing a trick in each side
suit.

However, North-South could have made three notrump.

THE ARGUMENT

North complained about South's rebidding a four-card suit—he felt that South should have bid two spades on his second turn.

South pointed out indignantly that bidding two spades would have been a "reverse," and would have indicated a holding of 19 points. It was North's diamond raise which derailed everything, claimed South. Had North bid two hearts, South insisted, she would have proceeded to game at notrump.

"Bid a three-card suit!" snorted North.

GOREN SETTLES THE ARGUMENT

North and South were each correct in some of their contentions. However, neither commented on the true cause of the problem, which happened to be South's choice of her opening bid.

Opening the bidding in a suit carries with it an obligation to bid once more, if your partner responds in a new suit.

A first bid must be chosen only after taking into consideration your partner's possible response. One should bear in mind that one's partner is likely to be long in the opener's shortest suit, and that the partner will probably make a response to the opening bid in the suit that the opener is weakest in.

With two biddable four-card suits which do not touch each other, open the suit below your short suit.

For this purpose, the sequence of suits runs as follows: spades, hearts, diamonds, clubs; and then once more: spades, hearts, etc. In this hand, the spades are under the club shortness.

Consider South's hand. If South opens one spade—the suit which directly follows his club shortness—

North's response of two clubs will not find South flat-footed. South can now safely bid two diamonds. This bid permits North to show a heart stopper—if he has one—with a bid of notrump.

If North had held hearts instead of clubs, he would have responded two hearts. Then South would simply raise to three hearts or four hearts, depending upon the strength of his hand.

Let us change the suits around, and give South this hand:

♠ K Q 7 3
♡ 9 5
◇ A K J 4
♣ 10 9 2

Now the correct opening bid is one diamond. If partner responds one heart, South will rebid one spade.

If North inconveniently responds two clubs, South would have to stretch a little, and raise to three clubs.

Also see: Arguments 6, 8, 9.

ARGUMENT 6

Holding three four-card suits, which suit do you bid first?

THE HAND

```
                    NORTH
                    ♠ A 8 7
                    ♡ 9 3
                    ◇ 7 6
                    ♣ K Q J 6 5 3
    WEST                               EAST
    ♠ K 9 4 3                          ♠ 5 2
    ♡ J 7 6 2                          ♡ A 8 4
    ◇ K 10 2                           ◇ Q 9 5 4
    ♣ 9 4                              ♣ A 10 7 2
                    SOUTH
                    ♠ Q J 10 6
                    ♡ K Q 10 5
                    ◇ A J 8 3
                    ♣ 8
```

THE AUCTION

SOUTH	WEST	NORTH	EAST
1 ◇	Pass	2 ♣	Pass
2 ♡	Pass	2 NT	Pass
3 NT	Pass	Pass	Pass

THE RESULT

North wound up with eight tricks.

THE ARGUMENT

"I suggested to my partner that his correct second bid was three clubs," writes South. "In response, he icily inquired whether I had learned my bridge from the

16

Marquis de Sade. Rather than waste time on a futile argument, we agreed to let you be the final arbiter. Who was to blame?"

GOREN SETTLES THE ARGUMENT

I fear South must take the blame for this debacle. The manner in which South bid his hand showed a powerful holding of about 19 points, with longer diamonds than hearts—it would seem to North that he held something like five or six diamonds and four hearts. With a stopper in spades, North cannot be blamed for looking for a nine-trick contract in notrump.

The correct opening bid on South's hand is one spade.

With three touching biddable suits of equal length, bid the suit below the singleton first.

I must interject at this point that when holding Q J 10 of a four-card suit (exceptionally, shaded to Q J 9), the suit is biddable even though it falls short of a strict 4 points in high cards.

After South's bid of one spade, North will respond with two clubs. Now South bids two diamonds, leaving the way open to finding a 4-4 fit in hearts. If North now bids hearts over South's diamonds, the partnership has found an eight-card trump fit.

In the actual deal, North does not hold four hearts, so he simply rebids three clubs. And South must pass. The hand is a misfit, and three notrump is against the odds.

Note that North can make nine tricks in a club contract. He loses, at most, two tricks in clubs, one in hearts, and one in diamonds.

If one of your suits is not biddable, ignore it when selecting your opening bid. For instance:

♠ Q 9 6 3
♡ A Q 10 3
◇ A J 8 3
♣ 8

Here, the spade suit is not biddable. You have only two biddable suits—hearts and diamonds. The correct opening bid is one heart: the higher-ranking of touching suits of equal length.

I would depart from these principles if I held an exceptionally strong hand, such as:

♠ A Q J 2
♡ K Q 10 5
♦ A K 8 3
♣ 8

My partner might hold the right cards for game yet be unable to respond if I opened the bidding with one spade. To give him the maximum amount of room, I would open this hand with one diamond, intending to raise a response of either major suit to game.

If the partnership has agreed to play five-card majors, then the opening bid on South's hand would have to be one diamond. If North responds two clubs, he presents South with an awkward rebid problem. One solution is to lie about the length of the diamond suit and rebid two diamonds. However, the preferred treatment in such a potential misfit situation is to make the "forced reverse" into two of a major suit.

Also see: Arguments 5, 8, 9.

ARGUMENT 7

When is it proper for third hand to open light?

THE HAND

```
                    NORTH
                    ♠ 7 4
                    ♡ K Q 6 5 4 3
                    ◇ 9 5
                    ♣ K J 7

WEST                                    EAST
♠ K Q 10 6                              ♠ 9 8
♡ 10 9 2                                ♡ A J 8
◇ Q 7 6 4                               ◇ A 10 8 2
♣ A 3                                   ♣ Q 9 6 2

                    SOUTH
                    ♠ A J 5 3 2
                    ♡ 7
                    ◇ K J 3
                    ♣ 10 8 5 4
```

THE AUCTION

NORTH	EAST	SOUTH	WEST
Pass	Pass	1 ♠	Pass
2 ♡	Pass	2 ♠	Pass
Pass	Dbl	Pass	Pass
Pass			

THE RESULT

The carnage was frightful. West led the ace of clubs, and continued with the 3 of clubs. The declarer went up with the dummy's king. The declarer then followed with the king of hearts. West took his ace and shifted to the 9 of trumps. The declarer was forced to duck, and a

19

trump continuation removed the dummy's last trump. With no way to get to the board, the declarer was forced to concede three trump tricks, one heart, two diamonds, and two clubs.

Result: down three, vulnerable, for a loss of 800 points.

South might have saved a trick by leading a diamond from the dummy at trick three, guessing to go up with the king and playing to ruff a third diamond. But going down 500 would have been no triumph.

THE ARGUMENT

North was fuming. "Did you consider your collection of garbage an opening bid?"

South defended himself vehemently. "It might not be an opening bid in first or second seat, but my hand was certainly adequate for a third-hand opening. Any book will tell you that, in the third seat opposite a passed partner, you can open with sub-minimum values."

South also suggested that North might have been better advised to respond one notrump, so as to allow for the possibility of an extremely light opening.

"With a six-card heart suit?" snorted North, incredulously.

GOREN SETTLES THE ARGUMENT

There are times when it is valid to open the bidding in third seat with insufficient values, but one should bear in mind that he is bidding in this risky manner *despite* the fact that he does not hold the required values and not *because* his hand is deficient.

The partner of a third-hand bidder does not know that the bidder does not hold a full opening bid. There is no electronic device that tips him off that the bid is abnormally weak. There is no law that says third hand may not open the bidding holding 13 or 14 points, or even 18 or 19 or more. The responder cannot distort the entire bidding structure just to allow for the bare possibility that third hand may have taken some unusual action.

When one opens very light in third seat, he should have some specific justification. Such a light opener should pass any bid his partner might make that is not 100% forcing. To rebid confirms a full opening bid.

A light third-hand opener must be prepared to handle any response his partner makes.

On the hand in question, South was certainly not prepared to handle a two-heart response from North.

A third-hand light opening should have definite lead-directing value in the event that the opponents buy the contract.

On this count, too, South could not be sure that some other suit might not prove to be a better lead. His suit is not sufficiently robust to warrant that spades would be the right lead.

There is a certain indignity to losing 800 points on a hand that might have been thrown in, or where the opponents would have had to struggle for a part score. Better judgment on South's part would have averted the bloodbath.

Also see: Arguments 1, 2, 3.

ARGUMENT 8

*Can a player who bids only five-card majors
find it right, on occasion, to open a four-card
major?*

THE HAND

NORTH
♠ J 7 3
♡ K 8 5
♢ J 4
♣ Q 10 8 6 3

SOUTH
♠ A K Q 10
♡ A Q 10 3
♢ 9 5 3
♣ 7 2

THE AUCTION

SOUTH	WEST	NORTH	EAST
1 ♢	Pass	1 NT	Pass
Pass	Pass		

THE RESULT

The defenders took the first four tricks in diamonds,
then followed with three more in clubs.

Down one.

Making two of either major suit would have been a
relatively easy matter.

THE ARGUMENT

South maintained that, though he did not relish opening the bidding on a three-card suit headed by the 9, to

do anything else would have meant breaking away from the system.

GOREN SETTLES THE ARGUMENT

On at least one point I must agree with South: there is something repugnant about having to open the bidding in a suit consisting of three cards headed by the 9. I can state categorically that I would not do so, were you to hold a gun to my head.

The originators of the five-card-majors theory took this problem into account when they developed their methods. They simply consider any very strong four-card suit as a five-card suit; and a suit that contains 100 honors would certainly qualify as an excellent suit anywhere in the world. Thus, this hand should have been opened with one spade, and the optimum contract of two spades would have been reached.

There is a sound basis for this solution. Let us consider cases where one's partner's support consists of something like 9 7 2. If one has opened with a major suit consisting of A K Q 10, he is certain of three tricks in the suit, perhaps four if the outstanding jack is guarded no more than twice. However, if one has opened with a suit consisting of A J 8 6 3, he will be fortunate indeed to make four tricks in the suit. The usual number of tricks such a hand could be expected to take is three—the same number certain to be taken in the first case with the four-card trump holding.

Even when playing five-card majors, a very strong four-card suit should be treated as if it were a five-card suit.

Also see: Arguments 5, 6, 9.

ARGUMENT 9

Is it ever right to bid a four-card suit before a longer suit?

THE HAND

```
                    NORTH
                    ♠ J 6 3
                    ♡ A 10 9
                    ♦ K 7
                    ♣ A J 9 7 4
    WEST                              EAST
    ♠ Q 10 8 5                        ♠ 9 2
    ♡ 8 4                             ♡ 7 6 2
    ♦ 10 9 8 3 2                      ♦ A Q 6 5
    ♣ Q 2                            ♣ K 10 6 5
                    SOUTH
                    ♠ A K 7 4
                    ♡ K Q J 5 3
                    ♦ J 4
                    ♣ 8 3
```

THE AUCTION

SOUTH	WEST	NORTH	EAST
1 ♡	Pass	2 ♣	Pass
2 ♠	Pass	4 NT	Pass
5 ♦	Pass	6 ♡	Pass
Pass	Pass		

THE RESULT

West led the ten of diamonds. When the smoke cleared, the declarer had lost two diamonds and a club. He managed to discard his two losing spades on the dummy's good clubs.

Down two.

THE ARGUMENT

South blasted North for leaping to slam when he didn't hold substantially more than a normal two-over-one response.

North sarcastically offered to treat South to a beginner's course at any bridge school.

South had reversed the bidding, hadn't he? And that showed a powerful hand of 19 points or better. Well, shouted North, the hand just wasn't that good.

GOREN SETTLES THE ARGUMENT

South *did* reverse the bidding.

A reverse bid indicates a hand of 19 points or better.

And South's hand didn't count up to 19 points, no matter how you tallied it.

Hands with touching suits where the lower-ranking suit is the longer often cause bidding problems. This is especially true where the suits involved are spades and hearts. Where the spade suit is good, I recommend opening one spade and then rebidding hearts at the two-level, unless my partner supports my first suit.

However, I hold no strong objection to opening hands of this type with a bid of one heart. After all, it is perfectly natural to want to bid your longer suit first. But you must be aware that this course of action can lead to rebidding problems, and may result in suppressing your spade suit.

If your partner responds one notrump to a heart opening, it is best to pass immediately. To rebid two hearts when your partner has failed to show adequate support can get you into a lot of trouble if your partner's hand is minor-suit oriented. You don't have the strength for a reverse, so you cannot rebid two spades; and besides, when your partner bypassed a response of one spade, he denied a reasonable four-card holding in that suit.

When, as in this hand, your partner responds in a minor, you must—if you don't hold 19 points—forget your spade suit and simply rebid your hearts.

Those who adhere to the system of five-card majors might find less difficulty with this hand, because one's partner is obliged to respond in almost any sort of four-card spade suit. The partner would still have to respond two clubs, because a jump raise would guarantee four trumps. But when the opener rebids two hearts, the responder would jump to four hearts and that would be that.

Also see: Arguments 5, 6, 8, 10.

ARGUMENT 10

In order to show strength, shoud one bid a short suit before a longer suit?

THE HAND

```
                    NORTH
                    ♠ 10 7 6
                    ♡ 7 6 3
                    ◇ Q J 7
                    ♣ A 10 6 2
    WEST                              EAST
    ♠ K 8                            ♠ 5 4 2
    ♡ Q 8                            ♡ J 9 5 2
    ◇ 6 5 4 2                        ◇ K 10 8
    ♣ K J 8 5 4                      ♣ Q 9 3
                    SOUTH
                    ♠ A Q J 9 3
                    ♡ A K 10 4
                    ◇ A 9 3
                    ♣ 7
```

THE AUCTION

SOUTH	WEST	NORTH	EAST
1 ♡	Pass	1 NT	Pass
2 ♠	Pass	3 ♡	Pass
3 ♠	Pass	4 ♡	Pass
Pass	Pass		

THE RESULT

The declarer went down one.
He lost a spade, a diamond, and two hearts.

THE ARGUMENT

South complained that four spades was a lead pipe cinch, and that North was to blame for getting her into the wrong contract.

By bidding hearts first and then spades, South countered, she had reversed the bidding. Her reverse showed she held at least 19 points. When she rebid her spades, North should have realized that South held four hearts and five spades. And South heatedly insisted that her partner's final bid should have been four spades.

North asked how she was to know that South held longer spades than hearts when she had opened the bidding with hearts. They wound up making a small wager on my decision.

GOREN SETTLES THE ARGUMENT

I'd say North wins in a breeze. I would have bid exactly as she did.

It is axiomatic that with two suits of unequal length, bid your longer suit first.*

South was partly right in her definition of a reverse bid—a reverse above the one-level does show a hand of at least 19 points. However, there is more to the definition of a reverse bid.

A reverse bid suggests that the first-bid suit is longer than the second.

The way South bid her hand, she was showing a holding of six hearts and five spades.

The correct way to bid South's powerful hand is to open the bidding with one spade. If her partner responds one notrump, then jump shift to three hearts. North would show her preference by returning to three spades, and South would go on to four spades. With

---

* Exception: See preceding Argument 9.

slight care in the play—ruffing a heart before drawing trumps—this contract can be brought home.

I can think of only one case where, holding two suits of unequal length, it is correct to open the shorter suit first.

When one has a relatively weak hand which is not good enough for a later reverse, the shorter suit should be bid first.

Here is an instance:

> ♠ 9 5
> ♡ A Q 10 2
> ◇ A J 10 8 3
> ♣ Q 5

With the above hand, it is correct to open the bidding with one heart, and to rebid two diamonds over either one spade or two clubs.

However, let us change the hand slightly:

> ♠ A Q 10 2
> ♡ 9 5
> ◇ A J 10 8 3
> ♣ Q 5

Now it is correct to open one diamond. If your partner responds one heart, you can, on your second turn, bid one spade. However, if your partner responds two clubs, you must suppress your spade suit for the moment, and content yourself with a rebid of two diamonds to show a hand with very little more than a minimum opening bid.

Also see: Argument 9.

ARGUMENT 11

With two good five-card suits, is reverse bidding the best method to show a strong hand?

THE HAND

```
                    NORTH
                    ♠ Q J 4
                    ♡ 6 5
                    ◇ K 9 7
                    ♣ A J 9 6 3
WEST                                    EAST
♠ 7 5 2                                 ♠ 9 6
♡ A 8                                   ♡ 10 7 4 3
◇ Q J 10 5 4 3                          ◇ 8 2
♣ 10 4                                  ♣ K Q 8 7 2
                    SOUTH
                    ♠ A K 10 8 3
                    ♡ K Q J 9 2
                    ◇ A 6
                    ♣ 5
```

THE AUCTION

SOUTH	WEST	NORTH	EAST
1 ♡	Pass	2 ♣	Pass
2 ♠	Pass	3 NT	Pass
4 ♡	Pass	Pass	Pass

THE RESULT

West led the queen of diamonds. As South was not clairvoyant, he played trumps in the normal way, trying to drop the 10 in three rounds. When this failed, he ended up losing two trump tricks.

The declarer made five on the deal.

It was obvious that twelve tricks could have been made in a spade contract.

THE ARGUMENT

South chided North for not correcting to spades. In spades, North held three-card support headed by two honors, whereas North held only a weak doubleton in hearts.

North maintained that, as far as he was concerned, South held six hearts and four spades and that there was good reason not to correct the contract.

South disagreed vigorously. He said his reverse showed a hand of at least 19 points, and that when he took the bid out of three notrump he was asking North to place the final contract. Therefore, North should have given preference to spades. South claimed he would then have tried for slam.

GOREN SETTLES THE ARGUMENT

The reverse bid in bridge seems to give rise to more disagreements than almost any other facet of bidding. Perhaps it is the name given it that causes all the confusion. In any event, let us once more set out the conditions for this bid.

When you hold a modest hand with touching suits, the normal way to bid the hand is to open the higher-ranking suit, and then rebid in the lower-ranking.

With very strong hands of about 19 points, you reverse the procedure by bidding a longer lower-ranking suit first. This shows a strong hand, for you might be forcing a partner with minimal values to give you preference at the three-level.

An examination of two auctions will make this point clear:

	[A]			[B]	
SOUTH		NORTH	SOUTH		NORTH
1 ♡		1 ♠	1 ◇		1 ♠
2 ◇			2 ♡		

The auction in *Hand A* is normal. North can give preference to two hearts or pass two diamonds with a weak hand and a fit for that suit.

In the auction in *Hand B,* North must go to three diamonds if he prefers South's first-bid suit.

Merely having a strong hand is not sufficient justification for a reverse bid. There are also certain requirements as to the shape of the hand.

When you reverse with a bid higher than the one-level, your second suit is invariably shorter than your first.

For the purposes of opening the bidding, South's hand is worth 20 points. However, if North has a fit for either of his suits, South's hand will revalue to better than 21 points. South should take this into consideration when planning the auction. The correct way for South to bid his hand with its two fine major suits is to open the bidding with one spade and then jump shift in hearts at his next turn. This procedure would have inevitably led to a contract of six spades—a bid which would have been made by the simple expedient of ruffing a low heart in the dummy before drawing all the trumps.

As South bid the hand, North was correct in passing four hearts. South had shown six hearts and four spades, and North had good reason to suppose that his hand was not a perfect fit for his partner.

CHAPTER 2

Opening Suit Bids of Two

ARGUMENT 12

*What is the minimum strength to justify
an opening suit bid of two?*

THE HAND

	NORTH	
	♠ 9 7 6	
	♡ Q 9 8 3	
	◇ A K 5 3	
	♣ 10 6	

WEST		EAST
♠ Q 10 5 4		♠ J 2
♡ 7 4		♡ J 10 6
◇ J 10 8 6 4		◇ Q 9 2
♣ J 3		♣ Q 9 8 5 4

	SOUTH	
	♠ A K 8 3	
	♡ A K 5 2	
	◇ 7	
	♣ A K 7 2	

THE AUCTION

SOUTH	WEST	NORTH	EAST
2 ♣	Pass	2 ◇	Pass
2 ♡	Pass	4 NT	Pass
5 ♠	Pass	5 NT	Pass
6 ♠	Pass	7 ♡	Pass
Pass	Pass		

THE RESULT

Though trumps behaved kindly, declarer had no play for his contract. He was forced to concede a spade trick.

Down one.

THE ARGUMENT

North was bitterly sarcastic about his partner's opening two-bid. He sardonically pointed out that South's hand contained seven losers.

South retorted that North had let one ace, one king, and one queen go to his head. The danger of opening his hand with a simple one-bid, South contended, was that North might pass and miss a sure game.

GOREN SETTLES THE ARGUMENT

Let us first lay one bogey to rest: If South were to open the bidding with one club and North were to pass, it is most unlikely that game could be made. The South hand, as North so correctly points out, contains seven losers, and North would almost certainly have to be able to respond to an opening bid, if game is going to be possible.

Losing tricks are a key factor in deciding whether to open a hand with a forcing two-bid. To bid in such a forceful manner, the hand should not contain more than four or five losers.

An opening two-bid in a suit is virtually forcing to game, and the responder is expected to keep the auction alive on the worst of hands. Therefore, the opening two-bidder must have almost enough strength in his own hand to guarantee game.

However, losing tricks are not the sole guide to opening with a two-bid.

♠ A K Q J x x x x
♡ x x
◇ A x
♣ x

This hand contains only four losers, yet it would be foolhardy to open it with two spades. The danger is that your partner, holding a fair hand, might drive the hand to an unmakeable level. Yet there is virtually no danger that a one-spade bid will be passed out.

The requirements for a demand bid in a suit include strictures on point count, as follows: with a five-card suit, the opener needs 25 points; with a six-card suit, the opener needs 23 points; with a seven-card suit, the opener needs 21 points. Naturally, these figures refer to high-card points —the distributional factor is reflected by lowering the high-card requirements.

If at all possible, avoid opening a strong two-bid with a four-card suit. However, I can picture a hand where there would be no alternative. For instance:

♠ A K Q J
♡ A K J x
◇ A Q J x
♣ x

This hand may properly be opened with a bid of two spades.

Also see: Arguments 13, 15, 16.

ARGUMENT 13

Does "game in hand" always justify a forcing two-bid?

THE HAND

NORTH
♠ A Q J 8 7
♡ J 4
♢ K Q J
♣ K Q J

SOUTH
♠ K 3
♡ A K Q 10 9 6 5 2
♢ A 7
♣ 8

THE AUCTION

SOUTH	WEST	NORTH	EAST
2 ♡	Pass	7 NT	Dbl
Pass	Pass	Pass	

THE RESULT

East led the club ace, and that was that.

THE ARGUMENT

It required a speechless moment for North to recover his voice, and then his remarks were vivid, indeed. He suggested that a pre-emptive bid of four hearts came closer to expressing the value of South's hand than did a two-bid.

South protested that he had practically game in hand; and if holding as powerful a hand as that did not qualify for a two-bid, then what in heaven's name did? Wouldn't he look silly if he had opened the hand with one heart, and then everyone had blithely passed? Besides, why hadn't North used Blackwood to check on aces?

North almost spluttered as he pointed out that his own hand totaled 19 points in high cards. Assuming that South held all the remaining high cards in the deck, that would bring South's point count to no more than 21 points. Surely one might depend on a two-bidder holding 21 points!

Eventually, the heated discussion was temporarily shelved so that the game could continue; a state of armed truce was declared until my verdict could be ascertained.

GOREN SETTLES THE ARGUMENT

It is never correct to use a two-demand bid if you hold fewer than 21 points in high cards; and with such a meager point count, your trump suit should be at least seven cards long. If your trump suit is shorter than seven cards, the high count requirement goes up: 23 points with a six-card suit; 25 points with a five-card suit.

On this point, North is unqualifiedly correct. However, that player must be verbally chastised for his intemperate jump to seven notrump. South is right when he points out that North could have used Blackwood to check for aces. No matter how strong North's logic was, there was nothing to lose by using a ready-at-hand convention to make *doubly* sure. What could North possibly have lost by using Blackwood to check for aces? If South had misread his hand, or had deliberately bid a phony, the situation wouldn't have been so irretrievably lost had South been given an opportunity to correct his first bid.

But getting back to the main point:

Game in hand is not one of the requirements for an opening forcing two-bid.

Let's take an extreme example: Suppose you find that you have been dealt twelve solid diamonds plus a singleton, what do you bid? Certainly not two diamonds. There is no question that you have game in hand—you even have enough for a small slam. Indeed, it might prove to be sound tactics to pass initially with such a hand in the hope of eventually being able to buy the contract at six diamonds—perhaps even doubled.

You can be sure of one thing: if you hold twelve diamonds, someone else holds a hand he is going to open. The likelihood of being passed out is practically nil.

Also see: Arguments 12, 15, 16.

ARGUMENT 14

What are the basic requirements for a weak two-bid?

THE HAND

NORTH
♠ K 10 9 5 4 2
♡ 8
♢ A 7 3
♣ A 8 3

SOUTH
♠ A Q 6
♡ K Q 10 9 5 4
♢ 9 4 2
♣ 7

THE AUCTION

SOUTH	WEST	NORTH	EAST
2 ♡	Pass	Pass	Pass

THE RESULT

The declarer lost two trump tricks and two diamonds. However, North-South hold a laydown for four spades. If the defenders do not open a diamond, North-South should make at least eleven tricks.

THE ARGUMENT

South, with high sarcasm, twitted his partner and asked North what kind of cards he'd have to hold to venture support of his partner's concededly weak opening. "Shall we give you Fort Knox? Aren't two aces and a king and a six-card spade suit enough?"

"Don't be so smart-alecky!" retorted North. "If the

hands happened to be a misfit my 11 points in high cards wouldn't go far. How could I visualize a game opposite a partner who, by his weak two-bid, denied the values for an opening bid of one in a suit?"

"But with your singleton in my suit," protested South, "you might at least have tried to improve our contract by bidding spades."

"Obviously you don't understand weak two-bids," North sneered. "Let's stop using them."

GOREN SETTLES THE ARGUMENT

The book by Howard Schenken, who popularized the weak two-bid back in the 1930's, subheads one of the chapters with "Warning: Dangerous if used improperly." I can only echo that warning.

Unlike other pre-emptive bids, the weak two-bid is as useful for its offensive potential as for its defensive aspects. A bid at the two-level has only a limited pre-emptive value, but such a bid does describe the hand quite accurately.

Here are the requirements for a weak two-bid:

1. A hand of less than opening bid strength. (About 6 to 10 points not vulnerable; 8 to 12 points, if vulnerable).

2. A six-card suit headed by no worse than Q-J-9. (Your partner may have only a singleton in your trump suit and it is embarrassing —and sometimes expensive—if the opponents take more tricks in your trump than you do.)

3. At least five playing tricks in your own hand.

4. About 1½ to 2 defensive tricks.

5. If you open with a weak two-bid in a major, you should not hold four cards in the other major.

6. If you open with a weak two-bid in a minor, the bid guarantees you do not hold four cards in either major.

When you open with a weak two-bid in a major, your partner should not have to worry about missing game in the other major, should he happen to hold a broken six-card suit in the other major.

In the hand under discussion, South's hand was too good for a weak two-bid. For one thing, he held solid defensive values—2½ quick tricks.

By every standard, South had a perfectly sound opening bid of one heart. His hand was worth 13 points, he had no rebid problems, and he had more than enough defensive strength. Had he made his proper opening bid, there is no doubt that four spades would have been reached.

Let us interchange South's diamonds and spades. Now the restriction about the other major no longer applies; nevertheless, in first or second seat South should open one heart. In third seat, however, the requirements are relaxed, and the hand may optionally be opened with a bid of two hearts. The fact that his partner has passed makes it unlikely that game will be missed, and the pre-emptive factor now carries more weight.

Also see: Arguments 17, 19.

ARGUMENT 15

Playing "weak twos," what strength is promised by an artificial and forcing two-club opening bid?

THE HAND

NORTH
♠ Q 7 6 2
♡ Q J 5 4
◇ 7 6 3
♣ 10 2

WEST
♠ K 10 9
♡ K 7 6 3
◇ K 10 4
♣ Q 9 5

EAST
♠ 5
♡ A 10 9 2
◇ J 5 2
♣ 8 7 6 4 3

SOUTH
♠ A J 8 4 3
♡ 8
◇ A Q 9 8
♣ A K J

THE AUCTION

SOUTH	WEST	NORTH	EAST
2 ♣	Pass	2 ◇	Pass
2 ♠	Pass	4 ♠	Pass
Pass	Pass		

THE RESULT

The declarer lost one spade, one heart, and two diamonds.

Down one.

THE ARGUMENT

"I thought we were playing two clubs forcing, not weak," remarked North sarcastically. He insinuated that South was part of a vicious plot to see that he didn't win a single rubber all week.

South defended his bidding rather vehemently. After all, he pointed out, it was North who had leaped to four spades on what, even in days of an energy crisis, could not be called more than the smell of an oil rag. If North had bid three spades, South could have passed.

North was far from ready to surrender. He had 7 points, arrived at in this fashion: 3 for the queen of spades (promoted 1 point because it was an honor in partner's trump suit); 3 points in hearts; 1 point for the doubleton in clubs. Facing any reasonable opening two-bid, seven points, he insisted, would be enough for game opposite a sound two-demand bid. Furthermore, his jump raise in trumps was exactly descriptive: good trump support but no ace, no king, and no singleton.

South turned a deaf ear. His hand was just too strong for a mere one-bid, and that was that.

GOREN SETTLES THE ARGUMENT

The strength required for an opening two-club bid, artificial and forcing, is the same as for an opening forcing two-bid in a suit in the Standard American system of bidding—with a single exception. You may open two-clubs with 23 or 24 points with a balanced hand. The reason for this is that the opener can stop at two notrump.

The fact that you are using two clubs as your forcing opening bid instead of a two-bid in other suits does not grant you a license to reduce the strength requirements any time you fear that partner may pass an opening one-bid.

North gets the decision on every one of his arguments, including the one he didn't bother to answer. South could not have passed if North had merely raised to three spades.

There *is* a situation where the bidding can die at two notrump or three of a major, but it does not apply to this case.

The negative response to a two-club forcing bid is two diamonds. A two notrump response is a positive bid made on a balanced hand of about 8 high-card points, including at least one king. Any other positive response to an artificial two-club bid requires an ace and a king, or the equivalent.

Using two clubs as the only forcing bid also allows a convenient notrump structure. Opening two notrump bids can now be shaded to 21 or 22 high-card points. With 23 or 24 high-card points and a balanced hand, the opener bids two clubs and rebids two notrump. This is the exception we spoke of earlier. In this case, the responder may pass the two notrump rebid, if he has fewer than 3 points.

ARGUMENT 16

After a strong two-club opening and a two-diamond response, is it necessary for the opener to jump to force his partner to bid again?

THE HAND

                    NORTH
                    ♠ 4 3 2
                    ♡ 6
                    ◊ Q 10 6 5 4 3
                    ♣ 8 4 3

WEST   EAST
♠ Q 10 9 6   ♠ K J 8 7 5
♡ 10 8 5 2   ♡ K 7
◊ J   ◊ 9 8 7
♣ Q 9 6 2   ♣ A 7 5

                    SOUTH
                    ♠ A
                    ♡ A Q J 9 4 3
                    ◊ A K 2
                    ♣ K J 10

THE AUCTION

SOUTH	WEST	NORTH	EAST
2 ♣	Pass	2 ◊	Pass
3 ♡	Pass	3 NT	Pass
4 ♡	Pass	Pass	Pass

THE RESULT

West opened the singleton jack of diamonds. If the declarer had known the lie of the cards, he could have won the first trick with the dummy's diamond queen, taken a heart finesse, dropped the king of hearts under the ace, and cashed the jack. This would leave West with the good 10 of hearts, but then South would lose only one trump trick and two club tricks.

However, it seemed wiser for South to try to preserve his entry in the dummy; so he won the diamond in his hand and led the ace and queen of hearts. East was able to win with the king and give his partner a diamond ruff.

West put East back on the lead with the ace of clubs, and a second diamond ruff cut the declarer off from the dummy. The defenders shifted to spades. In the end, South had to lose the queen of clubs.

Down two!

THE ARGUMENT

"Tough luck," North sympathized.

"Luck?" screamed South. "Why didn't you show your diamonds? We could have made at least five. With the king of hearts dropping on the second lead, you might conceivably have even made six!"

"I would have showed my diamond suit if you had given me the chance," retorted North, heatedly. "But you jumped in hearts, and I was afraid to take the bidding past three notrump. Why did you jump?"

"I didn't want you to pass out two hearts," was South's rejoinder.

It was futile for North to reply that he could not have passed.

South insisted that North would have passed out two hearts and should have passed out two hearts.

GOREN SETTLES THE ARGUMENT

It is not necessary for the player who has opened with a strong artificial two-club bid to jump after a two-diamond response, if he wants to keep the bidding going. Although the responder has shown weakness, the responder is nevertheless bound to make at least one more bid. And if the opener's

third bid is anything but a simple rebid of his first
suit, the responder is bound to bid once more.

One of the advantages of using the artificial two-
club bid as the strong opening bid is that there is
often room for an exchange of information at one level
lower than if a major had been opened at the two-level.

In the hand in question, South should merely have
rebid two hearts over the artificial weakness response
of two diamonds. Now, if North bids two notrump, in-
dicating extreme weakness and a distaste for hearts,
South would risk a pass only if he rebid three hearts.
He should, in fact, hold a slightly stronger hand to
entitle him to jump to game.

Had South rebid two hearts, North—having already
expressed his weakness—would have shown his six-
card diamond suit. South would then have raised the
diamonds, and the diamond game would be reached.

After a two-club opening and a two-diamond response, the opener can be passed out only if his
rebid is two notrump. If the opener rebids in a
suit, the responder must bid again. Then, if the
responder's rebid is discouraging, the opener
must bid a new suit to insure still another bid by
the responder.

Also see: Arguments 12, 13, 15.

CHAPTER 3

Opening Suit Bids of Three, Four, or Five

ARGUMENT 17

What is the minimum strength to justify an opening suit bid of three in a major suit?

THE HAND

```
              NORTH
              ♠ A 4
              ♡ A 9 5 4
              ◇ A K Q 8 4 3
              ♣ 10
WEST                            EAST
♠ K J 5                        ♠ 10 8
♡ K 7                          ♡ J 8 6 3
◇ 7 6 2                        ◇ J 10
♣ A 9 7 3 2                    ♣ K Q J 6 5
              SOUTH
              ♠ Q 9 7 6 3 2
              ♡ Q 10 2
              ◇ 9 5
              ♣ 8 4
```

THE AUCTION

SOUTH	WEST	NORTH	EAST
3 ♠	Pass	6 ♠	Pass
Pass	Dbl	Pass	Pass
Pass			

THE RESULT

West led the ace of clubs. She then sat back to wait for two trump tricks. Since North-South were not vulnerable, the loss was 300 points plus the value of the lost game.

THE ARGUMENT

North stated categorically that anyone who opened South's hand with a pre-emptive bid must be either very rich or very sick.

South averred that she promised nothing with her opening except what she had. Who had asked North to jump to six spades? Hadn't North ever heard of a pre-empt? Five quick tricks just weren't enough with which to push to slam.

GOREN SETTLES THE ARGUMENT

A pre-emptive opening bid should be governed by the Rule of 2 and 3. When not vulnerable, the preemptive bidder guarantees that his hand will produce within three tricks of his bid; when vulnerable, his hand will make within two tricks of his bid.

Applying this principle to an opening bid of three in a suit, it means that the non-vulnerable opener holds a hand that will develop about six tricks; the vulnerable bidder, about seven. The bid is generally made with a seven-card suit; rarely with a suit that includes more than two losers. Judged by this standard, North was well within his rights to leap to six spades.

In the first and second seats, I would abide rigidly by this rule. Therefore, South was way off base to open with three spades.

In third seat, however, I might be inclined to relax this stricture. The reason is that an opening three-bid puts a tremendous amount of pressure on the opponents. Once your partner has passed, the chance of his getting your side too high is rather slight, and you stand to gain more than you stand to lose by making life difficult for your opponents.

Beware of opening pre-emptively when you hold a secondary major suit.

Consider this hand:

♠ K Q 10 x x x x
♡ Q 10 x x
♢ x
♣ x

Your partner might pass on opening bid of three spades and might leave you in an impossible contract when he has a heart fit, and your side can make four hearts.

As a general rule, an opening three-bid shows a hand of less than opening bid strength with a dearth of defensive values, and a hand usually not of much use offensively in any suit other than the one that has been bid. The purpose of the bid is to shut out everyone, and this generally includes your partner.

I therefore deem it very important to limit a three-bid to a hand that lacks defensive potential. Seldom, if ever, should one pre-empt with a hand containing two aces. A partner must be allowed to know whether or not you are likely to hold defensive tricks. Otherwise, he might take an unwarranted sacrifice against an opposing game contract that can be defeated.

Also see: Arguments 14, 19.

ARGUMENT 18

Does a pre-emptive three-bid in a minor promise a solid suit?

THE HAND

NORTH
♠ 6
♡ 863
♦ KJ98532
♣ A7

WEST
♠ KJ85
♡ J972
♦ A
♣ 10963

EAST
♠ Q9432
♡ Q10
♦ Q76
♣ J42

SOUTH
♠ A107
♡ AK54
♦ 104
♣ KQ85

THE AUCTION

NORTH	EAST	SOUTH	WEST
3 ♦	Pass	3 NT	Pass
Pass	Pass		

THE RESULT

West led his fourth-best spade. East played the queen and the declarer held up. Spades were continued until the declarer won with the ace. When West gained the lead with the ace of diamonds, the defenders cashed two more spade tricks. They still had to score a trick with the queen of diamonds.

The declarer was down two.
Five diamonds is a sound contract.

THE ARGUMENT

South couldn't believe that North had opened three diamonds with such a ragged suit. He stated emphatically that a pre-empt in a minor guaranteed a solid suit.

North claimed that the correct bid on the South cards was five diamonds. The South hand might take care of as many as five losers.

GOREN SETTLES THE ARGUMENT

It is all well and good to play that a minor suit pre-empt shows a solid suit, provided you have a partnership agreement to that effect.

Failing a specific understanding as to the quality of a three-bid in a minor suit, the player should treat such a bid exactly the same as he would a three-bid in a major suit. The Rule of 2 and 3 applies.

South was at fault in this deal. With his strong hand, there had to be a play for game in the bid suit even opposite a hand such as North held; for with most of South's strength in prime controls, he should have elected to bid five diamonds.

Even if North turned up with seven solid diamonds and nothing else and three notrump was cold as ice, it should be clear that making five diamonds on the hand would be no problem.

And on any other type of hand, there might be some play for game in a suit bid, but hardly any chance at all in three notrump. Opposite a weak pre-empt, a retreat into notrump with insufficient stoppers is a quest for disaster.

Observe that players who use the "gambling" three notrump bid do not have this dilemma. They would open with three notrump on a hand with seven solid cards in a minor suit. Hence, for them, an opening bid of three in a minor indubitably shows a broken suit.

Also see: Arguments 18, 20, 21.

ARGUMENT 19

On what kind of hand should a player open the bidding with four of a major?

THE HAND

```
            NORTH
            ♠ K Q 7 3
            ♡ 8
            ◇ A 7 6 2
            ♣ 9 8 4 3

            SOUTH
            ♠ A 8 2
            ♡ A K Q 10 9 4 3 2
            ◇ 9
            ♣ 2
```

THE AUCTION

SOUTH	WEST	NORTH	EAST
4 ♡	Pass	Pass	Pass

THE RESULT

West led the king of clubs. That was the only trick for the defense.

THE ARGUMENT

Slightly miffed at missing a slam, South suggested that North might have taken some action, though he was at a loss to suggest just what.

North professed surprise that his partner made twelve tricks with what little he, North, had to contribute to the campaign.

54

GOREN SETTLES THE ARGUMENT

An opening bid of four in a suit is similar to a pre-emptive bid of three. It generally promises an eight-card suit, or a solid seven-card suit. In first and second seat, the bid denies the values for an opening bid of one in a suit.

Such a bid guarantees that the hand, no matter what partner holds, will not go down more than three tricks if not vulnerable, nor more than two tricks if vulnerable.

The bid is generally made to ward off an incipient sacrifice bid by non-vulnerable opponents.

Typical hands for an opening bid of four hearts not vulnerable could be:

[A]	[B]
♠ x	♠ x
♡ A Q J x x x x	♡ A K Q J x x x
◇ x x	◇ x x x
♣ x x	♣ x x

If one's partner has already passed, the third-seat bidder is permitted some liberties with hands of this type. However, a bidder should not have less than the minimums shown to open four in the third seat.

However, many good hands that have no real hope for slam opposite a passed partner can be opened with a bid of four in the third seat. Here's a typical example:

> ♠ x
> ♡ A K Q 10 x x x
> ◇ A J 10 x
> ♣ x

Opposite a partner who could not open the bidding, there is not much hope of making a slam. A bid of four hearts has much to recommend it. Someone at the table rates to hold quite a few spades, and a bid of four hearts might pre-empt the opponents out of their spade suit.

South must take the blame for missing the slam. His hand is too strong for an opening bid of four hearts; he should have opened with a bid of one heart.

With a hand as strong as South has, even if North held only the king of spades and nothing else, the combined hands would be enough for a game in hearts. Yet, there is little danger, if North passes South's one-heart opening bid with such a three-point holding, that game will be missed. For if North and West both pass, it is most unlikely that the auction will end there. East will almost surely have the strength and distribution to enter the bidding, which will afford South the opportunity to bid four hearts.

After North responds one spade, getting to slam is not automatic. But a one-spade response fits South's hand so well that he might gamble on slam possibilities by immediately checking for aces via Blackwood. When he finds that North holds one of the needed aces, the slam is practically assured.

Also see: Arguments 14, 17.

ARGUMENT 20

What is the minimum strength to justify an opening bid of four in a minor?

THE HAND

NORTH
♠ K 10 7 3
♡ Q J 5
◇ 8 5
♣ A Q 7 5

SOUTH
♠ 8
♡ 6 2
◇ A K J 10 9 7 6 2
♣ 6 4

THE AUCTION

SOUTH	WEST	NORTH	EAST
4 ◇	Pass	Pass	Pass

THE RESULT

West led the jack of clubs. The finesse of the queen lost to the king. The defenders cashed the ace and king of hearts and ace of spades.

Down one.

North-South had good chances for making three no-trump.

THE ARGUMENT

"Your hand is much too strong for a four-diamond opening bid," suggested North. "I would prefer an opening bid of three diamonds."

"Too strong?" snickered South mirthlessly. "My hand should take seven tricks at a diamond contract and is worthless in defense. Applying the Rule of 2 and 3, I barely have enough for a not vulnerable opening bid of four diamonds!"

GOREN SETTLES THE ARGUMENT

Strange as it seems, an opening bid of four in a minor suit indicates less strength than an opening bid of three in a minor.

Let us consider some of the reasons why. Unlike an opening bid of four in a major suit—which is a game bid—an opening bid of four in a minor is designed purely as an obstructive tactic. The opening bidder usually has a long ragged suit and is hardly interested in getting to game unless his partner has a very good hand.

South would indeed have done better either to pass or to open three diamonds.

A typical hand for an opening bid of four diamonds, not vulnerable, would be:

♠ x
♡ x
◇ Q J 10 x x x x
♣ Q J 10

If vulnerable, the hand must be strengthened by a playing trick, for example, by adding a minor-suit king in place of the jack of that suit.

There are many hands with solid seven-card minor suits or semi-solid eight-card minor suits that can make game at notrump opposite some stoppers in one's partner's hand. A player should be reluctant to rule out a three notrump contract with his opening bid.

Because an opening bid of four in a minor bypasses a possible contract of three notrump, this

bid is made on a hand totally unsuited to notrump play, and with little or no defensive strength.

Even though the responder to an opening pre-empt of four of a minor suit holds a powerhouse, he should predicate his bid on the fact that the opening bidder is unlikely to have an entry in his hand, except in the bid suit.

Also see: Arguments 18, 21.

ARGUMENT 21

When should the opener bid five of a minor suit?

THE HAND

NORTH
♠ A 8 7 6 4
♡ 4 3
◇ Q 8
♣ A Q 5 2

SOUTH
♠ 9
♡ A 8 7
◇ A K J 10 6 5 3
♣ K J

THE AUCTION

SOUTH	WEST	NORTH	EAST
5 ◇	Pass	Pass	Pass

THE RESULT

The defenders led a heart and never took a trick. Even with a spade lead, South would surely have made at least twelve tricks.

THE ARGUMENT

"Good gracious!" commented South, "you are a conservative player. You hold a full opening bid, and my hand was good enough to contract for an eleven-trick game on my own—yet you did not raise me!"

"Don't you know you pre-empted?" retorted the

lady who sat North. "I was just hoping I was bringing you enough stuff to enable you to make game."

"A pre-empt at the *five*-level? Oh! Mrs. Cadwallader! You shock me!"

GOREN SETTLES THE ARGUMENT

Mrs. Cadwallader knows her bridge. South should have opened with a bid of one diamond.

An opening bid of five of a minor suit is pre-emptive. Like any other pre-empt, it denies the values for an opening bid of one in a suit, and it is governed by the Rule of 2 and 3.

Typically, the hand will have an eight- or nine-card suit. Such a hand may have even less strength defensively than an opening bid of three.

Not vulnerable, here is a typical five-diamond opening bid.

♠ x
♡ x x
◇ K Q J 10 x x x x x
♣ x

The hand should take eight tricks playing in diamonds, but might not take one in defense. The purpose of the bid is to shut out the opponents. By opening at a high level, the pre-emptive bidder takes away so much bidding space that he forces the enemy to guess instead of allowing his opponents room to get the best result through a constructive auction.

In third or fourth seat, you can beef up your opening bids of five in a minor. The fact that your partner and at least one opponent have passed gives the bid a different tactical objective. The purpose is still pre-emptive, but the chance of missing a slam is greatly diminished.

Consider this hand:

♠ x
♡ x
◇ A x x
♣ A K J x x x x x

In third position, after two passes, an opening bid of five clubs is in order. True, you have three quick tricks, but the length of your club suit robs two of these tricks of much of their defensive value. To make a slam, your partner needs at least one ace and some values in diamonds. He may hold these cards and still have validly passed his hand, but the odds are against this.

To make five clubs, he need hold only diamond values.

By pre-empting, you achieve two purposes. You may keep the opponents from finding the right major suit contract. Or, if fourth-hand holds good strength and the opponents get into the auction, you may give your partner a chance to double for a big set.

True, in some cases, you may not be able to make five clubs, but on balance, you will gain more by this bid than you will lose.

Also see: Arguments 18, 20.

CHAPTER 4

Opening Bids of One Notrump

ARGUMENT 22

Is it ever wrong to open one notrump when you hold a balanced 16-point hand?

THE HAND

```
                    NORTH
                    ♠ 10 7 6 2
                    ♡ J 7 4
                    ◇ A 8 7
                    ♣ K Q 5
    WEST                              EAST
    ♠ Q 9 5                           ♠ J 4
    ♡ K 10 8 6 3                      ♡ Q 9 2
    ◇ Q 10                            ◇ K J 6 4 3
    ♣ 8 7 4                           ♣ 9 6 3
                    SOUTH
                    ♠ A K 8 3
                    ♡ A 5
                    ◇ 9 5 2
                    ♣ A J 10 2
```

THE AUCTION

SOUTH	WEST	NORTH	EAST
1 NT	Pass	3 NT	Pass
Pass	Pass		

THE RESULT

West led the six of hearts. The dummy played low, and East made the fine play of the nine of hearts, which forced the declarer's ace. When the declarer ran his clubs, West made the excellent discard of the ten of diamonds.

The declarer was eventually forced to surrender a trick to the queen of spades, whereupon the defenders cashed four heart tricks to set the contract one trick.

THE ARGUMENT

The dummy had hardly hit the table when South started muttering about players who had not yet learned the simplest convention, namely, the Stayman Convention to check for a four-card major suit after a notrump opening bid.

North tried valiantly to defend himself. He said he thought nine tricks might prove easier to make than ten, since his hand was perfectly balanced.

GOREN SETTLES THE ARGUMENT

I find no fault with North's choice of three notrump. Three notrump, speaking in the simplest terms, is a contract for one trick less than four spades; therefore, in many cases, it is easier to bring home. As it was, three notrump was defeated only because East made a fine play at Trick One. Had East thoughtlessly played the queen of hearts instead of the 9, the declarer would have been home. Some would say this was South's bad luck.

The point I mean to stress is that I am not at all happy about South's opening bid of one notrump. True, he held 16 points and a hand that is relatively balanced —but almost all his points are concentrated in prime controls: that is, in aces and kings. Hands of this type are generally better fitted for suit play than for notrump.

An opening bid of one notrump should be avoided with a 16-point hand if it contains an unstopped suit and fewer than seven honor cards.

I would further generalize by saying that where an opener holds no tenaces, there is little advantage in letting the lead come up to *his* hand. Indeed, if the final contract is to be notrump, it is probably better that his partner become the declarer.

In the hand before us, South has two good suits. There is really no reason why he should not plan to bid them both. Indeed, there are many hands where game in a major might be achieved on a 3-4 fit, when a final contract of three notrump would have no play at all.

As I see it, South should have opened with one club. Then, most assuredly, the 4-4 major fit would have been uncovered and four spades would have been the final contract. And in the proper contract of four spades, South would not have been subject to "bad luck."

For in this hand, four spades can be made against any lead. The declarer wins the first trick, cashes the ace and king of spades, and then plays four rounds of clubs. On the fourth club, he discards one of dummy's diamonds. It matters not whether West ruffs this trick. The declarer would lose only one spade, one diamond, and one club.

Also see: Arguments 23, 24.

ARGUMENT 23

Can an 18-point hand be too strong for a bid of one notrump?

THE HAND

```
              NORTH
              ♠ 10 8 3
              ♡ K 10 9 2
              ◇ 10 4 2
              ♣ A 8 6
WEST                          EAST
♠ A J 9 7 2                   ♠ 6 4
♡ 7 3                         ♡ A J 6 5
◇ Q 8 5                       ◇ 7 6
♣ J 10 5                      ♣ Q 7 4 3 2
              SOUTH
              ♠ K Q 5
              ♡ Q 8 4
              ◇ A K J 9 3
              ♣ K 9
```

THE AUCTION

SOUTH	WEST	NORTH	EAST
1 NT	Pass	Pass	Pass

THE RESULT

West led a low spade, and whether North's 8 or 10 was played, the declarer had scant difficulty in establishing nine tricks.

THE ARGUMENT

"With 7 points and three 10s, couldn't you have raised me to two notrump?" South roared at his partner. "And why didn't you probe for a 4-4 heart fit by bidding two clubs? That would also have got us into game."

"You do open peculiar notrumps," retorted North icily. "If you had simply opened one diamond, we would have arrived in a proper contract. Who ever heard of opening one notrump with a five-card suit?"

To prevent incipient mayhem, the two other players suggested that the case be referred to me for adjudication.

GOREN SETTLES THE ARGUMENT

North was right, but for the wrong reasons.

There is nothing wrong in opening one notrump with a five-card suit.

An opening bid of one notrump shows a hand of 16-18 points that is balanced: that is, a hand with either a 4-3-3-3 pattern, or a 4-4-3-2 pattern, or a 5-3-3-2 pattern. The five-card suit could even be a major.

The fault here lay in South's wooden valuation of his hand. True, his point count is 18 in high cards—the upper limit for an opening bid of one notrump. However, his powerful five-card suit makes the hand actually worth more than 18 points.

Though distributional points are not counted in notrump valuation, South's diamond suit gives the hand additional trick-taking potential. Factors of this type should be borne in mind when opening the bidding.

Keep in mind that aces and kings are slightly undervalued in the point count. Note that South's hand contains four such major honors.

When a hand counts 18 points in high cards, but might count more than 18 if opened with a suit bid, you should add one point for a good five-card suit. Any hand worth more than 18 points is too strong for an opening notrump bid.

A hand worth more than 18 points but opened with one notrump may stifle a partner who has only minimum values. A partner with 6 or 7 points is bound to respond to a suit bid, but might easily pass out a notrump bid; and the 7-point hand—opposite a 19-point hand—might easily have enough strength to bring home a three notrump contract.

Accordingly, with this hand, South should have opened one diamond, intending to rebid two notrump if North responds in a major suit. The two notrump bid, in such a situation, is virtually forcing to game. If North holds a strong five-card major, he will bid three of his suit over South's two notrump. If his holding is a four-card suit, he will close out the bidding at three notrump.

Also see: Arguments 22, 24.

ARGUMENT 24

Is it wrong to open one notrump holding a six-card suit?

THE HAND

```
                    NORTH
                    ♠ 10 6 4
                    ♡ J 7 6 4 2
                    ◇ A J
                    ♣ K 8 7
    WEST                                EAST
    ♡ K 9 8 2                           ♠ J 7 5 3
    ♡ A 9                               ♡ Q 10 8
    ◇ Q 7 5                             ◇ 8 6
    ♣ J 6 5 3                           ♣ Q 9 4 2
                    SOUTH
                    ♠ A Q
                    ♡ K 5 3
                    ◇ K 10 9 4 3 2
                    ♣ A 10
```

THE AUCTION

SOUTH	WEST	NORTH	EAST
1 ◇	Pass	1 ♡	Pass
3 ◇	Pass	3 ♡	Pass
4 ♡	Pass	Pass	Pass

THE RESULT

East led the three of spades. The declarer finessed the queen, and lost to West's king. Now the fate of the contract rested on not losing more than two trump tricks.

Unfortunately, the declarer led a low heart to his

king. West won with his ace, and East was still going
to win two trump tricks behind North's jack.

The declarer was down one.

THE ARGUMENT

South blew his top. He did not mind his partner
misguessing the trump position—*but they were in the
wrong contract,* he screamed. Three notrump could not
be beaten. South gave his opinion about someone who
rebids such a moth-eaten heart suit rather than three
notrump.

North wanted to know why South, with 16 points in
high cards, hadn't opened one notrump. Then all the
trouble would have been avoided.

GOREN SETTLES THE ARGUMENT

Three to the king is normally more than adequate
support for a suit that has been rebid freely. But here
North's rebid was almost automatic. It was South's
choice of an opening bid that got the auction off on
the wrong foot.

Let us consider South's hand carefully. It has 16
points in high cards, a stopper in every suit, and no
singleton and no void. Despite the fact that it contains
a six-card diamond suit, it is in essence a balanced
hand. I would therefore recommend an opening bid of
one notrump.

Let us look at some of the advantages of such a
bid. Making the descriptive bid of one notrump relieves
one of the pressure of having to strain to find a suitable
rebid over your partner's one-over-one response. Also,
a nine-trick game is generally easier to fulfill than an
eleven-trick game. Moreover, holding the ace-queen
of spades and the king of hearts, it might be vital to
protect these holdings from an opening lead *through*
them, as would happen if your partner became the
declarer at three notrump. So my rule is:

With 16 points in high cards, and a balanced hand—no singletons, no voids—bid notrump holding a six-card *minor*.

But a word of caution:

Never open one notrump with a six-card major suit. The chances of ending in an inferior three notrump contract rather than the superior major suit game outweigh the problem of finding a satisfactory rebid.

If, by chance, your partner *does* have an excellent fit for your six-card minor, this will solidify the suit and enable you to run the suit in a three notrump contract.

Also see: Arguments 22, 23.

ARGUMENT 25

Is an unbalanced hand unsuitable for notrump play?

THE HAND

NORTH
- ♠ A 9 5
- ♡ K 9 8 2
- ◇ A Q 6
- ♣ K 7 6

SOUTH
- ♠ K 8 3
- ♡ Q
- ◇ K J 10 8 2
- ♣ J 10 5 2

THE AUCTION

NORTH	EAST	SOUTH	WEST
1 NT	Pass	3 ◇	Pass
4 ◇	Pass	5 ◇	Pass
Pass	Pass		

THE RESULT

West led the queen of spades.

Though the declarer managed to discard his losing spade on the king of hearts, he could not make his contract. He was forced to concede two club tricks and the ace of hearts.

As the cards lie, three notrump would have been a relatively simple contract, and each partner was quick to blame the other for the debacle.

THE ARGUMENT

It was South's contention that North should have rebid three notrump to show a minimum opening bid.

North claimed that, with his excellent support for his partner's suit and his wealth of controls, it would have been a dereliction of duty to deny his partner's suit.

GOREN SETTLES THE ARGUMENT

In response to an opening bid of one notrump, a jump response in a suit conveys to the opener that the hand can be played in the responder's long suit at the game level, or perhaps even in slam.

Once North had shown a balanced 16-18 points, South knew that his side had the values for game. Unfortunately, he let his five-card diamond suit and his singleton heart sway his judgment when he elected to jump to three diamonds.

Though he held a 5-4-3-1 pattern, South had an honor card in every suit. His singleton heart queen rated to be an important card for his partner at a notrump contract. Since nine tricks are easier to make than eleven, South should simply have raised to three notrump.

For purposes of a suit contract, the value of the singleton heart was hard to determine. South· should have made allowances for the fact that North might hold a minimum 16 points for his notrump opening. If we add this to South's 10 high-card points, it is easy to see that a five-level contract could be in jeopardy.

No blame attaches to North for his raise to four diamonds. He had excellent support for the suit in which his partner had jumped. Moreover, all his side points were in aces and kings. As far as he was con-

cerned, he held an ideal hand for a diamond slam.
Therefore, it was imperative that he agree on the suit
at the first opportunity, to allow South to investigate
the slam possibilities of the combined holding.

CHAPTER 5

Opening Bids of Two Notrump

ARGUMENT 26

Should you open two notrump holding a five-card major suit?

THE HAND

```
                    NORTH
                    ♠ 10 4 3
                    ♡ J 4
                    ◇ 8 7 6 3
                    ♣ K 7 4 2

   WEST                            EAST
   ♠ A 7                           ♠ K 9 8 6 5
   ♡ Q 9 3 2                       ♡ 10 5
   ◇ Q J 10 5 4                    ◇ 9 2
   ♣ 9 3                           ♣ J 10 8 6

                    SOUTH
                    ♠ Q J 2
                    ♡ A K 8 7 6
                    ◇ A K
                    ♣ A Q 5
```

THE AUCTION

SOUTH	WEST	NORTH	EAST
1 ♡	Pass	Pass	Pass

THE RESULT

West led the queen of diamonds, won by the declarer's king. South led a heart to the jack, which won. The declarer was thus able to hold his losses to one trump, two spades, and one club. He made nine tricks.

At the completion of play it was noticed that, provided the declarer made the same play in hearts, North-South could make nine tricks at notrump.

THE ARGUMENT

North lashed out at South for not opening the bidding with a demand bid of two hearts, which would certainly have gotten their side to game.

South was positive that his hand did not measure up to the standards required for a forcing two-bid. In his opinion, the fault lay with North. After all, North had a king, a jack, and a doubleton. Had he scraped up any sort of response, South would have leaped to game.

GOREN SETTLES THE ARGUMENT

I do have some sympathy for North; he did nothing wrong, yet his partner tried to blame him for missing the game. But North is way off base in suggesting that South should have opened with a demand bid. The South hand is almost a king short of the requirements for a strong two-bid.

Neither player mentioned the winning solution, which is to open with a bid of two notrump.

Possession of a five-card major is no bar to opening with a bid of two notrump.

Observe how the South hand meets all the qualifications for a two notrump opening bid: the hand is balanced; it contains 23 points in high cards; it has stoppers in all suits.

Had South made his correct opening bid, North would have enough to scrape up a raise to game. Just a modicum of care in the play would have earned a handsome reward.

Also see: Argument 27.

ARGUMENT 27

May you open two notrump with fewer points when you have a good five-card suit or a good six-card suit?

THE HAND

                    NORTH
                    ♠ 9 5
                    ♡ A 9 8 3
                    ◇ 1 0 8 4 2
                    ♣ 6 3 2

                    SOUTH
                    ♠ A 8
                    ♡ K 6
                    ◇ Q J 3
                    ♣ A K Q J 5 4

THE AUCTION

SOUTH	WEST	NORTH	EAST
1 ♣	Pass	Pass	Pass

THE RESULT

The declarer had no difficulty fulfilling his contract.

He lost one trick in spades and two in diamonds, to make four.

But there was no way that a contract of three no-trump could have been defeated.

THE ARGUMENT

"When I open one club, a bid that enables you to show any suit at the one-level, the least you can do is keep the bidding open for one round," barked South.

"After all, it's not as if you had nothing; you held a four-card heart suit headed by the ace. One peep out of you and we would have been in game."

"If you wanted to hear from me you should have opened with a demand bid," came back North. "Anyone will tell you that I did not have the values for a response. You were nearer a two-club opening bid than I was to a one-heart response."

GOREN SETTLES THE ARGUMENT

I sympathize with North. I doubt whether I would have responded to a one-club opening bid. I would place full blame for missing game on the shoulders of South.

No, I do not advocate opening the South hand with two clubs. If there is one thing in bridge I dislike doing, it is tampering with the values for a forcing two-bid in a suit; this throws constructive slam bidding off kilter. However, I do suggest that South might have considered opening the bidding with two notrump.

To open with a bid of two notrump, the opener should hold 22 to 24 points in high cards. He should also have every suit stopped. If the opener holds a solid six-card suit, he may add two additional points for that holding.

The hand in question meets all the criteria for a two notrump opening bid. Despite the fact that it contains a six-card suit, it is essentially a balanced hand, and we have seen earlier that holding a six-card suit, if it is a minor, is no bar to opening with a notrump bid.

Had South elected to open the bidding with two notrump, North would surely have gone on to game.

Also see: Argument 26.

CHAPTER 6

Opening Bids of Three Notrump

ARGUMENT 28

What are the requirements for a three notrump opening bid?

THE HAND

```
                    NORTH
                    ♠ 7
                    ♡ Q 10 5 4
                    ◇ J 8 7 3
                    ♣ 10 9 5 2
  WEST                                  EAST
  ♠ K 10 9 5 4                          ♠ J 8 6 2
  ♡ K 6 3                               ♡ 9 8 7 2
  ◇ 4                                   ◇ 10 2
  ♣ Q 8 7 6                             ♣ K 4 3
                    SOUTH
                    ♠ A Q 3
                    ♡ A J
                    ◇ A K Q 9 6 5
                    ♣ A J
```

THE AUCTION

SOUTH	WEST	NORTH	EAST
3 NT	Pass	Pass	Pass

THE RESULT

Even if clubs were led, the declarer could make

79

eleven tricks by forcing out the king of hearts, for the
diamonds would provide at least two entries to dummy.

No lead could stop six diamonds.

THE ARGUMENT

North commented savagely on the rather unusual
distribution that South had for his opening bid.

South counter-attacked that his hand was essentially
balanced despite the six-card minor suit. Besides, what
about his 150 aces? With his singleton, North should
have known that they were in the slam zone if a fit
could be found, so it was up to him to move.

North said he wanted to move on to a new partner,
and called on me for support.

GOREN SETTLES THE ARGUMENT

**An opening bid of three notrump shows a bal-
anced hand of 25-27 points. Since the bid consumes a great amount of bidding space, thus
making it difficult to probe for the optimum contract, the bid should be avoided if the hand contains a good five-card suit. It should rarely be
employed when holding a six-card suit.**

If there is one lesson to be learned from the continued success of the Italian bidding methods, it is
how stultifying jump bids in notrump can be. The
perennial world champions almost never jump in notrump—they go out of their way to find some other bid.

This hand points up the reason why. South's hand is
worth 25 points for notrump purposes, but if a diamond fit can be found, the hand revalues to 32 points,
almost enough for a slam on its own! (You must add
3 points for the extra length.)

Had South made his natural bid of two diamonds,
slam could have been reached very quickly. Here is a
possible auction:

SOUTH	NORTH
2 ◇	2 NT
3 NT	4 ◇
6 ◇	

Also see: Argument 29.

ARGUMENT 29

When your partner has passed, can you relax the requirements for an opening three notrump bid?

THE HAND

```
                      NORTH
                      ♠ Q 8 5 4
                      ♡ 9 2
                      ◇ 7 4
                      ♣ J 6 4 3 2
      WEST                                EAST
      ♠ A 6                               ♠ J 10 9 3 2
      ♡ A Q 10 5 4 3                      ♡ J 8 7
      ◇ 10 5 3                            ◇ 6
      ♣ Q 9                               ♣ K 10 8 7
                      SOUTH
                      ♠ K 7
                      ♡ K 6
                      ◇ A K Q J 9 8 2
                      ♣ A 5
```

THE AUCTION

NORTH	EAST	SOUTH	WEST
Pass	Pass	1 ◇	1 ♡
Pass	2 ♡	3 NT	4 ♡
Pass	Pass	Dbl	Pass
Pass	Pass		

THE RESULT

The play was immaterial. The declarer guessed the location of the jack of clubs and picked up the king of hearts. He lost only one trick in each side suit, for an excellent score.

82

THE ARGUMENT

North was scathing in his denunciation of South's double. In his opinion, South's double was atrocious: the king of hearts was bound to be worthless, the long diamonds might be worth one trick—and maybe not that—and the king of spades was just a big if. South should have bid five diamonds over four hearts.

But, South claimed, with half the deck in his hand it was sheer bad luck that West made his contract. To bid five diamonds had to be wrong. How could he contract for eleven tricks opposite a partner who rated to have nothing? That was just asking to be doubled and then to go down two or three tricks.

GOREN SETTLES THE ARGUMENT

North was right about South's double. His double of four hearts was the height of optimism. However, I disagree with North's suggestion that his partner should have sacrificed in five diamonds.

South's approach to the hand was that of a short-order cook rather than a master chef. He abided rigidly by point count instead of using his imagination.

In theory, an opening bid of three notrump in third or fourth seat shows the same strength as in first or second seat, namely 25 to 27 high card points, but there is no law that says you cannot exercise your judgment once your partner has passed.

South's hand has eight running tricks, plus two kings. If either one of these kings is led up to, that would produce the ninth trick there and then. Though the high-card count is only 20, practical considerations dictate that a bid of three notrump must be the winning decision. Besides the probability that this would be a makeable contract, the bid has tremendous pre-emptive advantages. Note that in the hand under discussion,

West would be taking his life in his hands if he ventured into the auction over a three notrump opening.

But, you say, isn't there the danger that your partner, thinking you have 25 to 28 points, might leap to a slam that is unmakeable? Perhaps, if your partner treats the hand in a wooden manner and does nothing but count points.

A responder should bear in mind that the opener in third seat who calls three notrump might be making a tactical bid. Rather than leap directly to slam, a responder who holds enough points to bring the combined count to 33 should simply make the forward-going bid of four notrump, thus allowing his partner to pass and to get out of the auction at a makeable level.

Note that an opening bid of two diamonds would be an unsatisfactory solution to the problem. It would get North to keep the bidding open with a weak hand, but if he became the declarer at three notrump, it would expose both of South's major suit kings to what could be a damaging lead through.

I am not altogether unmindful of the fact that with a hand such as South has, he stands the chance of being sandbagged and macerated. West might open with a spade. If East holds the ace of spades, properly analyzes the position, and then shifts to hearts through South's king, the defense could run five or six or even seven tricks before South could catch his breath. But that is a chance South takes bidding three notrump with this type of hand—a chance that I think, on balance, will pay off.

Also see: Argument 28.

ARGUMENT 30

What are the proper responses to an opening "gambling" three notrump?

THE HAND

NORTH
♠ A K 9 8 2
♡ A K 7
♢ 10 6
♣ J 7 2

SOUTH
♠ 6
♡ Q 8 3
♢ A K Q J 7 5 4
♣ Q 5

THE AUCTION

SOUTH	WEST	NORTH	EAST
3 NT	Pass	6 NT	Pass
Pass	Pass		

THE RESULT

West led a club, and the defenders cashed their two tricks in the suit, and cheerfully conceded the rest of the tricks to the declarer.

Down one.

THE ARGUMENT

"If I knew you opened THAT sort of hand with a gambling three notrump bid, I would never have agreed to play the convention with you," barked North.

"If I thought for a moment you expected anything

more, I wouldn't have dreamed of asking you to play it," was South's retort courteous. The argument grew heated and only the promise of arbitration restored order.

GOREN SETTLES THE ARGUMENT

The difficulty here is that North and South are each talking from a different viewpoint. South was playing what is known as a weak gambling three notrump. In this convention, now generally accepted, the bidder holds a solid minor of seven cards or more, with hardly anything else. This bid has pre-emptive value.

Moreover, if the bidder happens to catch his partner with a smattering of high cards—let's say an ace in one suit, a king in another, possibly a queen-jack in a third suit—and the lead is favorable, it is quite possible that he can steal a hand and come home with nine tricks, against opponents who might have scored at least a partial in a major suit.

On its face, this kind of bid seems risky, but the fact is that it is fairly sound, for it is hedged with safeguards. Consider the following:

The proper responses to a gambling three notrump opening are:
1. **Bids of four hearts or four spades are natural, showing a good suit and a desire to play there.**
2. **Four clubs is an escape bid. It asks opener to pass if his suit is clubs, or to convert to diamonds if that is his suit.**
3. **Five clubs is similar, asking partner either to pass or convert to five diamonds.**
4. **Four notrump is Blackwood, but since opener has already promised the ace of his minor suit, he scales down his responses one step. Thus, five clubs shows one ace, five diamonds show two aces, etc.**
5. **Four diamonds is an idle bid. Some play that**

it requests opener to pass if his suit is diamonds, but to bid game if his suit is clubs. Such a bid might be useful on a hand including a singleton diamond and three or four clubs.

In the hand we're discussing, North believed that South was playing the *other* variety of gambling three notrump—the stronger variety—a solid seven-card minor with stoppers in two of the other three suits. The bidder is gambling that his partner can plug the other hole, and that he can bring home a game where his partner holds cards which he would deem insufficient to bid on.

Let us say the opener holds seven tricks in a minor suit, plus one outside ace. He might find his partner with one single lone ace floating in a sea of 3s, 4s, 6s and 7s, a miasma of garbage with no redeeming feature. Yet this dismal holding might be enough for the declarer to bring home nine tricks. Suppose the gambling three-notrumper's hand looks like this:

♠ K x
♥ A x
♦ A K Q J x x x
♣ x x

If this were the case, North would have been correct in jumping to a slam, for South would have to hold either the ace or king of clubs to justify his opening bid, along with a queen-jack of hearts or a queen-jack of spades.

Where partners have agreed on playing a strong gambling notrump, it is implicit that a three-notrump bid by third hand after his partner's pass foreswears all hope of slam. The three-notrump bidder is sticking his neck out just so far, and doesn't wish to be dragged up to rarefied heights.

CHAPTER 7

Responses to Opening Suit Bids of One

ARGUMENT 31

Should you ever pass your partner's opening bid of one club?

THE HAND

```
                NORTH
                ♠ A943
                ♡ 72
                ◊ K9
                ♣ AK863

WEST                            EAST
♠ Q10                           ♠ KJ762
♡ KQ105                         ♡ J96
◊ QJ85                          ◊ A63
♣ Q104                          ♣ J5

                SOUTH
                ♠ 85
                ♡ A843
                ◊ 10742
                ♣ 972
```

THE AUCTION

NORTH	EAST	SOUTH	WEST
1 ♣	Pass	1 ♡	Pass
1 ♠	Pass	Pass	Pass

THE RESULT

East led a low spade. The only tricks the declarer

made were the ace-king of clubs, the ace of hearts, and the ace of trumps.

Since North-South were vulnerable, the loss was 300 points.

THE ARGUMENT

North blamed South for the debacle. He felt that his partner should have taken him back to his first-bid suit.

South reminded North that they were playing five-card majors, and that he had no way of knowing whether North held five clubs or three. Moreover, he had done all he could by responding one heart—his holding certainly did not merit two bids.

GOREN SETTLES THE ARGUMENT

There is no doubt that South did all he could by responding one heart—in fact, far more than he should!

The fact that one plays five-card majors does not justify a response to an opening bid on sub-minimum values, simply because the responder holds four cards in one of the majors.

One should realize that the more cards he holds in a suit, the fewer his partner is likely to hold in that suit. Therefore, in the hand in question, it is far more likely that North will hold four spades rather than four hearts. South should have asked himself what he would do if North's second bid turns out to be one spade.

I cannot stress too often how important is this "principle of anticipation," both in opening the bidding and in responding. A legion of bridge crimes could be avoided if players just gave more thought to their *second* action, rather than just to their initial bid.

There is little need to fear the consequences of a pass to your partner's bid of one club. Just because you play five-card majors doesn't mean that your partner cannot have a club suit when he opens one club. Even if your right-hand opponent makes a takeout double, you should not run. If your left-hand opponent passes for penalties, your partner can redouble to ask you to rescue, if his club suit is indeed "short."

There are some types of hands where I would bid over my partner's one-club opening. For instance:

♠ x x x
♡ x x x x
♢ A x x x x
♣ x

It is perfectly safe to respond one diamond to your partner's opening bid of one club, as you are prepared to pass his rebid of one heart or one spade.

A simple change of suit by the opener at the one-level, or a simple rebid in a lower-ranking suit at the two-level, is not forcing.

Also see: Argument 32.

ARGUMENT 32

What is the absolute minimum holding with which one should respond to a one-bid?

THE HAND

```
                    NORTH
                    ♠ K 10 5 2
                    ♡ 10 6
                    ◊ A K 8
                    ♣ A K Q 4

    WEST                                EAST
    ♠ J 7                               ♠ Q 9 6
    ♡ K Q 7 3                           ♡ A 9 5 4
    ◊ J 7 2                             ◊ Q 10 9 4
    ♣ J 9 8 3                           ♣ 10 6

                    SOUTH
                    ♠ A 8 4 3
                    ♡ J 8 2
                    ◊ 6 5 3
                    ♣ 7 5 2
```

THE AUCTION

NORTH	EAST	SOUTH	WEST
1 ♣	Pass	1 ♠	Pass
4 ♠	Pass	Pass	Pass

THE RESULT

West led the king of hearts, and the declarer had but one chance for his contract—that the clubs would divide 3-3 so that he could sluff a diamond. Unfortunately, the actual distribution followed the odds, and the declarer lost one spade, two hearts, and a diamond.

THE ARGUMENT

"Why is it that every time I have a good hand I have to take a minus score?" ranted North. "Don't you know that you need 6 points to respond to an opening bid?"

"I held the master suit," protested South. "This was going to be the only chance to show it to you. Besides, my bid has pre-emptive value. Why didn't you content yourself with a raise to three spades? I would have gone on to game if I had anything!"

GOREN SETTLES THE ARGUMENT

Beware of making a shaded response on a hand that has no distributional assets. It leaves your side with little or no room to maneuver. As a rule of thumb, deduct 1 point from your count when you hold a balanced hand as a responder.

North could not afford to raise to only three spades. That bid would not be forcing, and as his hand revalued to 21 points in support of spades, he could not risk having his partner pass below game with a bare 5 or 6 points.

Whenever you respond to an opening bid, your partner is going to presume that you hold at least 6 points. If you do not have the values in high cards, you should have compensating distributional values.

I would not insist that you pass your partner's one club opening bid with:

♠ x x x
♡ K x x x x x
♢ x x x
♣ x

It is relatively safe to respond one heart. If your partner raises hearts, your hand has considerable trick-taking ability, and even four hearts should play quite well.

However, your partner is more likely to have spades than hearts. If he rebids one spade, you can afford to pass as you have three-card support for spades—it should be a better contract than clubs. At worst, your partner will rebid one notrump or bid his clubs again. This time, you have to pass, and hope for the best. If you are doubled at one notrump, you should retreat to two hearts.

Also see: Argument 31.

ARGUMENT 33

Does a raise to two in your partner's opening suit bid promise a holding of four trumps?

THE HAND

NORTH
♠ K 4
♡ J 10 8 6 3
◇ A Q 4
♣ K 7 6

WEST
♠ Q J 9 6 2
♡ 7 4
◇ J 8 5
♣ A 9 2

EAST
♠ A 10 7
♡ 9 5 2
◇ K 10
♣ Q J 8 5 3

SOUTH
♠ 8 5 3
♡ A K Q
◇ 9 7 6 3 2
♣ 10 4

THE AUCTION

NORTH	EAST	SOUTH	WEST
1 ♡	Pass	1 NT	Pass
Pass	Pass		

THE RESULT

West led the queen of spades. The declarer covered with the dummy's king, and East won the trick with his ace. The defenders proceeded to clear the spade suit, making five tricks.

West now led a low diamond. The queen was finessed and the king won. The diamond ten forced the ace. When West got on lead with the ace of clubs, he cashed the jack of diamonds.

94

Down two.
North-South could have made two hearts.

THE ARGUMENT

North was scornful of a player who would not raise partner when his support consisted of the three top trumps.

South insisted that, playing four-card majors, it was mandatory to hold four trumps to support the opening bid.

GOREN SETTLES THE ARGUMENT

This hand brings to mind a story about the late Fred Kaplan, one of this country's finer players, with high standards, and a low boiling point. He insisted that his partners should never raise him without four-card support.

Playing at his club one day, his partner gave him a single raise holding only the A-K-Q of trumps. Fred gazed intently at the dummy, pawed the cards for a moment, dug into his pocket, carefully placed his watch on the table in front of him, and remarked: "Partner, I give you just ten seconds to produce a fourth trump!"

This position is rather extreme. If you hold the three top cards in your partner's suit, you can bet your bottom dollar he holds a five-card suit—for without the ace, or king, or queen he cannot hold a biddable four card suit. Thus, the three master trumps constitute excellent support.

If you play four-card majors, you should have four-card trump support to raise your partner's opening bid. However, three trumps with a top honor furnish adequate trump support.

The responding partner who holds three trumps should at least hold the king in the suit. If he holds the queen and two small, he might get by, but a supporting bid is risky. Jack and two small must be considered shaded.

Yet there are even circumstances where one might have to raise his partner on a holding of only three low trumps. Consider this hand:

♠ 9 8 2
♥ A K J
♦ 8 7 6 5 4
♣ 6 3

Your partner opens the bidding with one spade. What do you do? Personally, I find it distasteful to respond one notrump with two suits unguarded and all my strength in one suit. I have three trumps and a ruffing value, so I prefer a raise to two spades. After all, just because we play four-card majors doesn't mean that my partner cannot hold five cards in the suit he opens. And if he does hold only four, we are unlikely to come to any great harm. Indeed, if my partner jumps to four spades, his strength in the other suits must be such that I would confidently expect him to make the contract, even if he held but four trumps.

ARGUMENT 34

Should a player ever bid a three-card suit in response to an opening suit bid?

THE HAND

```
                    NORTH
                    ♠ A K J 9
                    ♡ 9 5
                    ◇ K J 5
                    ♣ J 10 8 6

WEST                                    EAST
♠ Q 7                                   ♠ 10 5 4
♡ A 10 6 4 3                            ♡ K J 7
◇ 10 9 7 2                              ◇ Q 6 3
♣ Q 2                                   ♣ A 7 4 3

                    SOUTH
                    ♠ 8 6 3 2
                    ♡ Q 8 2
                    ◇ A 8 4
                    ♣ K 9 5
```

THE AUCTION

NORTH	EAST	SOUTH	WEST
1 ♣	Pass	1 NT	Pass
Pass	Pass		

THE RESULT

West led a low heart, and the defenders took five tricks in the suit. Later in the play, the declarer finessed in clubs, and as a result lost two tricks in the suit.

The contract failed by one trick. North-South could have made nine tricks in spades.

THE ARGUMENT

North was quick to insist that South's correct response to his one-club opening bid was the cheapest bid of one spade—not one notrump.

South argued that Goren in his book stated that on a balanced hand of 9 to 11 points—exactly what he held—the proper response to a one-club opening bid is one notrump. Besides, South insisted, his spade suit was not biddable.

North retorted that this style of bidding went out with the ark. The modern approach was to respond one spade. His remarks about players who went by the book were hardly complimentary.

South suggested North should have opened one spade —his club suit was anything but robust, whereas his spades were excellent.

North countered that a two-heart response would then leave him in an awkward position. If South hadn't bid one spade over the one-club opening, he was denying a holding of four cards in the spade suit. Therefore, there was no purpose in North introducing that suit at any further point in the auction.

GOREN SETTLES THE ARGUMENT

A response of one notrump over an opening one club is never made if the responder holds a four-card major.

That does not mean that I endorse a one-spade response on the hand shown. No matter what modern bidding scientists say, I find it unappetizing to respond one spade on a suit headed by the 8. I realize that this has become mandatory with those who espouse the initial opening of a major suit only if it is at least five cards long, but that does not make such a bid any more appealing to me.

I realize full well that this leaves me with a problem

with the South hand. However, I do have a solution—
one that requires judgment rather than mere rote. As I
have to tell a little white lie about my hand, I would
choose to "miscount" the length of one of my suits.
Accordingly, I would pretend that I have four diamonds, and simply respond one diamond as a waiting
bid. This solution would be most appropriate on the
hand shown, for North would then bid one spade, and
I could raise to two spades.

I have several sound reasons for disliking to bid a
bad suit when I have a weak hand: It is frequently
pointless to do so unless my partner himself can introduce that suit into the auction. In many cases, it might
be advantageous to have my partner—the opening
bidder and therefore the stronger hand—as the declarer, *with the lead coming up to him.* Also, the contract might be more difficult to defend if the stronger
hand is concealed.

There are many occasions where the bid of the next
suit can solve the responder's problems on awkward
holdings.

Here is another example:

♠ x x
♡ A K x
◇ x x x
♣ x x x x x

Your partner opens the bidding with one diamond.
You do not have the values for a bid at the two-level
in your best suits, clubs, yet you have to respond. If
you were to select one notrump, very few would quib-
ble. Yet, in many ways, a response of one heart is far
more descriptive of your holding. It pinpoints where
your strength is for lead-directing purposes, and is unlikely to come to serious harm.

Suppose your partner were to raise you to two
hearts. He would almost certainly have four trumps,
and you would be playing a 4-3 fit—or "Moysian" fit,
as it has become known, after the late *Bridge World*

editor, Sonny Moyse, who wrote several articles on its advantages. If you have to take any spade ruffs, you will be doing so in the short trump hand. A contract of two hearts should present no great problem.

ARGUMENT 35

Which is the more encouraging response to an opening bid: a bid of one notrump or a single raise of your partner's suit?

THE HAND

```
                    NORTH
                    ♠ A Q 9 5 2
                    ♡ K J 4
                    ◇ K J 6 2
                    ♣ 6
      WEST                              EAST
      ♠ 10 7 3                         ♠ J 4
      ♡ 9 5 3                          ♡ A 10 6
      ◇ 10 8 3                         ◇ Q 9 5 4
      ♣ A K J 7                        ♣ Q 8 3 2
                    SOUTH
                    ♠ K 8 6
                    ♡ Q 8 7 2
                    ◇ A 7
                    ♣ 10 9 5 4
```

THE AUCTION

NORTH	EAST	SOUTH	WEST
1 ♠	Pass	1 NT	Pass
2 ◇	Pass	2 ♠	Pass
Pass	Pass		

THE RESULT

The declarer came to ten tricks simply by ruffing one diamond in the dummy.

THE ARGUMENT

North launched the attack: "With a fit for both my suits, could you do no better than give me a simple preference? How do you expect to win if you bid so meekly?"

South launched her own assault by pointing out tartly that she held a balanced hand and that North had made a minimum rebid.

GOREN SETTLES THE ARGUMENT

In theory, South has a perfect notrump response to an opening bid of one spade: a balanced hand and 9 points, with only three-card support for her partner's suit. However, there is more to responding to an opening bid than finding a category into which your hand fits neatly.

A responder should always strive to make that response most likely to encourage his partner. While a single raise of your partner's suit and a response of one notrump show hands of roughly the same strength, the simple raise is apt to be more encouraging, and should therefore be preferred wherever possible.

Once a fit has been located, the opener will revalue his hand in the light of the additional information he has received. Such revaluation will often allow him to jump straight to game, or to make a game try in some other suit.

In this case, South should have realized that her K-x-x in spades were important cards. Her partner would prefer to hear about the values in that suit, rather than merely to learn that South's hand was balanced with 6 to 10 points. In addition, South's doubleton diamond gave her a ruffing value with spades as trumps, and so the hand could play a trick better in the suit than at notrump.

After a two-spade response, North can, in the light of his five-card trump holding and his 15 points, probe with three spades. Now South, unconcerned about the trump situation, would reconsider her 11 points, and bid the game.

Note that those who adhere to bidding only five-card major would have little trouble with this hand —the raise to two spades on the South hand would be automatic.

South might also have drawn a further inference from her partner's bids; that North, having shown two suits, was unlikely to have many cards in the unbid suits. Also, missing the king of spades and the ace of diamonds, North probably had some high-card values in clubs and hearts, or a counter-balancing singleton or void.

Also see: Argument 44.

ARGUMENT 36

Should the responder bid the higher-ranking of two suits equal in length?

THE HAND

```
                     NORTH
                     ♠ A 7 4
                     ♡ K J 5
                     ◇ A K 10 3
                     ♣ K Q 5
     WEST                              EAST
     ♠ Q 10 6 5                        ♠ 9 2
     ♡ 6 3                             ♡ A 9 8 2
     ◇ 9 6 4                           ◇ J 8 5 2
     ♣ A 10 8 4                        ♣ 9 7 3
                     SOUTH
                     ♠ K J 8 3
                     ♡ Q 10 7 4
                     ◇ Q 7
                     ♣ J 6 2
```

THE AUCTION

NORTH	EAST	SOUTH	WEST
1 ◇	Pass	1 ♠	Pass
2 NT	Pass	3 ♡	Pass
4 ♠	Pass	Pass	Pass

THE RESULT

The trump position was rather unlucky. The declarer had to lose two trump tricks in addition to the two side-suit aces he was missing.

Down one.

THE ARGUMENT

North watched the play with polite amazement. When the result was scored, she mentioned that three notrump would have been a superior contract.

South felt that North should have been content to raise to three spades, since she held only three-card support.

North retorted that South's bidding had shown an unbalanced hand, and that three spades would have been a gross underbid that might have resulted in a missed slam—after all, nearly all her points were in prime controls.

GOREN SETTLES THE ARGUMENT

When your partner opens the bidding with one of a minor suit and you hold four cards in each major, it is generally proper to respond in the lower-ranking one—hearts—regardless of the comparative strength of the two suits. This virtually insures reaching a 4-4 fit if there is one, for your partner can bid one spade over one heart if he holds four spades.

This accords with the theory of the cheapest response. With more than one four-card suit, usually respond in your lowest-ranking suit.

Abiding by that principle, if your first response is in spades and you bid hearts on your next turn, you are showing longer spades than hearts—probably five spades and four hearts—but it could even be six spades and four hearts.

The principle of bidding the lower of two four-card majors always applies when the responding hand is not worth two forward-going bids; that is, when the responder has an average hand or worse.

I can visualize instances where one might want to depart from this principle. Consider this holding:

♠ K Q J x
♡ A Q 9 x
◇ x x x
♣ x x

Your partner opens the bidding with one diamond. If you respond one heart and your partner rebids one notrump, you cannot be sure what to do. Certainly, the hand is worth an effort toward game, but how would you go about it?

If you raise to two notrump and your partner goes on to game, there might be a killing weakness in the club suit. This could easily be a hand where a 4-3 fit in a major suit might play better than notrump.

To allow for that possibility, an original response of one spade might lead to a smoother auction. Over your partner's rebid, you can then show your hearts. True, your partner might expect to find you with five spades, but the quality of your suit is compensation.

Also see: Arguments 38, 41.

ARGUMENT 37

When should the responder prefer a double raise to a bid in a new suit?

THE HAND

NORTH
- ♠ Q J 10
- ♡ A Q J 7 3
- ◇ Q 3
- ♣ Q 10 6

WEST
- ♠ A 6 3 2
- ♡ 8 5
- ◇ 6 2
- ♣ A 8 7 4 2

EAST
- ♠ K 9 5 4
- ♡ 6 4
- ◇ J 10 9 8
- ♣ K J 3

SOUTH
- ♠ 8 7
- ♡ K 10 9 2
- ◇ A K 7 5 4
- ♣ 9 5

THE AUCTION

NORTH	EAST	SOUTH	WEST
1 ♡	Pass	2 ◇	Pass
2 ♡	Pass	4 ♡	Pass
Pass	Pass		

THE RESULT

East led the four of spades. The defenders took the ace and king of spades and had no problem finding the killing club shift. Two tricks there spelled a one-trick defeat for the contract.

107

THE ARGUMENT

North maintained that South should not have bid more than three hearts on his second turn.

South held that North, loaded with "quacks," a term often used by those desiring to impress others —"quacks" means queens and jacks—should have elected to rebid two notrump. South said that a contract of three notrump might have made, as East would probably have led a spade. Unless the defenders found the club shift in a hurry, the declarer would have had his nine tricks.

A friendship of 30 years seemed likely to bend, if not break, on the rocks of a game of cards, and my moderating influence was requested.

GOREN SETTLES THE ARGUMENT

I do not have a twinge of doubt in rendering this verdict.

The fault lies not in either player's rebid, but rather, in South's initial response of two diamonds. For one thing, South held ample support for his partner's opening major suit bid. Why didn't he support it? *Quo vadis?* Where was he going? Was his hand that powerful that he could immediately go looking for slam?

In support of hearts, South's hand is worth 13 points —10 points in high cards, 1 point for each doubleton, and 1 point extra in the trump suit for revaluing an honor in his partner's suit.

The way to show a hand strong enough to open the bidding and containing a four-card fit for your partner's major is to double raise the opening bid.

South's correct response was three hearts. North would then raise to game.

However, I would guess that, on this sequence, four hearts would be made. With nothing to go on, East would almost surely lead the jack of diamonds. The declarer would need no more. He can establish the diamond suit with the help of one ruff, and obtain two discards. Thus, his losses would be limited to three tricks in the black suits.

South's fault was that he ignored a basic precept. When there is one bid that accurately describes your hand, make it.

South indulged in a needless excursion when he introduced his diamond suit. That bid simply did his side no good. Instead, it warned an opponent off a lead that would have been helpful to the declarer.

To translate South's action into more mundane terms: It is rather like taking a short cut from New York to Miami by way of Los Angeles!

ARGUMENT 38

Holding two suits of unequal length, which suit should the responder bid first?

THE HAND

```
                        NORTH
                        ♠ 7 4 3
                        ♡ A K Q 9 5
                        ◇ 7 6
                        ♣ A J 9
    WEST                                    EAST
    ♠ Q 9 5 2                               ♠ 10 8
    ♡ 10 3                                  ♡ J 8 6 4
    ◇ K Q 8 4 3                             ◇ A J 10 2
    ♣ 10 7                                  ♣ 8 4 3
                        SOUTH
                        ♠ A K J 6
                        ♡ 7 2
                        ◇ 9 5
                        ♣ K Q 6 5 2
```

THE AUCTION

NORTH	EAST	SOUTH	WEST
1 ♡	Pass	1 ♠	Pass
2 ♡	Pass	3 ♣	Pass
4 ♠	Pass	Pass	Pass

THE RESULT

The defenders started off with two diamond tricks and then shifted to a heart. The fate of the contract hinged on the trump suit. Even when the trump finesse failed, all was not lost. A 3-3 division would still have allowed the declarer to get home with the loss of two diamond tricks and a trump trick.

However, the odds favored a 4-2 division, and so it turned out. A second trump trick had to be lost.

Down one.

THE ARGUMENT

"I suppose that's one of your new-fangled ideas," exploded North. "In the old days, we used to bid five-card suits before we bid four-carders, not the other way round."

South tried to explain that he was trying to keep the bidding low by first showing spades at the one-level.

But North was on his favorite subject of comparing the "scientists" of today with the "artists" of yesterday. No matter how much South tried to explain his logic, North merely kept on railing against the modernists.

GOREN SETTLES THE ARGUMENT

At the risk of appearing like an old fuddy-duddy, I am going to side most emphatically with North: South's first bid should have been two clubs, his five-card suit.

It seems to be common practice, particularly with players who favor five-card majors, to respond in a four-card major suit at the first opportunity. They appear to have an inherent fear of missing the right contract if they fail to show a major suit at the first opportunity. In their eagerness to avoid missing the 4-4 major fit, they sometimes miss the hand.

The answer to the question of which suit a responder should bid first depends on the strength of the responding hand, not on whether it is a major suit or minor suit. On a good responding hand, a responder can afford to bid naturally: he can show his longer suit first, and then later show his shorter suit. Economy of space becomes a factor only when the responding hand is not good enough for *two* forward-going bids.

As an example, let's change the responder's holdings to:

♠ A J x x
♡ x x
◇ x x
♣ K x x x x

Assume the bidding is opened with one heart. The above hand is not good enough for two bids. South has to decide between two clubs and one spade. However, the strength of the hand and the quality of the suit are not quite good enough for a two-over-one response. Two clubs is out. The response of one spade is recommended.

Wherever possible, bid naturally. If you do decide to distort the picture either of the strength of your hand or the shape of your hand, you should have a very strong reason for doing so. Just a whim is not enough!

Note that in the hand before the bar, five clubs would make with careful play. The declarer cashes the club king and leads to the dummy's ace. When trumps divide, two high hearts are cashed, and a low heart is ruffed with the club queen. The club jack serves as a re-entry to the dummy, at the same time drawing the enemy's last trump. Now two discards are available for the declarer's losing spades. So South loses only two diamond tricks in all.

Also see: Argument 36.

ARGUMENT 39

Does a jump shift absolutely guarantee support for your partner's opening suit?

THE HAND

NORTH
♠ A K 7 6 3
♡ 9 5
♢ 7 2
♣ A 6 5 4

SOUTH
♠ 8
♡ A Q J 4
♢ A K J 4 3
♣ Q 8 3

THE AUCTION

NORTH	EAST	SOUTH	WEST
1 ♠	Pass	3 ♢	Pass
3 ♠	Pass	4 ♡	Pass
4 ♠	Pass	Pass	Pass

THE RESULT

Trumps behaved well, dividing 4-3. Nevertheless, the declarer lost two trump tricks and two clubs, for down one.

The best spot for North-South was three notrump.

THE ARGUMENT

North compared South to the game fish that gave up the sprat in favor of a tasty mackerel, only to find himself on the angler's hook. He maintained that South

113

was so impressed by the large reward given to a slam
that he overlooked the small profit of a game, and ended
up with a loss. The hand, it was clear, he bellowed, was
a potential misfit, and South did not allow him to get
out at any point. The veriest beginner knew that a
jump shift promised at least a partial fit in the opener's
suit.

South declared that he had never heard such rub-
bish. His hand was worth 19 points, and the only way
to show such strength was to jump shift.

GOREN SETTLES THE ARGUMENT

Let me disillusion South; his hand was not worth
19 points in my book. His singleton was a singleton in
his partner's suit. To assign a full 2 points to that
singleton so early in the auction—before a fit has
been located—is the height of optimism.

However, that doesn't mean that I wholeheartedly
endorse North's point of view that a jump shift absolutely guarantees trump support.

**You should jump shift on any hand where you
can visualize slam possibilities the moment your
partner opens the bidding.**

On the South hand, there is no way that the responder can start thinking in terms of slam, because
of his shortness in his partner's suit. Neither is his own
suit self-sustaining. To make the game in diamonds, he
requires trump help in his partner's hand.

Let us rearrange the cards slightly, to make the
hand:

♠ x
♡ A K Q 10 x
◇ A K J 9 x
♣ x x

Now there is a good chance for slam if the opener
holds a modicum of support for either hearts or dia-

monds. The only way to get the message across is with an immediate jump shift to three hearts, despite the singleton spade.

With a very solid long suit, I would even relax the rule of 19 points. Consider this hand:

> ♠ x
> ♡ A K Q J x x x
> ◇ A x x
> ♣ x x

Even opposite a one-spade opening bid, this hand does not require much to make a slam. South's heart suit is completely solid, and as little as two aces and a king in the opener's hand would make a slam a near laydown. If you do not immediately jump shift to three hearts with a hand like this, you will never be able to convey to your partner the tremendous trick-taking potential of your hand.

The rule, therefore, would shape up like this:

A responder's jump shift indicates (1) A strong hand of no less than 14 high card points with a solid suit of no less than seven cards in length headed by top honors; or (2) A strong hand of no less than 19 points in playing strength with good support in one's partner's trump suit; or (3) A strong two-suited hand of no less than 17 points in high card strength.

ARGUMENT 40

When a responder has previously passed, is his jump shift forcing?

THE HAND

```
                    NORTH
                    ♠ A K 10 6 2
                    ♡ A 8 3
                    ◇ 9 5
                    ♣ K 9 4

    WEST                                EAST
    ♠ Q                                 ♠ 7 4
    ♡ K J 9 6 2                         ♡ Q 10 5 4
    ◇ Q 8 3                             ◇ 7 6
    ♣ J 10 6 3                          ♣ A Q 8 7 2

                    SOUTH
                    ♠ J 9 8 5 3
                    ♡ 7
                    ◇ A K J 10 4 2
                    ♣ 5
```

THE AUCTION

SOUTH	WEST	NORTH	EAST
Pass	Pass	1 ♠	Pass
4 ♠	Pass	Pass	Pass

THE RESULT

When the dummy came down, North moaned in anguish. East had led a heart. The declarer raked in all thirteen tricks.

THE ARGUMENT

"How can you pass with a hand like that?" he

116

screamed. "By any system that's 13 points and two defensive tricks. In addition, the offensive potential of the hand is awesome. Had you opened the bidding, there was no way we would have stopped short of six spades."

South was not too happy with the result, but he was quick on the trigger. He claimed that, as he was a passed hand, no bid he made could be forcing, so unless he bid game, even that result might not have been reached.

Opinion at the table was divided as to whether or not South should have opened. But the consensus was that there was no way to reach slam unless South opened the bidding—a claim I was asked to verify.

GOREN SETTLES THE ARGUMENT

In the days when I used to play rubber bridge, I never held such good cards that I could afford to pass a hand like South's. In my book, South should surely have opened. However, to each his own. It is to the contention that there was no way to get to slam that I want to address myself.

A jump shift by a passed hand shows a hand of near opening strength in the bid suit, plus a fit for one's partner's suit. The bid is forcing to at least the level of three in the opener's suit.

Thus, South could have created a forcing situation by a jump shift to three diamonds. As this bid would also show spade support, North would probably jump to four spades to show a better than minimum hand. Three spades might conceivably be passed.

The ball would now be in South's court. If he had courage, he would first try Blackwood, and then jump to six spades when North showed two aces.

Alternatively, he could have tried five spades.

To think that all this back-and-forth folderol could have been avoided by the simple expedient of opening the bidding!

ARGUMENT 41

Holding two five-card suits, which should the responder bid first?

THE HAND

```
                        NORTH
                        ♠ 8
                        ♡ K 9 5
                        ◇ A K Q 10 9 8
                        ♣ Q 10 5
        WEST                                EAST
        ♠ Q 7 3                             ♠ A J 6 2
        ♡ Q J 4                             ♡ 8 3
        ◇ 5 3                               ◇ 7 6 4 2
        ♣ K 9 8 3 2                         ♣ A 7 6
                        SOUTH
                        ♠ K 10 9 5 4
                        ♡ A 10 7 6 2
                        ◇ J
                        ♣ J 4
```

THE AUCTION

NORTH	EAST	SOUTH	WEST
1 ◇	Pass	1 ♡	Pass
3 ◇	Pass	3 ♠	Pass
4 ♡	Pass	Pass	Pass

THE RESULT

The declarer lost three tricks in the black suits, and a trump trick for down one.

THE ARGUMENT

North felt his partner was to blame for missing their side's best contract of three notrump. He maintained that South had bid his suits in the wrong order, and as a result he had expected a far stronger hand.

South claimed to be following the principles espoused by one Charles Goren. All he was doing was bidding his suits "up the line"—that is, the lowest ranking first—therefore, no blame should attach to him for the disaster.

GOREN SETTLES THE ARGUMENT

I do not know where my correspondent gets the idea that I advocate responding on mediocre hands in the lower of two equal-length major suits. Certainly this is the case with two four-card majors, but not with two major suits of five cards each or longer.

When the responder holds two major suits, both of them longer than four cards, he should apply the same principles he would apply in choosing the suit were he the opening bidder. With two equal-length major suits of at least five cards, respond in the high-ranking suit first.

Let's see how that would work on the hand sent in by our reader. After North's one-diamond opening, South responds one spade. North now might not deem his hand worth a three-diamond rebid. But even if he does, South has a comfortable three-heart rebid. When North elects to bid three notrump, South should refrain from bidding four hearts to show that he is 5-5. His minor honors in clubs and diamonds should prove useful in a notrump contract. Quite likely, North has a running diamond suit to contribute most of the nine tricks needed for the notrump game.

Also see: Argument 36.

ARGUMENT 42

Is a bid of four notrump always Blackwood?

THE HAND

```
                    NORTH
                    ♠ K 3
                    ♡ Q 7
                    ◇ A Q 8 7 3
                    ♣ K 8 4 2
WEST                                    EAST
♠ Q 9 8 4 2                             ♠ J 7 6
♡ 10 5                                  ♡ A J 6 4 3
◇ J 10 2                                ◇ 6 5
♣ 10 6 3                                ♣ 9 7 5
                    SOUTH
                    ♠ A 10 5
                    ♡ K 9 8 2
                    ◇ K 9 4
                    ♣ A Q J
```

THE AUCTION

NORTH	EAST	SOUTH	WEST
1 ◇	Pass	1 ♡	Pass
1 NT	Pass	4 NT	Pass
Pass	Pass		

THE RESULT

This proved to be less than the optimum contract, for twelve tricks were made rather easily.

THE ARGUMENT

South sailed in to the attack. "I thought every bridge player had heard of the Blackwood convention! Partner, when I ask you for aces, you just tell me how

120

many you have. I'll see to it that we land in the right spot."

"It is a sad comment on your bridge education if you think that your bid was Blackwood," replied North. "As far as I am concerned—and indeed that goes for anyone who plays bridge—your bid was a quantitative raise in notrump."

The discussion became acrimonious, my correspondent says, and it was decided to send the case to me.

GOREN SETTLES THE ARGUMENT

North is absolutely right.

Unless a suit has been agreed upon, either specifically in the auction or implicitly, a jump to four notrump is a quantitative raise in notrump and not a request for partner to show his aces. Such a bid requests one's partner to bid six notrump, if he has maximum values for his previous bidding.

Under these circumstances, North was correct to pass four notrump, for though he had 14 points and a five-card suit, he did not have so much as a 10 or 9 to give his hand some body.

Had South wanted to ask for aces, he should have used the Gerber Convention.

In the Gerber Convention, a jump to four clubs over one's partner's notrump bid requests him to show aces by steps, in the same way as in Blackwood.

There is a bid available that describes South's hand exactly.

A jump response of three notrump directly after an opening suit bid of one shows a perfectly balanced hand (4-3-3-3 in shape) with 16 to 18 points.

Because this bid paints such a vivid picture of the

holding, it should be preferred to showing a major suit. This is one of the few cases where a major suit should be suppressed in favor of a notrump bid.

Had South elected to bid three notrump at his first turn, North would undoubtedly have moved toward slam. With an announced fit for both his suits, North's wealth of controls and distributional values should make slam appear attractive, and a four-club bid would be recommended.

ARGUMENT 43

With a very good balanced hand, do you support your partner's opening bid or jump in notrump?

THE HAND

```
                    NORTH
                    ♠ K 9 3
                    ♡ 6 3
                    ◇ K 4 2
                    ♣ A K 9 5 2

    WEST                                EAST
    ♠ J 7 2                             ♠ Q 10 6 5
    ♡ A 9 8 5 4                         ♡ J 7 2
    ◇ A 9 5                             ◇ J 10 8 3
    ♣ 8 3                               ♣ 7 4

                    SOUTH
                    ♠ A 8 4
                    ♡ K Q 10
                    ◇ Q 7 6
                    ♣ Q J 10 6
```

THE AUCTION

NORTH	EAST	SOUTH	WEST
1 ♣	Pass	3 ♣	Pass
5 ♣	Pass	Pass	Pass

THE RESULT

East led a spade. By finessing the ten of hearts, the declarer managed to obtain a spade discard. However, he still had to lose two diamonds and the ace of hearts.
  Down one.

THE ARGUMENT

North rose from the table and bellowed: "How come we're in a ridiculous club game? We can't lose three notrump!"

"How come we're in a ridiculous club game?" retorted South. "Because you bid it, that's why! Had you simply responded either three diamonds or three spades to show a stopper, I would have converted to three notrump."

"In the days when I learned to play bridge, your proposed sequence of bidding would have shown a strong two-suited hand," sneered North. "The fact is that you held a balanced hand, with 14 points in high cards, and stoppers—in—every—suit! Your proper bid was two notrump. Opposite my dead-minimum of 13 points, together we hold 27 points in high cards. Couldn't you see we had a cold three notrump?"

"And suppress my excellent fit for your suit?"

Shortly before matters reached a stage of pistols at sunrise, the argument was referred to me.

GOREN SETTLES THE ARGUMENT

South is all wet—or perhaps I should say far at sea. Holding between 13 and 15 points, and with all suits covered, the responder should have bid two notrump —not three in a minor.

With a perfectly balanced hand in the 13 to 15 point range, a response of two notrump to an opening minor suit bid of one is most descriptive.

Facing an opening bid, a response of two notrump is forcing. Such a hand is strong enough to open the bidding. The same is true if the responder gives the opener's suit a double raise.

What differentiates the two bids? Generally, a jump raise of one's partner's suit is made on hands that have a ruffing value—hands that are slightly unbalanced. I

would have more sympathy for South's bid if his hand
were set up as follows:

       ♠ A x
       ♡ K Q 10
       ◇ Q x x x
       ♣ Q J 10 x

Note that with this hand, five clubs stands a fair chance
of success. If the heart ace is onside or the finesse of
the 10 of hearts works, the declarer will be able to
discard a diamond on a high heart, and thus limit his
losers to the two missing aces.

When the fit is in a major suit, there is more justification for a double raise. To make game at notrump,
you need to take nine tricks. For game at a major
suit, you need ten tricks, and the 4-4 or better fit in the
major generally produces at least one trick more in a
suit contract than at notrump.

ARGUMENT 44

What is the minimum strength required to respond in a new suit at the two-level rather than raise your partner's opening bid?

THE HAND

```
                    NORTH
                    ♠ Q 9 3
                    ♡ K Q J 8 7
                    ◇ Q 6 4
                    ♣ A 5
WEST                                    EAST
♠ K 10 7 2                              ♠ A J 8 4
♡ 5 4 2                                 ♡ 10 3
◇ 10 2                                  ◇ K 9 5
♣ Q 10 8 7                              ♣ K 9 4 3
                    SOUTH
                    ♠ 6 5
                    ♡ A 9 6
                    ◇ A J 8 7 3
                    ♣ J 6 2
```

THE AUCTION

NORTH	EAST	SOUTH	WEST
1 ♡	Pass	2 ◇	Pass
2 ♡	Pass	3 ♡	Pass
4 ♡	Pass	Pass	Pass

THE RESULT

East led a low club. The declarer had no play for his contract. Even though the king of diamonds was onside and the finesse for it succeeded, the declarer was forced to concede two spade tricks, and a trick in each minor suit.

Down one.

THE ARGUMENT

"You never stopped bidding your minimum," cried South viciously. "I guess you would have been looking for a slam, had you held another jack!"

"You were not shy, either," shot back North. "I think you promoted your jack of clubs to a king— that's the only justification I can find for *your* bidding."

GOREN SETTLES THE ARGUMENT

I find South at fault.

It is often a close decision whether to bid your own suit at the two-level or to raise your partner's suit. On the hand in question, South held 11 points if diamonds were the trump suit; yet his hand counted only 10 points in support of hearts. Though you add 1 point for the doubleton spade, you must deduct 1 point because the hand is flawed—it has only three-card trump support.

Is the South hand good enough to make two bids? There is a simple guideline to follow.

If the responder's hand is above average strength —11 or 12 points—it is too strong for a single raise over the opener's bid of one. Such a hand is worth two bids.

South's hand, we have seen, is worth only 10 points in support of hearts. It, therefore, rates only one bid— a raise to two hearts.

A raise of your partner's suit will cause him to re-value his hand, and will encourage him to bid again, if there is a chance for game.

Conversely, where the responder's raise is minimal, the prudent opener who himself has initiated the bidding with a minimum holding will hear loud and clear that the chances of making game do not exist.

Let us change South's hand slightly, and make it:

♠ x
♡ A x x x
◊ A 10 x x x
♣ x x x

Now South's hand is worth 11 points in hearts (8 points in high cards and 3 for the singleton spade). The hand is now too good for a single raise, yet not strong enough for a jump raise. South can show such a hand by responding two diamonds, then supporting hearts on his next turn. Note that although we have removed 2 points in high cards from South's hand, making four hearts now depends only on limiting the diamond losers to one.

On the actual hand, North was quite right, on the bidding, to proceed to four hearts. According to South's bidding, the combined total count of the two hands was at least 26 points. In addition, North's diamond fit improved his hand.

Also see: Argument 35.

ARGUMENT 45

When do you jump to game in response to an opening bid of one?

THE HAND

```
                    NORTH
                    ♠ J 7 4 2
                    ♡ A K 9 5 4
                    ◇ A 8 3
                    ♣ J

WEST                                    EAST
♠ A 9 8 3                               ♠ K Q 10 5
♡ J                                     ♡ 6
◇ K 10 7 6 2                            ◇ Q J 4
♣ Q 9 6                                 ♣ K 10 7 3 2

                    SOUTH
                    ♠ 6
                    ♡ Q 10 8 7 3 2
                    ◇ 9 5
                    ♣ A 8 5 4
```

THE AUCTION

NORTH	EAST	SOUTH	WEST
1 ♡	Pass	2 ♡	Pass
Pass	Pass		

THE RESULT

North had no trouble making eleven tricks.

THE ARGUMENT

No sooner had the dummy hit the table than North exploded: "Your weak, namby-pamby single raise lost us an easy game. You should have, at least, bid three hearts."

South sat back and let the storm roll over her. She then quietly explained: "Even revaluing my hand in support of hearts, and giving me 3 points for my singleton, my hand is still worth only 10 points. That's all I have. A raise to three hearts would show a full opening bid, and I'm a long way off from that."

North and South continued to argue about the merits of two hearts versus three hearts. To stop the furore and get the game on the rails again, the players decided to refer the matter to me.

GOREN SETTLES THE ARGUMENT

South was guilty of over-dedication to the point count. She was technically correct in claiming that her hand was worth a maximum raise to two hearts. What South failed to take into account was the trick-taking capacity of her hand, and its lack of defensive power.

An immediate jump to game—four hearts over an opener's one heart—is not a strength-showing bid. It is a pre-emptive action.

There are those who erroneously maintain that the jump to four is even stronger than a raise to three, and that such a jump invites partner to go on to slam. I unqualifiedly disagree.

Let me point out that a bid of three hearts would be entirely out of order.

A raise to three in a major suit over an opening bid of one in that suit shows at least 12 points and implies that the responder holds the equivalent of an opening bid. Such a bid is forcing to game.

The reason a responder immediately bids four is twofold: (1) to shut out opposition bidding; and (2) to discourage slam exploration.

ARGUMENT 46

Can a double raise of your partner's opening suit bid be played as non-forcing?

THE HAND

NORTH
♠ 10 3
♡ A Q 9 7
◇ K 5 4
♣ A 4 2

SOUTH
♠ A 9 5 4
♡ K 10 4 3
◇ Q 9 8
♣ J 7

THE AUCTION

NORTH	EAST	SOUTH	WEST
1 ♡	Pass	3 ♡	Pass
4 ♡	Pass	Pass	Pass

THE RESULT

North lost a spade, two diamonds, and a club. Down one.

THE ARGUMENT

South asserted that North had no business going on to game holding a minimum opening. "My bid of three hearts said that I thought we could make nine tricks if you had no better than 13 or 14 points," he argued.

North protested vociferously that a jump raise was forcing the game.

"Back in the time of the ark, it might have been," responded South. "The modern trend is to play it as a limit bid, and I believe everyone now plays it that way."

GOREN SETTLES THE ARGUMENT

I fear that South is going to be a greatly disappointed man. Not everyone, even in these super-scientific days, plays a jump raise of the opener's suit as a limit bid. There are legions of players, from internationalists down to neophytes, who still play that a double raise in a suit is forcing to game.

The limit raise is not new to bridge. Until 1934, when it was displaced by the forcing jump raise, the limit raise was part of the original Culbertson System. The word "limit" accurately describes this kind of raise.

The limit raise is not forcing but highly encouraging. The opener is expected to pass with a minimum. The normal range for the bid is 9 to 11 points, including distribution. The bid guarantees at least four-card support in the trump suit (even if the partnership has agreed to only bid five-card majors).

Below are minimum and maximum hands for a limit jump raise of an opening one heart bid:

	[A]		[B]
♠	A x x x	♠	A x x x
♡	K x x x	♡	K x x x
◇	x x x x	◇	J x
♣	x	♣	Q J x

Besides its descriptive value, the bid also has considerable merit as a pre-emptive maneuver. On most hands where the opener passes the limit raise and fails to fulfill his contract, the opponents are likely to have passed up a more profitable spot for themselves.

However, a limit raise is not the sort of bid to spring on one's partner as a surprise.

A limit raise is a convention that must be discussed before you start to play. The vast majority of players still use a forcing jump raise.

Lacking prior agreement, North was quite correct in assuming that his partner was playing the bid in the generally accepted style.

ARGUMENT 47

How does the responder evaluate a singleton in the opener's suit?

THE HAND

```
                    NORTH
                    ♠ A 9 4
                    ♡ A K Q 6 5
                    ◇ 7
                    ♣ 10 9 5 4
    WEST                            EAST
    ♠ K 10                          ♠ Q J 6 5 2
    ♡ J 8 4 3 2                     ♡ 10 7
    ◇ A Q 10 4                      ◇ 9 3
    ♣ Q 2                           ♣ K 8 7 6
                    SOUTH
                    ♠ 8 7 3
                    ♡ 9
                    ◇ K J 8 6 5 2
                    ♣ A J 3
```

THE AUCTION

NORTH	EAST	SOUTH	WEST
1 ♡	Pass	2 ◇	Pass
2 ♡	Pass	3 ◇	Dbl
Pass	Pass	Pass	

THE RESULT

West got off to the inspired lead of the king of spades. The declarer took the dummy's ace and tried to get two spade discards on the hearts. Unfortunately, East ruffed the third heart with the nine of diamonds. Eventually, the declarer had to play clubs from his

134

hand, and ended up losing three trump tricks, one spade, and two clubs.

Down two.

THE ARGUMENT

North flayed South for his bidding. "How could you ever have the presumption to bid that Swiss cheese full-of-holes suit, again and again?"

South said his hand was worth 11 points; he said he could rebid his six-card suit since he held only a singleton heart.

The discussion became loud and vituperative. In deference to the host's request, it was decided to call for arbitration from this source.

GOREN SETTLES THE ARGUMENT

Players who bid three diamonds on this type of holding must be out to prove the theory that the ego is mightier than the wallet. South let rote take the place of good judgment—a poor tactic at the card table.

A singleton in an opener's long suit is, at best, a doubtful asset. A responder should not assign to the singleton any distributional value until such time as it has been determined that there is a fit somewhere else in the hand.

South was guilty of a severe case of over-optimism. There was no reason to suppose that it would be better to play the hand in his suit at the three-level than in his partner's suit at the two-level.

The moment North could do no more than rebid his hearts, South should have realized that game on the hand was unlikely but that trouble was not. His singleton heart now became a liability—the portent of a misfit. Accordingly, South would have been wise to shut up shop, for to bid on, in the face of a misfit, is to court disaster.

ARGUMENT 48

Should the responder count his distributional points when he responds to an opening bid with two of a new suit?

THE HAND

```
                    NORTH
                    ♠ J 6
                    ♡ K Q J 8 5
                    ◇ A 8
                    ♣ A J 10 3

WEST                                    EAST
♠ A Q 7 5                               ♠ 10 8 4 3 2
♡ 10 3                                  ♡ A 9 7 4
◇ Q J 7 6                               ◇ 9 2
♣ 9 8 4                                 ♣ K 6

                    SOUTH
                    ♠ K 9
                    ♡ 6 2
                    ◇ K 10 5 4 3
                    ♣ Q 7 5 2
```

THE AUCTION

NORTH	EAST	SOUTH	WEST
1 ♡	Pass	2 ◇	Pass
3 ♣	Pass	4 ♣	Pass
5 ♣	Dbl	Pass	Pass
Pass			

THE RESULT

East led a spade and the defenders took two spade tricks. There was no way to avoid losing two more tricks to East's ace of hearts and king of trumps.

As North-South were vulnerable, they lost 500 points.

THE ARGUMENT

As the facts were reported to us, it seems North was upset by his partner's raise to four clubs. He felt that, as South held a minimum for his first bid, he should either have passed three clubs or have rebid three notrump.

South was indignant that anyone should think he could have passed three clubs—surely that bid was forcing. And to bid three notrump with such a weak spade holding did not seem right, so four clubs was the only bid.

South offered a small wager as to which bid in the auction was worst, and the matter was referred to this department for determination.

GOREN SETTLES THE ARGUMENT

Both North and South were overly aggressive in the auction. However, as I must select the worst bid, I would nominate South's initial response of two diamonds.

True, the hand values to 10 points with diamonds as trumps. But to follow that point of view blindly is to let point count take control where judgment should be exercised.

At the outset of the bidding, it is wrong to count a distribution point for a doubleton in your partner's suit.

To respond two diamonds to an opening bid of one heart misrepresents the hand. South should have had either more high-card values or a better suit.

I would have chosen one notrump for my initial response. While South's shape may not be ideal for the bid, he does have stoppers in all the unbid suits.

If in your bidding you must misrepresent either the strength of your hand or the shape of your

hand, it is generally wiser to show its strength correctly.

By first responding one notrump, you give yourself the opportunity to raise the opener's two-club rebid to three clubs, showing a four-card fit and maximum values for your initial notrump response. The auction would have ended there, for North did not hold quite enough for further action.

If more reasons are required for South to assign minimum values to his hand, one very sound reason would be his lack of first-round controls. He is the proud possessor of two kings and a queen; but until North's bid of three clubs was made, South's queen of clubs might have been of no value whatsoever.

CHAPTER 8

Responses to Opening Suit Bids of Two

ARGUMENT 49

What constitutes a positive response to a forcing two-bid?

THE HAND

```
              NORTH
              ♠ A 8 4
              ♡ A K Q 9 4
              ◇ A K 3
              ♣ K J


              SOUTH
              ♠ Q 9 5 3 2
              ♡ 7 2
              ◇ Q J 5 4
              ♣ Q 3
```

THE AUCTION

NORTH	EAST	SOUTH	WEST
2 ♡	Pass	2 ♠	Pass
4 NT	Pass	5 ♣	Pass
6 ♠	Pass	Pass	Pass

THE RESULT

The defenders cashed the ace of clubs at trick one. As the cards lay, the declarer still had to lose two trump tricks.

Down two.

THE ARGUMENT

North suggested that South see his optometrist about getting new spectacles—the pair he had on apparently revealed aces and kings that weren't there. Only faulty eyesight could excuse responding positively on South's miserable collection of cards.

South retorted that "Goren said" 7 points were enough for a positive response to a two-demand bid. South had that many points in high cards, without even counting his distributional values. Since he was correct in his response, the onus for getting to the ludicrous slam obviously rested upon North.

GOREN SETTLES THE ARGUMENT

South was off the beam.

No positive response to a two-demand bid should ever be made with a hand that does not contain at least a king.

The minimum for a positive response to an opening demand bid is a holding of 7 points in high cards.

With 7 points, the responder should hold one quick trick; with 8 points, the responder needs only one-half a quick trick. If the responder does not hold one-half a quick trick, he should initially make a negative response.

A positive response in a suit promises a five-card suit.

With 8 points fairly evenly distributed and no five-card suit, the responder should jump to three notrump.

South's hand contains nothing but queens and jacks. Whenever this is the case, a player should exercise conservatism and caution.

South's correct first response should have been the negative bid of two notrump. After North's rebid of three hearts, South would now show his five-card spade suit. North would then raise to four spades to end the auction.

Also see: Argument 51.

ARGUMENT 50

Is a jump raise of an opening two-bid strong?

THE HAND

```
                    NORTH
                    ♠ A K Q 8 4
                    ♡ K J 7
                    ♢ A Q
                    ♣ A J 5
WEST                                  EAST
♠ 6                                   ♠ 9 2
♡ A 9 6 3                             ♡ 10 5
♢ J 8 4 3                             ♢ K 10 7 6 2
♣ Q 10 7 6                            ♣ K 8 4 3
                    SOUTH
                    ♠ J 10 7 5 3
                    ♡ Q 8 4 2
                    ♢ 9 5
                    ♣ 9 2
```

THE AUCTION

NORTH	EAST	SOUTH	WEST
2 ♠	Pass	4 ♠	Pass
4 NT	Pass	5 ♣	Pass
6 ♠	Pass	Pass	Pass

THE RESULT

There was absolutely no play for the contract. The declarer lost a trick in each side suit.

Down two.

THE ARGUMENT

North was thoroughly incensed. He accused South of deliberately throwing away money, of sabotaging

142

the game, of conduct unbecoming anyone who knew anything about bidding.

South retorted that if North's bridge ability could match his lack of couth, North might become one of the world's great players. Anyone who knew the rules would realize that South's four-spade response was a weakness bid.

GOREN SETTLES THE ARGUMENT

It is an old wives' tale that every jump raise of a partner's opening bids shows a strong hand. A jump raise of an opening one-bid to three does; a jump raise of an opener's two-bid to four does not.

The jump raise of a two-demand to four indicates a very specialized type of hand. It promises excellent trump support, but denies any first- or second-round control.

In other words, such a bid is a warning—not an encouragement.

Had the opener understood this, he would have realized that slam was a virtually hopeless proposition. South had denied holding any ace, or king, or singleton, or void. The declarer would have to lose at least one heart trick. He then would need a successful diamond finesse, plus the queen of clubs and the queen of hearts in his partner's hand. Additionally, the declarer would have to win the club finesse.

With a good hand and good spade support, there is no need for the responder to jump. It is insufficient for the responder to raise his partner's suit. Such a bid would be positive and forcing, and would leave the maximum room for exploration of the full possibilities of the hand.

ARGUMENT 51

Does a positive response to a two-bid guarantee the ace in the suit bid?

THE HAND

NORTH
♠ J 7 6
♡ 6
♢ Q 10 9 8 5 4
♣ A K 5

SOUTH
♠ A K Q 3
♡ A K Q J 5 4 3
♢ K J
♣ —

THE AUCTION

SOUTH	WEST	NORTH	EAST
2 ♡	Pass	3 ♢	Pass
7 ♡	Pass	Pass	Pass

THE RESULT

West led the ace of diamonds. The declarer took the rest of the tricks.

Down one.

THE ARGUMENT

"Don't you know that when you responded three diamonds, you promised the ace of diamonds!" thundered South. "If you had what you guaranteed, the grand slam would have been a laydown."

"All I told you was that I had enough for a positive

144

response and that I held a five-card diamond suit," countered South. "I did not have to hold the ace of diamonds."

"Anyone who leaps straight to a grand slam on your hand is either a masochist or a fool. Haven't you ever heard of cue-bidding?"

GOREN SETTLES THE ARGUMENT

Once upon a time it was very popular to show aces in response to your partner's opening two-bid. There still are a number of die-hards who use that method. However, the ace response to a two-demand bid is no longer a taken-for-granted response.

In the absence of any prior understanding, no one should assume that his partner is showing aces in response to a demand bid. The normal method is to show a long suit if you have the value for a positive response. There are no stipulations as to what that suit must be headed by.

I will readily admit that there are some hands, like this one, where it might be convenient to show aces over a two-bid. It could be useful where the opener has a void suit, and a long, strong suit of his own, and is therefore not interested in playing in any other suit. However, such hands are relatively few and far between.

On most hands, where the auction starts with a strong two-bid, the showing of aces wastes a precious round of bidding. As a result, it is easy to miss a fit in a secondary suit, or to bypass a sound three notrump contract that could be the only makeable bid with the combined hands.

Also see: Argument 49.

ARGUMENT 52

Should the opening two-bidder's partner show a new suit or raise his partner's suit?

THE HAND

```
                    NORTH
                    ♠ A Q
                    ♡ A K 9 8 6 3 2
                    ◇ Q 5
                    ♣ A Q
WEST                                    EAST
♠ K J 10 5 3                            ♠ 8 7 6 4 2
♡ 5                                     ♡ J 7
◇ 7 2                                   ◇ K 10 8 4
♣ K 10 5 3 2                            ♣ J 8
                    SOUTH
                    ♠ 9
                    ♡ Q 10 4
                    ◇ A J 9 6 3
                    ♣ 9 7 6 4
```

THE AUCTION

NORTH	EAST	SOUTH	WEST
2 ♡	Pass	3 ◇	Pass
3 ♡	Pass	4 ♡	Pass
Pass	Pass		

THE RESULT

The play was a formality. A spade was opened into North's ace-queen. The declarer then drew trumps, and followed with finesses in the minor suits.

These succeeded and the declarer made all thirteen tricks.

146

THE ARGUMENT

North was most upset that his side had not reached the laydown small slam. In strong terms, he suggested that South could have found a better bid on his second turn than a mere raise in hearts.

South maintained he had done all he could when he made two progressive bids on his hand.

GOREN SETTLES THE ARGUMENT

South is the main culprit; but it was his first bid rather than his second that was off target.

When your partner opens with a demand bid, it is often crucial to decide on the trump suit as soon as possible. This allows the opener to revalue his hand, and to assess the possibilities of slam at an early stage.

To raise an opening bid of one, it is desirable to hold four trumps, for the opener might be bidding on a four-card suit. This does not hold true when raising an opening two-demand bid. It is only in the most exceptional of cases that the demand bidder will open in a four-card suit. His suit is expected to be at least five cards long, quite likely six cards in length. Therefore, three cards to an honor in the responder's hand represents good trump support.

It is far more relevant to the auction for the responder to show adequate trump support for the two-demand bid than to bid a weakish five-card minor suit of his own.

Consider the effect of an immediate response of three hearts in preference to a bid of three diamonds. After his suit is raised, the opener revalues his hand to 28 points—5 additional points for his unusual trump length. Since the responder has shown at least 7 points, the combined holdings are in the slam zone.

Indeed, with his wealth of controls, the opener might immediately check on aces and kings, with the intention of bidding seven hearts if all suits are doubly controlled.

Let us look at an alternative holding for South:

♠ J x
♡ x x
◇ A Q x x x
♣ x x x x

With this holding, South would bid as he actually did. And with this holding, a heart slam is a poor proposition, indeed.

ARGUMENT 53

*After a two-demand bid, can either partner
stop short of game?*

THE HAND

NORTH
♠ 84
♡ J 7 4 3
◇ J 9 5 2
♣ 10 7 2

WEST
♠ 10 3
♡ Q 10 8 2
◇ Q 10 7 4
♣ K 8 6

EAST
♠ 7 6 2
♡ 9 6 5
◇ K 6
♣ A J 5 4 3

SOUTH
♠ A K Q J 9 5
♡ A K
◇ A 8 3
♣ Q 9

THE AUCTION

SOUTH	WEST	NORTH	EAST
2 ♠	Pass	2 NT	Pass
3 ♠	Pass	3 NT	Pass
4 ♠	Pass	Pass	Pass

THE RESULT

The declarer inevitably lost two tricks in each of the
minor suits.

Down one.

THE ARGUMENT

After West had opened the two of hearts and dummy's dubious assets were revealed, South began muttering to himself.

Then North observed: "Well, anyway, you had 100 honors. But why didn't you leave me in three notrump? It's cold if the opponents don't open clubs."

"But they *would* have opened clubs," shrieked South. "And I would still have had my 100 honors if you had had sense enough to pass three spades! We'd easily have made our contract."

"I couldn't pass!" was North's horrified rejoinder. "You opened with a game-forcing two-demand bid."

GOREN SETTLES THE ARGUMENT

In almost every case, an opening two-bid in a suit is forcing to game. No matter how weak the responder is, he must keep the bidding open until a game contract has been reached, or until the opponents have entered the auction, or until either side has been doubled for penalties.

However, there is one exception to this rule. If over the responder's negative bid, the opener continues with a simple rebid of his own suit, the responder may pass—if he can contribute absolutely nothing further of value.

The opener might have started with as few as nine playing tricks when he opened with a strong two-bid. If the responder is absolutely broke, it is illogical that his side should be compelled to take a loss simply because they are unable to call a halt somewhere below the game level. There should be a safety valve, and there is.

Two warning notes:

The responder is allowed to stop short of game

only if the opener rebids his own suit. Any other rebid makes the sequence forcing to game.

The responder, after his initial negative response, can pass only if he has no semblance of a trick; otherwise he likely will be missing a game.

Consider this hand:

♠ x x x
♥ x x
♦ Q x x x
♣ x x x

The opener bids two spades and the responder two notrump. The opener now rebids three spades. Should the responder pass?

Definitely not! The responder has two potential sources of a trick for his partner: (1) the queen of diamonds, and (2) a ruffing possibility in hearts. His hand is likely to produce the one additional trick the opener needs to make his game.

On the hand in question, South does not have anything resembling a trick in support of spades. Therefore, he should have passed three spades and earned a plus score.

ARGUMENT 54

After your partner opens with a weak two-bid, how can you check more particularly on his actual strength?

THE HAND

```
                    NORTH
                    ♠ 94
                    ♡ KQ10876
                    ◇ 93
                    ♣ Q76

        WEST                        EAST
        ♠ KJ6                       ♠ Q1052
        ♡ 53                        ♡ A4
        ◇ Q1052                     ◇ 864
        ♣ A542                      ♣ KJ109

                    SOUTH
                    ♠ A873
                    ♡ J92
                    ◇ AKJ7
                    ♣ 83
```

THE AUCTION

NORTH	EAST	SOUTH	WEST
2 ♡	Pass	4 ♡	Pass
Pass	Pass		

THE RESULT

The defenders attacked in clubs, winning the first two tricks in that suit. Then East shifted to a spade. When the ace of trump was won, the spade winner was cashed.

Down one.

THE ARGUMENT

North suggested with elaborate courtesy that there was a step that existed between two hearts and four hearts. Had South simply raised to three hearts, he pointed out, he (North) would have passed, since he held a minimum.

South burst out in scornful laughter. He thought everyone knew that a simple raise of partner's opening weak two-bid was pre-emptive and would assuredly be passed. How could he, holding 14 points, refuse to bid to game, especially when he held three quick tricks, and three trumps including an honor?

GOREN SETTLES THE ARGUMENT

Despite South's guffaws and elaborate rationale, North is right.

Looking at the South hand in isolation, that hand could very well produce game opposite a North hand which is near the top of the limit for a weak two-bid. But opposite a quite weak but valid "weak two-bid," game is not in the cards. And there is no way of knowing just what the strength of your partner's opening bid really is.

Generally speaking, a raise of the weak two-bidder's suit to the three-level serves a more useful function if that raise is used pre-emptively.

There are several methods available for checking on how strong the opening weak two-bidder is. Some play that any new suit bid by the responder is forcing. However, this often leads to unnecessary complications in the subsequent bidding.

For the sake of simplicity, my recommendation is:

In response to a weak two-bid, use two notrump as the only forcing bid. The bid is artificial, and

does not necessarily describe a balanced hand. It simply asks the opener to clarify his holding.

A popular way to do this is for the opener to show a feature of his hand if there is such a feature to be shown. With the North hand, there is nothing to show; his rebid would be three hearts, which would deny any extra values. However, if North held the ace of clubs, or even the king of clubs, instead of the queen of clubs, North would rebid three clubs to show a good value in that suit.

An alternative method—and I think a more effective method—was devised by my friend and long-time teammate, Harold Ogust.

The Ogust responses to partner's forcing bid of two notrump over a weak two-bid are as follows:

1. **A rebid of three clubs shows a minimum "weak-two bid."**
2. **A rebid of three diamonds shows a maximum "weak-two opener." (If diamonds is the trump suit, a bid of three hearts is used for this purpose.)**
3. **A rebid of the trump suit shows a suit which is strong enough to play even opposite partner's singleton; e.g. K Q J x x x.**
4. **A rebid of three notrump shows that opener has a solid suit—at least as good as A K Q x x x—that can reasonably be expected to produce six tricks at a notrump contract opposite a low doubleton.**

CHAPTER 9

Responses to Opening Suit Bids of Three, Four, or Five

ARGUMENT 55

When do you raise your partner's pre-empt to game?

THE HAND

```
                    NORTH
                    ♠ 6 3
                    ♡ K Q J 7 6 5 2
                    ◇ 8 2
                    ♣ 8 6

    WEST                              EAST
    ♠ Q 10                            ♠ K 9 8 5 4
    ♡ 9 4 3                           ♡ A 10
    ◇ A J 4                           ◇ 9 7 6 5
    ♣ K 10 9 7 2                      ♣ J 3

                    SOUTH
                    ♠ A J 7 2
                    ♡ 8
                    ◇ K Q 10 3
                    ♣ A Q 5 4
```

THE AUCTION

NORTH	EAST	SOUTH	WEST
3 ♡	Pass	3 NT	Pass
Pass	Pass		

THE RESULT

West led the seven of clubs. Though he gained a trick on the lead, South was not happy. He was never able to get to the dummy.

Down four.

THE ARGUMENT

Everyone seemed agreed that with 16 points in high cards South had to take some action. But as to what South should have bid—here opinions were at great variance.

GOREN SETTLES THE ARGUMENT

I disagree with all the players at the table. I suggest that South's best action was to pass.

Before converting an opening pre-empt to no-trump, the responder must consider whether there is a sure bridge between the hands. Without guaranteed communication, the best bid is usually to pass, even with great strength.

The overwhelming fact here is that South has a trump singleton. In a notrump contract, South may never be able to get into North's hand. I therefore would pass, but I would not criticize a bid of four hearts too heavily.

The one bid that is out of the question is three notrump. If North is bidding soundly, there just cannot be a source of nine tricks on South's holding.

Let me add one further bit of advice and warning:

Unless you don't need your partner's suit to make nine tricks, do not bid notrump without some assurance that his suit can be used.

The responder should have A-x, K-x, or at least

Q-x in his partner's suit. Otherwise, either pass or raise your partner's suit—even with a singleton—as your values dictate.

Also see: Arguments 56, 57.

ARGUMENT 56

When may you respond in notrump to your partner's pre-empt?

THE HAND

```
                    NORTH
                    ♠ A Q J 9 8 4 3
                    ♡ 9 4
                    ◇ 10
                    ♣ Q 8 3

WEST                                    EAST
♠ 10                                    ♠ 6 5 2
♡ A 10 6 5 2                            ♡ K 7
◇ 8 7 2                                 ◇ A J 6 4 3
♣ K J 9 4                               ♣ 7 5 2

                    SOUTH
                    ♠ K 7
                    ♡ Q J 8 3
                    ◇ K Q 9 5
                    ♣ A 10 6
```

THE AUCTION *(North-South are vulnerable)*

NORTH	EAST	SOUTH	WEST
3 ♠	Pass	4 ♠	Pass
Pass	Pass		

THE RESULT

East led a club, and the defenders took four tricks. Down one.

THE ARGUMENT

West's innocent remark that he thought the opposition could make three notrump stirred up a hornets'

nest. For now North stung South furiously for not trying the nine-trick game. South could only muster up
the defense that being vulnerable, North's bid had
promised seven tricks. His hand, he claimed, surely
looked good enough for three tricks.

GOREN SETTLES THE ARGUMENT

True, seven plus three equals ten, but there is more
to bridge than just that. A pre-emptive bidder almost
never has more than one ace, and often doesn't even
have one.

**It is not the number of winning tricks you have
that determines whether you should raise partner's
opening pre-emptive bid, but the number of possible losers you hold. To raise his partner's opening pre-empt, a responder should have aces and
kings, not a collection of high-card points without
basic controls.**

Queens and jacks in combination with kings are
usually hallmarks of a hand that is oriented toward
notrump. South's hand is suited for a bid of three notrump.

Holding the king in his partner's suit, South should
reason that the suit will be good for seven tricks, or
that, if his partner is missing the ace, there must be
one outside entry in the opening hand. Otherwise the
bidding would not have been opened at the three-level
when vulnerable. In either case, the combined holding
would be enough to yield nine tricks.

To illustrate the power of aces in this game, let us
change South's holding slightly, giving him:

♠ 10 x
♡ K Q J
◇ A x x x
♣ A x x x

With this hand, three notrump will probably fail

unless the spade finesse succeeds, yet four spades will almost surely roll home no matter who holds the king.

A hand with 14 quality high-card points is worth more for suit play than one that counts 15 but includes too many quacks.*

Also see: Arguments 55, 57.

---

* Queens and jacks, which are slightly overvalued, if only because they lack the quality of immediacy.

ARGUMENT 57

Is a new-suit response to a pre-emptive bid forcing?

THE HAND

NORTH
- ♠ J 10
- ♡ A Q J 10 5 2
- ♢ Q 6
- ♣ A Q 5

WEST
- ♠ A 8 6 5 4
- ♡ 6 3
- ♢ K 9 5
- ♣ 10 7 4

EAST
- ♠ Q 7 3
- ♡ K 9 8 4
- ♢ 2
- ♣ K J 9 6 2

SOUTH
- ♠ K 9 2
- ♡ 7
- ♢ A J 10 8 7 4 3
- ♣ 8 3

THE AUCTION

SOUTH	WEST	NORTH	EAST
3 ♢	Pass	3 ♡	Pass
Pass	Pass		

THE RESULT

East led the diamond deuce. The declarer took the trick with the dummy's ace. In an attempt to prevent ruffs, the declarer now led a heart to the ace. He continued with the queen of hearts to East's king.

A spade was now led to West's ace. After cashing the king of diamonds, West led the five of diamonds. North ruffed high, setting up a trump trick for East.

Since the diamonds were established and the king of spades was still in the dummy, the declarer just made his contract.

THE ARGUMENT

North vociferously protested South's pass. He maintained that three notrump could have been made.

South couldn't understand what all the fuss was about. Didn't all the books say that a pre-emptive bidder has described his hand with his one bid, and that from that point on it is up to his partner to take any further action?

GOREN SETTLES THE ARGUMENT

South is correct up to a point.

A pre-emptive bidder should not bid his hand twice.

However, that principle does not apply in this particular case.

A new suit bid by the responder after a preempt is unconditionally forcing on the opening bidder. In some rare cases, such a bid might not even be a real suit, but the opening move in a slam auction in the opening bidder's very own suit.

It is not easy to lay down the rules for a rebid by the pre-emptive bidder after getting a forcing response from his partner, for hands vary so widely. As a general rule, the opener should try to show the salient features of his hand.

On the given hand, South should have rebid three spades to show his value there, in case that was the information his partner needed to contract for a game in notrump. Note that this bid cannot be held to imply a four-card spade suit.

It is a cardinal rule that one does not pre-empt in a minor when he holds a secondary major suit.

With no side feature and a good trump holding, the opener can merely rebid his original suit. With light trump support for his partner's call and a ruffing possibility somewhere, the opener should raise the responder's suit.

Change one of South's clubs to a heart, and his bid should have been four hearts.

With both kings on the wrong side of North's aces, the declarer would probably go down one, but that result wouldn't make three-notrump a poor contract —simply an unlucky one.

Also see: Arguments 55, 56.

ARGUMENT 58

Are you ever justified in raising your partner's pre-empt with a weak hand?

THE HAND

	NORTH	
	♠ A Q 10 9 7 4 3	
	♡ 8	
	◊ 8 4 3	
	♣ 7 2	

WEST	EAST
♠ 6	♠ J
♡ A K 10 4 2	♡ Q J 9 6 5
◊ K 10 9	◊ A Q 5
♣ Q 8 5 4	♣ K 10 9 3

	SOUTH
	♠ K 8 5 2
	♡ 7 3
	◊ J 7 6 2
	♣ A J 6

THE AUCTION   [*East-West were vulnerable.*]

NORTH	EAST	SOUTH	WEST
3 ♠	Pass	Pass	Dbl
Pass	4 ♡	Pass	Pass
Pass			

THE RESULT

The declarer lost two tricks: one to the ace of spades, and the other to the ace of clubs. He took a winning position by playing South for the jack of clubs.

Eleven tricks were taken.

THE ARGUMENT

North suggested that should South care to remove his shirt, it would be obvious to one and all that he had a yellow streak a yard wide running down his back—possibly the result of an intelligence leak from the brain.

Four spades would have been defeated by only two tricks. Even five spades doubled would not be a bad sacrifice over a bid of five hearts. The very least South should have done was to bid four spades over East's four hearts.

South defended himself by saying it would have been unreasonable for him, with a hand that might produce only one trick for his partner, to have taken any action over four hearts, especially since he had some defensive values.

Once North had announced weakness by his opening a pre-empt, there was surely no point to offering the opponents a fat penalty.

GOREN SETTLES THE ARGUMENT

I must agree with South on one point—but only on one point—it would have been senseless for him to have bid four spades once the opponents had already bid four hearts. That is simply giving the opponents two bites at the cherry. They then could have bid on to five hearts if they were confident of making that contract; or if not, they could have doubled four spades for a tidy penalty.

This hand brings up an interesting point that is often overlooked by players of considerable experience.

The right time to sacrifice is *before* the opponents have found their best contract. When partner has pre-empted and you have a weak hand with support for his suit, raise defensively to whatever level you consider safe. This action, known in the trade as an "advance sacrifice," often will succeed

in putting pressure on the opponents, and force them to guess at a relatively high level.

Consider what might have happened had South elected to bid four spades at his first opportunity. With his side vulnerable, West would have had a most unpleasant decision to make. If South's action was preemptive, then East-West obviously must have a fair play at a five-level contract.

But what if South had all the outstanding strength and was bidding to make the game? In that case, East would be broke and any action by West would lead to disaster.

West might come up with the right answer and double for penalties. However, on many hands where the missing strength is divided between the two opponents, South will steal the contract undoubled.

CHAPTER 10

Responses to an Opening Bid of One Notrump

ARGUMENT 59

Should the holder of a four-card major who is responding to an opening notrump always bid Stayman?

THE HAND

NORTH
- ♠ A 8 7 6
- ♡ Q J 6
- ◇ Q 9 2
- ♣ A K 8

WEST
- ♠ J 4
- ♡ K 10 7 2
- ◇ 10 8 5 4
- ♣ 7 6 2

EAST
- ♠ 9 3 2
- ♡ A 9 5
- ◇ K 7 3
- ♣ Q 10 4 3

SOUTH
- ♠ K Q 10 5
- ♡ 8 4 3
- ◇ A J 6
- ♣ J 9 5

THE AUCTION

NORTH	EAST	SOUTH	WEST
1 NT	Pass	2 ♣	Pass
2 ♠	Pass	4 ♠	Pass
Pass	Pass		

THE RESULT

East led a trump. Though the diamond finesse succeeded, the declarer could win only nine tricks. He had to lose two hearts, and a trick in each minor suit.

Down one.

THE ARGUMENT

North-South thought nothing of the matter until East, more renowned for his card play than for his tact, sparked the fire by remarking that three notrump could not have been defeated. However, no one was quite sure how to get there, once the 4-4 spade fit had been located.

GOREN SETTLES THE ARGUMENT

Just because you have a tool in your shed doesn't mean that you have to use it—no matter what.

South launched into Stayman over his partner's notrump opening bid simply because he held a four-card major suit. He did not consider that with a perfectly balanced hand nine tricks at notrump might be easier to make than ten tricks in a major.

Let us ponder a moment over the reasons for trying to locate a 4-4 fit. With a combined holding of eight cards in a suit, this leaves but five in the opponents' hands. Five cards usually divide 3-2, which means that all the opponents' trumps can be extracted in three rounds, leaving one trump remaining in both the declarer's hand and in the dummy. These trumps can then be scored separately by means of ruffs, thus allowing the declarer to win one more trick in the major suit contract than he could win at notrump.

However, for this to come about, there must be a short suit to ruff. When this circumstance does not exist, the declarer will usually make the same number of tricks in the suit contract as he would in notrump.

When the declarer can make ten tricks at either contract—in notrump or in a major—it is of little importance where the hand is played. But when only nine tricks can be made, it is the difference between going down in a suit contract or making game in notrump.

Holding 10 points or more in high cards and a 4-3-3-3 distribution, a responder to one notrump should immediately raise to three notrump, and avoid bidding Stayman.

Also see: Arguments 60, 61, 62, 63.

ARGUMENT 60

Is a two-club response to a notrump opening forcing to game?

THE HAND

```
                NORTH
                ♠ K 9 8 2
                ♡ A Q
                ◇ A 10 7 3
                ♣ K 9 8

WEST                            EAST
♠ 6 4                           ♠ Q J 3
♡ 10 5 4                        ♡ 9 8 7 2
◇ K Q 8 4                       ◇ J 6
♣ A 7 3 2                       ♣ Q 10 5 4

                SOUTH
                ♠ A 10 7 5
                ♡ K J 6 3
                ◇ 9 5 2
                ♣ J 6
```

THE AUCTION

NORTH	EAST	SOUTH	WEST
1 NT	Pass	2 ♣	Pass
2 ♠	Pass	3 ♠	Pass
Pass	Pass		

THE RESULT

North made ten tricks.

East led the jack of diamonds, which the declarer won. He then cashed the ace and queen of hearts, and the king and ace of spades. On the dummy's king and jack of hearts, the declarer discarded two of his diamonds. With the ace of clubs onside, his only losers

170

were one trick in each minor suit, and the queen of spades.

Four spades made.

THE ARGUMENT

North-South were playing that a conventional bid of two clubs, inquiring for major suits, was forcing. Under those circumstances, South felt that North was obliged to bid until game was reached.

But North maintained that with a minimum no-trump opening bid, there was no reason for him to bid again. The forcing situation no longer existed once South had raised his response.

GOREN SETTLES THE ARGUMENT

The idea of using a two-club response to a one no-trump opening bid as a request for the opener to show a four-card major was first devised in England. However, it was codified and developed by U. S. internationalist Sam Stayman, and has become known worldwide as the Stayman Convention.

Why is the bid not forcing to game? Let us consider the logic of the situation.

Let us assume that the opener has a minimum 16 points for his notrump bid and that the responder has the 8 points required for his Stayman inquiry. The combined count of the two hands is only 24 points—not enough to contract for game. There must be some machinery to allow for stopping below game.

A raise of the opener's major says: "Partner, I have a minimum 8-9 points for my bid, plus four-card support for your major. If you have a maximum notrump, go on to game; if you are minimum, you can pass."

With a hand better than a minimum—that is, with more than 8 points—it is up to the Stayman bidder to contract for game. He is the one who can

judge the potential of the hand, for his partner's bid has limited his holding within fairly narrow confines.

On the hand in question, South's hand is worth 10 points in support of spades. As the combined count of the two hands totals at least 26 points, South should have avoided putting pressure on his partner by jumping directly to four spades.

However, North is not entirely in the clear. His hand is worth 17 points at a spade contract. With almost all his points in aces and kings, he might have plucked up the courage to go on to four spades, even though his partner had shown no more than 9 points.

Also see: Arguments 59, 61, 62, 63.

ARGUMENT 61

Can you employ Stayman after the opponents enter the auction?

THE HAND

```
            NORTH
            ♠ K J 8 3
            ♡ Q 6 2
            ◇ A Q 7
            ♣ K Q 6


            SOUTH
            ♠ Q 10 7 2
            ♡ K J 8 5 3
            ◇ 9 5
            ♣ A 7
```

THE AUCTION

NORTH	EAST	SOUTH	WEST
1 NT	2 ◇	3 ♣	Pass
Pass	Pass		

THE RESULT

How many tricks South went down in his frightful contract is immaterial.

It was obvious to everyone that North-South could have made a game in either major suit.

THE ARGUMENT

Had the participants been able to regard the whole matter as a bidding misunderstanding, all would have been well. Unfortunately, South launched a few acerbic remarks about players who did not know when to respond to a Stayman inquiry.

North scornfully volunteered that his seven-year-old daughter would have bid the hand better than South did.

For a while it seemed as if it might come to pistols at sunrise.

GOREN SETTLES THE ARGUMENT

Only a few players employ the convention that once partner has opened a notrump and the opponents compete, a club bid—even at the three-level—is a Stayman request for a major suit. The vast majority of players employ the three-club bid in its natural sense: as nonforcing, and showing a club suit.

If an opponent enters the auction over your partner's one notrump opening bid, the only way to force your partner to bid a major suit, if he has one, is to cue-bid the enemy suit.

Bidding at bridge is a language. As in everyday speech, different people speak different dialects. There are many areas of bridge where the same bid can be accorded different interpretations; some of these interpretations are considerably removed from standard practice. Woe to the partnership who talk to each other in two different idioms.

This hand is a case in point. Lacking a specific agreement that any club bid in a notrump sequence was to be interpreted as a Stayman response, North was quite right in assuming that South was showing a club suit in a weakish hand.

To get his partner to show a major suit, South should have bid three diamonds after East had overcalled in that suit.

North would have responded three spades, and the laydown game would have been reached.

Also see: Arguments 59, 60, 62, 63.

ARGUMENT 62

Can you sign off in clubs after making a Stayman response?

THE HAND

```
                    NORTH
                    ♠ K J 7 2
                    ♡ A J 9
                    ◇ K J 5 4
                    ♣ A 7
    WEST                              EAST
    ♠ Q 8 4                          ♠ A 10 6 3
    ♡ Q 10 5 2                       ♡ K 8 4
    ◇ A 9 3                          ◇ 10 8 7 6
    ♣ J 8 2                          ♣ K 6
                    SOUTH
                    ♠ 9 5
                    ♡ 7 6 3
                    ◇ Q 2
                    ♣ Q 10 9 5 4 3
```

THE AUCTION

NORTH	EAST	SOUTH	WEST
1 NT	Pass	3 ♣	Pass
3 NT	Pass	Pass	Pass

THE RESULT

It would be most kind to draw a veil over the proceedings.

Suffice it to say that North went down four tricks, vulnerable.

THE ARGUMENT

North was seething over South's three-club response.

175

South maintained that he could not bid two clubs for that bid would have been Stayman.

While his partner agreed with that, she insisted that South's only recourse was to pass and let her struggle in one notrump.

South refused to believe that there was no way to play a club partial with his hand.

GOREN SETTLES THE ARGUMENT

Over a partner's notrump opening bid, a responder who has a weak hand with a club suit can sign off in the suit by first bidding two clubs, and then over any bid by the opener, rebidding three clubs.

The responder must use this sequence with care, for he is forcing the bidding to the three-level.

It is generally unwise to try to sign off in clubs with a five-card suit. Let's say you hold:

♠ x x
♡ J x x
◇ x x x
♣ K J x x x

If your partner opens the bidding with one notrump, your wisest course is to pass. Since you have some values, your partner might find it easier to scrape together seven tricks at one notrump than you would nine tricks in three clubs.

But let us say you have the following hand opposite your partner's opening bid of one notrump:

♠ Q 5 3
♡ 7
◇ 9 8 2
♣ Q J 9 8 5 4

This hand, with not a single sure entry, offers a better

prospect of making nine tricks at clubs than seven tricks at notrump.

If we change the suits in a previous example to:

♠ x x
♡ K J x x x
◊ x x x
♣ J x x

Now it would be correct to respond two hearts over partner's one notrump opening.

After a one-notrump bid, a response of any suit at the two-level (other than clubs) shows a desire to play in that suit.

Also see: Arguments 59, 60, 61, 63.

ARGUMENT 63

Should you still play Stayman when two clubs is enough for game?

THE HAND

> NORTH
> ♠ A J 8 3
> ♡ K 10 9
> ◇ A Q 4 3
> ♣ K 5
>
> SOUTH
> ♠ 7
> ♡ 8 6 5
> ◇ J 5 2
> ♣ J 9 8 4 3 2

THE AUCTION

NORTH	EAST	SOUTH	WEST
1 NT	Pass	2 ♣	Pass
2 ♠	Pass	3 ♣	Pass
Pass	Pass		

THE RESULT

The declarer lost two heart tricks, one diamond trick, and two club tricks.

Down one.

THE ARGUMENT

South was incensed at not being able to close out the rubber. He intended his two-club bid as a final bid—not as Stayman. Since North-South had 60 points on score, two clubs, South reminded North, was enough for game. The only reason to bid two clubs would be to improve the contract. North should have realized this.

North stubbornly retorted that a convention is a convention.

GOREN SETTLES THE ARGUMENT

I do not play two clubs in this situation as a final bid, though I can see the merit of South's argument. There are a number of old timers who, when playing rubber bridge, play the two-club bid as a weakness bid and not as a Stayman inquiry.

The question is: In the long run, how can the bid of two clubs be most gainfully employed? Should two clubs over one notrump show a bust hand with a club suit even when only two clubs are needed, because a team has a 60 point partial, to make game? Or should two clubs *always* be used as the beginning of a constructive auction, even when only 40 points are needed to make game? I think the latter use is more frequent —therefore, more productive than the first method— and that therefore the bidding should be based on that presumption. I don't see why a partnership need give up the many constructive sequences that might start with a Stayman inquiry in favor of those relatively few hands where the responder might want to play the hand in two clubs, and believes one notrump is too risky.

South should have realized the possibility of North's misinterpreting his bid. To maintain partnership confidence, South should have passed.

If you want to employ a bid that partner might misconstrue, be sure to discuss such a bid with your partner before the start of play.

Your opponents are also entitled to an explanation of your methods. One of them might want to act over a two-club bid if he but knew in advance that the bid signified a weak hand with a long club suit.

Also see: Arguments 59, 60, 61, 62.

CHAPTER 11

Responses to an Opening Bid of Two Notrump

ARGUMENT 64

After a two notrump opening, is a three-club response a sign-off?

THE HAND

```
                    NORTH
                    ♠ A Q 8 2
                    ♡ A K 5 3
                    ◇ K Q 9
                    ♣ K J

        WEST                          EAST
        ♠ J 10 3                      ♠ K 9 6 5 4
        ♡ J 10 9 6                    ♡ 4 2
        ◇ J 5 4                       ◇ A 10 6 3
        ♣ 8 7 3                       ♣ A 6

                    SOUTH
                    ♠ 7
                    ♡ Q 8 7
                    ◇ 8 7 2
                    ♣ Q 10 9 5 4 2
```

THE AUCTION

NORTH	EAST	SOUTH	WEST
2 NT	Pass	3 ♣	Pass
3 ♠	Pass	4 ♣	Pass
4 ♡	Pass	5 ♣	Pass
Pass	Pass		

THE RESULT

The final contract was not all that bad, even though the declarer was down one.

Had the spade finesse been successful, the declarer would have been able to discard one of his losing diamonds; or had the ace of diamonds been onside, the declarer would have lost only one trick in each minor suit.

However, three notrump was an easy contract, for the queen of hearts would have been an entry to South's clubs.

THE ARGUMENT

South maintained that he had shown nothing but a weak club suit with his bidding.

North contended that this would have held true if he had opened one notrump and South had then bid clubs twice; but over two notrump, South's three clubs was Stayman. The bid guaranteed a four-card major.

No reference book offered an answer to the problem.

GOREN SETTLES THE ARGUMENT

All responses to an opening bid of two notrump are forcing to game. With a long minor suit and a bust, the responder must pass, and let the opener manage as best as he can.

A bid of three clubs over an opening two notrump is a Stayman inquiry which asks for a four-card major suit.

The sequence of bidding employed by South on this hand promised a four-card holding in one of the major suits—not a long club suit.

Nevertheless, South's hand is not the one with which we would choose to pass partner's opening two notrump bid. The opener has promised 22-24 points with his bid, and South holds 4 points and a six-card suit. He should go on to three notrump, in the fond hope that his partner will be able to make use of the long club suit.

Let us weaken South's hand slightly, and make it:

> ♠ x
> ♡ Q x x
> ◇ x x x
> ♣ x x x x x x

Now South does not have the values to raise two no-trump to game. Almost certainly, the hand will play better at a club partial than at notrump. However, there is no way to stop the bidding below game if South responds with three clubs, so he must pass.

Let us switch around the suits in the above hand:

> ♠ x
> ♡ x x x x x x
> ◇ x x x
> ♣ Q x x

Again game is doubtful, but there is more chance of making ten tricks at a heart contract than eight or nine at notrump. So South should bid three hearts. If partner rebids three notrump, South should correct to four hearts.

With a long minor and a near bust, pass the opener's bid of two notrump. With a near bust and a six-card or longer major, the responder should bid three of the major.

Also see: Argument 66.

ARGUMENT 65

Does raising the opener's two notrump to four notrump ask for aces?

THE HAND

NORTH
♠ K Q 5
♡ A J 7 3
◇ A 5
♣ A K J 7

SOUTH
♠ A J 10 7 6 2
♡ K 9 5
◇ 7 6 2
♣ 3

THE AUCTION

NORTH	EAST	SOUTH	WEST
2 NT	Pass	4 NT	Pass
Pass	Pass		

THE RESULT

After a diamond lead, the declarer took eleven tricks in notrump.

However, six spades was there for the taking, via a diamond ruff with a high trump.

THE ARGUMENT

South inquired whether North knew the responses to the Blackwood Convention.

North responded by asking whether insanity was hereditary in South's family.

Politely ignoring this grievous slur, South held firm to his conviction that any jump to four notrump asked for aces. He declared he was willing to pay if he was wrong.

GOREN SETTLES THE ARGUMENT

A raise of the opener's two notrump opening to four notrump is not a request to show aces. It is a quantitative raise of notrump, requesting the opener to go on to slam if he holds a 24-point hand.

There is one way to ask for aces over a notrump opening bid, and that is to employ the Gerber convention. A bid of four clubs asks the opener to show how many aces he holds, with the responses coming in steps, exactly as in Blackwood. Thus an answer of four diamonds would show either no aces or all four aces; four hearts would show one ace; etc.

This does not mean that, on this hand, South should have employed Gerber. For South does not know at this point where the hand is to be played. Granted that it seems that spades will be the final contract. But might not notrump prove a safer contract?

I can see no reason why South should not simply have responded three spades to his partner's two notrump opening. That bid would leave the maximum room for exploration.

Any suit response to a two notrump opening is forcing.

ARGUMENT 66

Can a player sign off by bidding three of a suit in response to a two notrump opening?

THE HAND

NORTH
- ♠ K Q 10
- ♡ K 8
- ◇ A K J 3
- ♣ A Q 7 6

WEST
- ♠ 9 7 6 4
- ♡ J 4 2
- ◇ Q 8 7 6
- ♣ 8 3

EAST
- ♠ A J 5
- ♡ A Q 9
- ◇ 10 2
- ♣ K 10 9 5 4

SOUTH
- ♠ 8 3 2
- ♡ 10 7 6 5 3
- ◇ 9 5 4
- ♣ J 2

THE AUCTION

NORTH	EAST	SOUTH	WEST
2 NT	Pass	3 ♡	Pass
4 NT	Pass	5 ♣	Pass
5 ♡	Dbl	Pass	Pass
Pass			

THE RESULT

West led the eight of clubs. The declarer played low from dummy, and East won the king and returned the suit. The declarer's jack won. He now led a trump to the king in dummy which was taken by East's ace. East played a third club. West ruffed as the declarer discarded a spade. The defenders still scored two trump tricks and the ace of spades.

Down four.

THE ARGUMENT

South wanted to know whether North had had a rush of blood to the head. He held only 22 points and a doubleton trump, so why charge into Blackwood?

North claimed that South had made a forward-going bid, and since all his points were in prime controls, he had every right to try for slam.

"A forward-going bid?" screamed South. "All I was trying to do was get out in three hearts! I thought the hand would play better in my five-card suit than in notrump."

GOREN SETTLES THE ARGUMENT

Using standard methods, there is no way to stop in three of a suit.

Any suit response to an opening bid of two notrump is forcing.

Such a response could even be the first move in a slam-going auction by a strong responding hand.

The sure way to stay out of game with South's hand is to pass two notrump and hope for the best. It happens that, if East makes his normal opening of a club, the result won't be too bad. South's jack will win the trick.

So will North's finesse of the jack of diamonds. Although the diamonds do not split, the declarer is bound to make two club tricks, three diamonds, one spade and at least one more trick because East is bound to be endplayed.

There is a special convention designed to allow you to play in three of a major, named after its originator, Jeremy Flint of England.

Under the Flint Convention, a bid of three

diamonds in response to an opening bid of two notrump demands that the opener rebid three hearts. If the responder's suit is hearts, he may pass. If the responder's suit is spades, he converts to three spades. The opener is expected to pass.

I must stress that this convention is not widely known or used, except by expert partnerships. If you want to play it, be sure to discuss it first with your partner. If it comes as a surprise to him, it could lead to disaster.

Also see: Argument 64.

ARGUMENT 67

In response to a two notrump opening, is a jump to game weak or strong?

THE HAND

```
        NORTH
        ♠ A K
        ♡ K 9 7 2
        ◊ A Q 10 4
        ♣ A Q J


        SOUTH
        ♠ Q J 8 7 6 3
        ♡ Q 3
        ◊ J 7 6
        ♣ 10 3
```

THE AUCTION

NORTH	EAST	SOUTH	WEST
2 NT	Pass	4 ♠	Pass
6 ♠	Pass	Pass	Pass

THE RESULT

West led the nine of clubs. Though it seemed from the lead that the finesse was going to lose, the declarer had no alternative. Even had he wanted to win the trick with the ace and take the diamond finesse in the hope of discarding a club, he had no entry to his hand.

East won with the king of clubs and cashed his ace of hearts.

Down one.

THE ARGUMENT

"You jumped the bidding on *that* collection?" stormed North. "I would almost prefer a pass! Wouldn't a bid of three spades have been sufficient?"

"Your bridge intelligence and your behavior seem to be on a par," responded South. "When I jumped to game I was making a shutout bid, and you should have passed."

North icily retorted that he could not see the point of trying to shut out a hand that had been announced as extremely powerful.

GOREN SETTLES THE ARGUMENT

Only to a limited extent would I agree with North. You cannot shut out a partner who has shown a very powerful hand—he must always be allowed to exercise his judgment about whether he should bid again. But South's signals were loud and clear.

In reponse to a two notrump opening bid, a bid of four of a *major* is weaker than a bid of three. The jump to four shows a good trump suit, but denies any first- or second-round controls.

Applying this principle to the hand in question, it is obvious that North's slam try is distinctly against the odds. His side is missing the ace of hearts, the king of diamonds, and the king of clubs. Thus, for slam to succeed, North has been warned by South's bid that both minor suit finesses must work.

North was bidding against the odds.

CHAPTER 12

Responses to an Opening Bid of Three Notrump

ARGUMENT 68

Can you use Stayman in response to a three notrump opening bid?

THE HAND

```
                    NORTH
                    ♠ K 9 5 4
                    ♡ A 10 8 2
                    ◇ 9 7 6 2
                    ♣ 6
WEST                                    EAST
♠ J 10 6 2                              ♠ Q 7 3
♡ 6 5 3                                 ♡ 9 4
◇ 10 3                                  ◇ J 8 5 4
♣ A 10 7 4                              ♣ 9 8 3 2
                    SOUTH
                    ♠ A 8
                    ♡ K Q J 7
                    ◇ A K Q
                    ♣ K Q J 5
```

THE AUCTION

SOUTH	WEST	NORTH	EAST
3 NT	Pass	4 ♣	Pass
4 ♠	Pass	6 ♠	Pass
Pass	Pass		

THE RESULT

The declarer lost two trump tricks and the ace of clubs.

Down two.

Six hearts would have been an excellent contract.

THE ARGUMENT

North and South had gotten their wires crossed.

North intended his four-club bid as the convention named after Sam Stayman. He was asking for four-card majors.

South thought North was using the ace-asking convention named for John Gerber: South's response of four spades showed two aces.

North insisted that a club bid over partner's notrump was always an inquiry for major suits.

"Absolute lunacy!" argued South. "There must be some way to check on aces, and four clubs in response to any opening notrump bid is always Gerber."

GOREN SETTLES THE ARGUMENT

Here's an interesting argument with a great deal of logic on both sides.

Playing with a strange partner, and lacking a previous agreement, a four-club bid over an opening three no-trump should be treated as Stayman.

Because the three notrump opening bid comes up so rarely, even experienced partnerships seldom discuss the responder's action. Yet it can be crucial on some hands, such as the one in question, to check on a 4-4 major fit. Note that in this hand six notrump fails, while a contract for six hearts comes home without a 3-3 diamond division or any similar good fortune.

However, there are other hands where the number of aces that the opener holds is the paramount matter.

Expert partnerships have developed a solution for this situation.

A response of four clubs over an opening three notrump bid checks on major suits; a response of four diamonds over an opening three notrump bid is a request for aces.

Also see: Argument 69.

ARGUMENT 69

Is a major-suit takeout of three notrump a slam try?

THE HAND

```
                    NORTH
                    ♠ K Q J
                    ♡ A Q 2
                    ◇ A J 2
                    ♣ A K Q 8
    WEST                              EAST
    ♠ A 10 5                          ♠ 8 7 6 4
    ♡ 6                               ♡ K J 9
    ◇ Q 10 6 5 3                      ◇ K 8 7 4
    ♣ J 9 7 4                         ♣ 5 3
                    SOUTH
                    ♠ 9 3 2
                    ♡ 10 8 7 5 4 3
                    ◇ 9
                    ♣ 10 6 2
```

THE AUCTION

NORTH	EAST	SOUTH	WEST
3 NT	Pass	Pass	Pass

THE RESULT

East led the four of diamonds to his partner's queen and the declarer's ace. The declarer played for his only chance—to find East with the doubleton king of hearts and the ace of spades. He led the ace and queen of hearts, in the hope that his deuce would become a means of entry to the dummy.

When this failed to materialize, he went down two.

Four hearts was a breeze, despite the fact that South would have had to lose two tricks in the trump suit.

THE ARGUMENT

"How could you leave me in three notrump with your worthless hand?" moaned North. "You were absolutely trickless at notrump, but you rated to produce at least three tricks in a heart contract. It was automatic for you to bid four hearts!"

"If you would play less automatically and use your noggin a bit more, we would both be better off," retaliated South. "Four hearts is a forward-going bid, and the one thing I certainly did not want you to do was to make another bid. I passed because I reckoned you had a better shot for nine tricks at notrump than I would have for eleven or twelve tricks in a heart contract."

GOREN SETTLES THE ARGUMENT

No matter what hearts North held for his opening three-notrump bid, one thing is certain: hearts was going to be a better spot than notrump. I fully concur with North when he suggested that his partner should have moved the contract to four hearts.

A move to four in a major over an opening bid of three notrump is not forward-going. Quite the contrary! It says: I doubt that you can make three notrump. I have a long suit and a bust hand, and I think we had better play in my suit.

How, then, can you investigate a possible slam? Suppose South's hand were:

♠ x x x
♡ K x x x x x
♦ K x
♣ x x

Do I mean to suggest that South should jump to five

hearts with such a holding? Of course not, but there is still a practical solution.

Where the responder holds some values, and if the hands happen to fit well, the responder should initiate the prospects of a slam with a Stayman inquiry.

Thus with the hand directly above, South would bid four clubs over the three notrump opening bid. He would then bid his heart suit on his next turn.

What if the diamond and heart suits were interchanged in the hand that caused the argument—should South remove to four diamonds?

No, he cannot do so, because a bid of four diamonds over an opening bid of three notrump is an ace-asking bid.

Besides, the responder would have no assurance that eleven tricks could be made in a minor suit contract. He should stick it out at three notrump and hope that, by some miracle, the declarer can scrape up nine tricks. If the three notrump contract were doubled, then of course the responder would and should run to four diamonds.

Also see: Argument 68.

CHAPTER 13

Opener's Rebids

ARGUMENT 70

After a one notrump response, does the opener's rebid of his original suit show a five-card suit?

THE HAND

```
                    NORTH
                    ♠ 10
                    ♡ Q J 10 9
                    ◇ Q 10 3 2
                    ♣ Q 10 9 7

    WEST                            EAST
    ♠ Q 9 8 6 4                     ♠ 5 2
    ♡ A 5 2                         ♡ K 8 6 3
    ◇ A 9                           ◇ 8 7 6 4
    ♣ 8 5 4                         ♣ A K 3

                    SOUTH
                    ♠ A K J 7 3
                    ♡ 7 4
                    ◇ K J 5
                    ♣ J 6 2
```

THE AUCTION

SOUTH	WEST	NORTH	EAST
1 ♠	Pass	1 NT	Pass
2 ♠	Pass	Pass	Pass

THE RESULT

In addition to their five tricks in aces and kings, the defenders collected two trump tricks.

The declarer went down two.

THE ARGUMENT

South, on the defensive, claimed he had to rebid his spades to show he held a five-card suit.

North maintained that one notrump could not be beaten, and that all South was showing was the gap in his bridge knowledge.

GOREN SETTLES THE ARGUMENT

The best place to play an indifferent hand when the opener's hand is relatively balanced is in a contract of one notrump. Usually, there is no reason for the opener who holds a minimum hand to disturb his partner's notrump response. Unless the opener is two-suited and wants to offer a choice of contracts, or unless his hand is relatively unbalanced, he should pass his partner's notrump response.

The bidding sequence of one spade, one notrump, two spades, almost invariably promises a six-card suit.

Let us assume that the opening bidder has an unbalanced hand, with a five-card spade suit and a singleton. That would give him seven cards in the other two suits. Ipso facto, he would hold a second suit of at least four cards. In that case, he would show his second suit over his partner's notrump response.

Also see: Argument 83.

ARGUMENT 71

Is a rebid in a new suit stronger than a rebid of one notrump?

THE HAND

```
                    NORTH
                    ♠ A J 10 7
                    ♡ K Q 10 2
                    ◇ J 6 3
                    ♣ K 4
WEST                                    EAST
♠ 9 4 3                                 ♠ 5 2
♡ 9 7 5                                 ♡ A 8 6
◇ K Q 9 4 2                             ◇ A 10 8
♣ 10 7                                  ♣ J 8 6 5 3
                    SOUTH
                    ♠ K Q 8 6
                    ♡ J 4 3
                    ◇ 7 5
                    ♣ A Q 9 2
```

THE AUCTION

SOUTH	WEST	NORTH	EAST
1 ♣	Pass	1 ♡	Pass
1 NT	Pass	3 NT	Pass
Pass	Pass	Pass	

THE RESULT

North-South could have taken ten tricks were it not for the fact that East-West took the first six—five in diamonds, plus the ace of hearts.

Down two.

THE ARGUMENT

South bellowed that North should have rebid two spades after the one notrump to check back.

North retorted that he would like to check back on South's mental history. Why in blazes, yelled North, didn't South follow North's one heart with a bid of one spade? That bid would have inevitably led to an unstoppable four-spade contract.

GOREN SETTLES THE ARGUMENT

I think I know what went through South's mind: "I have an absolute minimum and a balanced hand. Before my partner gets any wrong ideas about the strength of my hand, I will show him my weakness with a rebid of one notrump."

However, in doing so, South overlooked the important principle of "bidding up the line." By passing over the spade suit, he denied holding four cards in that suit.

When two alternative bids are available, bid the "cheapest" bid. By implication, a response of one spade over an opening bid in a minor denies a holding of four hearts.

There was no reason for North to "check back" on South's holding with a bid of two spades. South had already told him that such action would be futile. By bidding two spades, North would be saying he held a five-card heart suit.

There was another reason why North did not—and should not—rebid two spades.

Never tell the enemy more about a hand than you need to.

Once North "knew" that there was no 4-4 major fit (of course, there actually *was*) it would have been folly to alert the defenders to where his outside strength lay. Such a bid might have warned the defenders not to make a helpful lead and might have steered them to their best defense.

Let's say South held:

♠ 9 3
♡ K 10 5 4
◇ K Q
♣ A Q 9 3 2

South opens the bidding with 1 club and North responds 1 spade. Now South's best rebid is one notrump. Either North has a weak hand and no heart suit, or he has a spade-heart two-suiter. In either case, there is no need for South to bid his hearts. If North's only major is spades, one notrump is probably the best spot to play the hand. If North also holds hearts, South can raise North's rebid of hearts.

A second bid in a new suit at the one-level is no stronger than a second bid of one notrump.

Indeed, because of distributional values, in a hand containing four spades and five diamonds, one might bid a new suit on his second turn with fewer high-card points than he would need to bid one notrump.

ARGUMENT 72

*Is it wise to show another suit after your
partner's raise of your original suit bid?*

THE HAND

```
                    NORTH
                    ♠ Q 85
                    ♡ J 873
                    ◇ K 7
                    ♣ 9854

   WEST                             EAST
   ♠ J 10 7 2                       ♠ K 943
   ♡ Q                              ♡ 954
   ◇ Q 10 3 2                       ◇ J 64
   ♣ A J 62                         ♣ K Q 10

                    SOUTH
                    ♠ A 6
                    ♡ A K 10 6 2
                    ◇ A 985
                    ♣ 73
```

THE AUCTION

SOUTH	WEST	NORTH	EAST
1 ♡	Pass	2 ♡	Pass
3 ♡	Pass	Pass	Pass

THE RESULT

West led the jack of spades, covered by the queen,
king, and ace. Trumps were drawn in three rounds.
The declarer ruffed a diamond in dummy, and conceded one spade, one diamond, and two clubs.

He just made his contract.

THE ARGUMENT

"I don't know which is worse," complained North, "your bidding or your play. We should have been in four hearts, and you could easily have made game."

"I bid it by the book," replied South. "Even if you revalue my hand by adding a point for the fifth trump, my hand is still worth only 18 points. To jump to game would be aggressive—all I could do was invite game. Of course, you had to pass with a minimum."

GOREN SETTLES THE ARGUMENT

North is right. Ten tricks can be made by the simple expedient of ruffing two diamonds in dummy. The declarer plays one round of trumps and then ruffs a diamond. He returns to his hand via a trump lead from dummy, and then ruffs out his last diamond with the jack of hearts. He thus holds his losers to two clubs and a spade.

South's prime controls make it very tempting to leap straight to game once he has received support. However, the hand contains too many losers. I therefore recommend that in a situation of this sort one proceed with caution.

The hand merits a try for game. The only question is: What is the best way to invite North to go on to game?

I do not think it is so much a question of whether North holds 8 points or 9 points, but *where his points are.* I can construct many 9-point hands—even 10-point hands—that offer no play for game; yet on the actual holding of a mere 7 points, ten tricks can be made.

The key to the hand is: Where does North's strength lie, and how can South locate it? South should invite game by pinpointing North's values—the place where North must furnish help if the hand is to play in game.

South should proceed with a rebid of three diamonds

on his second turn. In effect, this is the same as a bid of three hearts, but it has the added value of highlighting a feature of South's hand.

When your partner has given you a minimum response, and it is imperative to find out where his strength lies, bid (if possible) a secondary suit. If the responder has an honor or ruffing values in that suit, his second positive response should yield the information needed to warrant a game try.

In this hand, if South bids three diamonds North should realize that his doubleton king of diamonds in addition to his four trumps greatly increases the value of his hand. Hence he should jump to four hearts.

The virtue of the three-diamond rebid can best be pointed up by rearranging North's hand slightly. Let's make it:

♠ Q x x x
♡ J x x x
◇ x x x
♣ K x

This hand has exactly the same count as North's actual hand, yet with this holding even three hearts might be difficult to bring home.

ARGUMENT 73

*Should you raise your partner's response
with three good trumps in his suit, or
rebid your own good five-card suit?*

THE HAND

NORTH
♠ A 8 7 6 2
♡ A 5 2
♢ Q 8
♣ 9 6 3

WEST
♠ J 9 5
♡ Q 10 7 3
♢ J 9 6 4
♣ A 8

EAST
♠ 10 4
♡ K J 8 4
♢ 10 2
♣ K Q J 7 5

SOUTH
♠ K Q 3
♡ 9 6
♢ A K 7 5 3
♣ 10 4 2

THE AUCTION

SOUTH	WEST	NORTH	EAST
1 ♢	Pass	1 ♠	Pass
2 ♢	Pass	Pass	Pass

THE RESULT

South made nine tricks.

THE ARGUMENT

It was North's contention that four spades could be

made with careful play, and that he would have preferred to have been there.

South declared spiritedly that he had no idea North held a five-card suit. Moreover, in his opinion, it was important to show that the diamond suit he had bid was a good five-carder.

GOREN SETTLES THE ARGUMENT

When a responder's holding is good enough for only one bid, he should make that bid which provides the most information to his partner. The same principle applies to the opener who has opened with a minimum, when he must rebid.

Since the purpose in bidding is to locate a fit, the existence of such a fit should be announced at the first opportunity. This is especially true of a fit in a major suit.

Had South in this hand reasoned in this manner, he would undoubtedly have come up with a two-spade rebid. With a fit established, North would have revalued his hand, which would then have been worth 12 points.

In addition, one of the responder's honor cards was in diamonds—the suit his partner had opened. Therefore, this queen was worth somewhat more than the value assigned to it by the point count.

North might not have bid four spades over South's raise to two, but North would certainly have made a strong move toward game by bidding three spades.

For those interested in how four spades can be made, let us describe the play. Let us assume the defenders take three club tricks and then shift to a trump, which is as good a defense as any. The declarer wins with the ace of spades, and draws another round of trumps with the dummy's king. The queen of diamonds is cashed, followed by a diamond to the king. Now a low diamond is led from the dummy and the declarer ruffs. When East cannot overruff, all that remains is for the declarer to cross to the dummy with a trump, drawing West's last trump in the process. The declarer now takes two heart discards on the dummy's good diamonds.

ARGUMENT 74

How strong a hand should you have to raise your partner's two-over-one response?

THE HAND

```
                    NORTH
                    ♠ 7 5
                    ♡ K Q 8 6 5
                    ◇ K 6 3
                    ♣ Q 10 5
    WEST                              EAST
    ♠ Q J 8 6                        ♠ 9 4
    ♡ 7 4                            ♡ 10 9 2
    ◇ 8 7 4 2                        ◇ A 9 5
    ♣ A 7 2                          ♣ K 9 8 6 4
                    SOUTH
                    ♠ A K 10 3 2
                    ♡ A J 3
                    ◇ Q J 10
                    ♣ J 3
```

THE AUCTION

SOUTH	WEST	NORTH	EAST
1 ♠	Pass	2 ♡	Pass
3 ♡	Pass	Pass	Pass

THE RESULT

The declarer had little trouble making ten tricks. He lost to the ace and king of clubs, and the ace of diamonds.

THE ARGUMENT

South fiercely challenged North's final pass. He

maintained that his bidding had promised at least 16 points; so North should have bid game.

North claimed that South had promised no more than a minimum holding.

The discourse became acrimonious, and I was drafted to pour oil over troubled waters.

GOREN SETTLES THE ARGUMENT

Had North responded to South's one-spade opening bid with a bid of two in a minor suit, a raise to the three-level in the minor by South would definitely have indicated a holding of at least 16 points.

Where the opening bid is in spades and the responder declares hearts, the requirement for a single raise from two hearts to three hearts is lowered to 14 points. Since it is always desirable to locate an eight-card combined holding in a major, the opener should strain to support the heart bid.

On this hand, North had done all he could when he made a two-heart response on his 10 points in high cards, and a doubleton in his partner's suit.

To avoid missing a game, South should have taken the strain off his partner. He knew from his hand that there had to be a play for four hearts, so he should have made that bid directly. North had to hold 10 points to go to the two-level. If South had but added North's 10 points to his own 16, he would have seen that, at worst, the hand would be close.

Also see: Argument 85.

ARGUMENT 75

Is a four-card suit ever rebiddable?

THE HAND

```
                    NORTH
                    ♠ J 10 5
                    ♡ Q 3
                    ◇ K Q
                    ♣ Q J 10 8 6 3

WEST                                    EAST
♠ 9 8                                   ♠ 6 4 3 2
♡ K 7 6 4                               ♡ A J 9 2
◇ J 10 5 4 2                            ◇ A 9 7 3
♣ 9 5                                   ♣ 7

                    SOUTH
                    ♠ A K Q 7
                    ♡ 10 8 5
                    ◇ 8 6
                    ♣ A K 4 2
```

THE AUCTION

SOUTH	WEST	NORTH	EAST
1 ♣	Pass	3 ♣	Pass
3 ♠	Pass	4 ♣	Pass
5 ♣	Pass	Pass	Pass

THE RESULT

West led the jack of diamonds. East won with the ace and shifted to the ace of hearts. West signalled with the seven. East continued with a heart to the king.

Down one.

THE ARGUMENT

In looking at all four hands, the players noticed that

209

four spades could have been made against any defense. This led to all sorts of speculation, but no one could come up with a sensible method of getting to the right contract. It was decided to write to me for an opinion.

GOREN SETTLES THE ARGUMENT

We have always been taught that five-card suits are rebiddable, and that four-card suits are not.

Many four-card suits that are solid, or nearly so, should be treated as if they were five cards long, and should be rebid under certain circumstances.

To make my point more strongly, let us consider two suit holdings in isolation:

[A]	[B]
Dummy	Dummy
x x x	x x x
Declarer	Declarer
Q x x x x	A K Q x

All other things being equal, wouldn't you rather hold the trump combination in *Hand B* than in *Hand A?* Yet almost everyone would rebid the declarer's holding in the first example; and few players would do so with *Hand B*.

I don't want to give the impression that a 4-3 trump fit is ideal: it can present grave problems. If the declarer is forced to ruff early in the hand, he may lose control of the proceedings. However, if he can keep his trump holdings intact until he draws trumps, he should do fine.

On the hand submitted, South should have realized that his spades would prove adequate under certain circumstances, even if his partner held only two-card support. Therefore, he might have tried a rebid of four spades rather than five clubs. North would have been delighted to pass, and a game would have rolled home.

I know some will say: "There's that Goren talking through his derby again. No one would ever find that bid at the table!"

In self-defense, I can only say that some years ago U.S. internationalist Bobby Jordan held a very similar hand in a world championship match against Italy. He bid four spades in this very situation, and made his contract for a large profit. What is more, the entire panel of commentators called the proper bid while Bobby was still thinking.

ARGUMENT 76

How much is a fit with your partner's suit worth?

THE HAND

```
              NORTH
              ♠ K 10 7 5 4
              ♡ A 9 4
              ◇ 7
              ♣ 8 6 3 2


              SOUTH
              ♠ A Q 8 3
              ♡ 8 7 6 2
              ◇ A K 10 9 2
              ♣ —
```

THE AUCTION

SOUTH	WEST	NORTH	EAST
1 ◇	Pass	1 ♠	Pass
2 ♠	Pass	Pass	Pass

THE RESULT

The hand was a laydown for four spades.

North scored three top tricks in the red suits. With the help of two club ruffs in dummy, he made a total of seven trump tricks—ten tricks in all.

THE ARGUMENT

North raved. He yelled that South had no bridge sense. He pointed out that after his response of one spade, South's hand had turned into a colossus, and that his partner was just too dumb to see that glaring fact.

212

South mumbled that his 13 points in high cards were still—despite all the shouting—still only 13 points.

GOREN SETTLES THE ARGUMENT

Despite his intemperate vehemence, North happens to be right.

When the opener counts his points, his distributional values are counted as 1 for a doubleton, 2 for a singleton, and 3 for a void. Holding a fit for his partner's bid, the responder counts 1 for a doubleton, 3 for a singleton, and 5 for a void. These added values are given to the responder because the declarer will be ruffing in the short trump hand, considerably increasing the combined trick-taking potential of the partnership assets.

Let us study the following trump holding for a moment:

Dummy
K J 9

Declarer
A Q 10 8 3

If the declarer takes two ruffs in his own hand and then draws trumps, he will realize only five tricks from the combined holding. However, if he takes the two ruffs in the dummy—the short trump hand—he will bring his total number of tricks in the trump suit to seven.

When the opener has an excellent trump fit with the responder, the roles become reversed. In effect, the opening bidder now becomes the responder. He must revalue his distribution, as if he were responding to an opening bid.

Thus, South should have counted his void as 5

points, bringing the total value of his hand to 18 points
in support of North's spade bid. That would be enough
for a jump raise to three spades. North would then
have been encouraged to go on to game.

ARGUMENT 77

Which is it more important to show first—good fit or great strength?

THE HAND

```
                    NORTH
                    ♠ J 10 8 7 5
                    ♡ Q J 10
                    ◇ J 10 4 2
                    ♣ Q
WEST                                    EAST
♠ Q 4 3                                 ♠ 6
♡ 7 3 2                                 ♡ 9 8 6 5 4
◇ A 7                                   ◇ 8 6 5 3
♣ A 10 8 3 2                            ♣ K 9 5
                    SOUTH
                    ♠ A K 9 2
                    ♡ A K
                    ◇ K Q 9
                    ♣ J 7 6 4
```

THE AUCTION

SOUTH	WEST	NORTH	EAST
1 ♣	Pass	1 ♠	Pass
2 NT	Pass	3 NT	Pass
Pass	Pass		

THE RESULT

West led a club. The defenders took the first six tricks.

Down two.

THE ARGUMENT

Even though he would have to lose a trump trick, North noted icily that four spades was "frigid."

North suggested that South should go elsewhere—perhaps to a warmer clime—if he wanted to play solitaire.

South protested that he had more than done his duty by showing a balanced 19-20 points. Hadn't North heard that a five-card suit was rebiddable?

GOREN SETTLES THE ARGUMENT

South felt satisfied that he had shown his balanced 20 points, but he forgot about the pre-eminent importance of showing a fit.

Once a 4-4 or better fit in a major suit has been established, it is generally sounder to play the hand in the suit rather than at notrump. There may be a fatal weakness in the hand at notrump, that would not be of much account if the hand were played in a trump suit.

A major suit fit often yields one more trick in play than can be made at notrump. The reason for this is that, once trumps are drawn, there is generally a trump left both in the dummy and in the declarer's hand. These trumps can be used *separately* for ruffing purposes. Thus, while the suit can produce no more than four tricks at notrump, it can produce five tricks or even six tricks in a suit contract.

North's raise to three notrump was eminently proper. He had stoppers in all the unbid suits, and a key card in his partner's suit. Once South, by his non-support, denied holding four spades, it looked as if notrump would prove an ideal spot.

Revalued for play at a spade contract, South's hand was worth 21 points. His proper action was to immediately bid four spades over North's one-spade response. Note that a bid of three spades, though highly invitational, would not be forcing to game.

We would stress that this preference for supporting one's partner's bid extends, in principle, to the major suits only. Switch the spade and diamond suits around, giving North a one-diamond response to South's one-club opener, and we would rebid two notrump with the South hand. The reason is obvious: with a balanced hand, it is often easier to make nine tricks at a notrump contract than eleven tricks in a minor.

ARGUMENT 78

When should you try to make your partner the notrump declarer?

THE HAND

```
                    NORTH
                    ♠ K Q 10 6
                    ♡ K 9 8 5 2
                    ◇ Q 4
                    ♣ Q 3
    WEST                                EAST
    ♠ 9 7 5 4                           ♠ A 3 2
    ♡ Q 4                               ♡ A 10 7 3
    ◇ J 10 8 7                          ◇ K 9 3 2
    ♣ 9 4 2                             ♣ 7 5
                    SOUTH
                    ♠ J 8
                    ♡ J 6
                    ◇ A 6 5
                    ♣ A K J 10 8 6
```

THE AUCTION

SOUTH	WEST	NORTH	EAST
1 ♣	Pass	1 ♡	Pass
2 ♣	Pass	2 ♠	Pass
2 NT	Pass	3 NT	Pass
Pass	Pass		

THE RESULT

West led the jack of diamonds, and in the fullness of time the defenders made three diamond tricks and two aces.

Down one.

THE ARGUMENT

Had the hand not occurred in a duplicate event, the play of the last trick might have ended the matter. However, when she opened the score sheet, South noted that several pairs had succeeded in making three notrump. Completely puzzled, South could not see how she could have made the contract after a diamond lead.

GOREN SETTLES THE ARGUMENT

The factor of position plays an important part in bridge. Many hands that are unmakeable from one side of the table cannot be defeated from the other side of the table. This hand is an excellent example.

When a notrump contract is contemplated, it is generally to the offensive side's advantage to have the lead come up to the hand holding the tenaces. It is equally important to have unprotected honors, i.e., K x or Q x x, protected against being led through at Trick One.

Let us consider a specific holding in isolation:

```
                    K x
      Q J 9 x                     A 10 x x
                    x x x
```

If South is the declarer at a notrump contract, the defenders can take four tricks in the suit right off the bat (if West leads the suit shown).

However, with North as the declarer, the defending side must give up a trick in this suit, if it elects to attack this suit at the opening gun.

Moreover, if the defenders decide to lead some other suit, the declarer might gain a vital tempo. Thus, the declaring side should do everything possible to see that the "right" hand becomes the declarer—in this case, the North hand.

On the deal in question, it should have been obvious to South that she stood to gain nothing by becoming the declarer. She did not hold a single tenace, nor did she hold an unprotected honor to shelter from the opening lead.

Therefore, South should have maneuvered to make North become the declarer in the three notrump contract. She could have accomplished this by bidding three diamonds rather than two notrump. She needn't have had any fear that North would have raised her bid in diamonds, for North had already shown at least nine cards in the major suits and, therefore, was unlikely to hold four diamonds. North certainly would not have raised South's secondary suit with only three-card support. It was much more likely that North would then have converted to three notrump.

From North's side of the table, there is no way the three notrump contract can be defeated.

ARGUMENT 79

If your partner's response to your opening bid is one notrump and your hand is quite strong, should your rebid be a jump in a new four-card suit?

THE HAND

```
                    NORTH
                    ♠ 10 5
                    ♡ 8 7 3
                    ◇ K Q 9 6
                    ♣ A 7 5 4

WEST                                    EAST
♠ 9 6 3 2                               ♠ 7 4
♡ A 6 2                                 ♡ J 10 9 5 4
◇ 7 4 3                                 ◇ 10 8
♣ Q 10 8                                ♣ K 9 3 2

                    SOUTH
                    ♠ A K Q J 8
                    ♡ K Q
                    ◇ A J 5 2
                    ♣ J 6
```

THE AUCTION

SOUTH	WEST	NORTH	EAST
1 ♠	Pass	1 NT	Pass
3 NT			

THE RESULT

After a heart lead, North had no trouble making eleven tricks.

But he was hardly pleased with the result, for a diamond slam was an absolute laydown.

THE ARGUMENT

North upbraided South for not bidding his diamonds over the notrump response.

South replied that, with only 21 points, he could not visualize a slam after North could respond with nothing stronger than one notrump.

GOREN SETTLES THE ARGUMENT

Two-suited hands should be treated as such. The holder of a two-suiter should endeavor to find a fit with his partner.

The beauty of the situation is that South can investigate slam possibilities without necessarily bypassing three notrump. His natural rebid of three diamonds, showing his second suit, also announces his great strength, and gives his partner several options: North can raise South's diamonds; North can now give preference to three spades; or North can show values in the unbid suits by rebidding three notrump, which South would then pass.

A jump by South to three diamonds would bring an energetic response from North. The technically correct bid on his hand would now be four clubs, showing an excellent diamond fit and the ace of clubs. A six-diamond contract would then become almost automatic.

ARGUMENT 80

Is the opening bidder's change of suit forcing?

THE HAND

NORTH
- ♠ K J 10 4
- ♡ J 3
- ♦ Q J 2
- ♣ A K 10 5

WEST
- ♠ 8 7 6
- ♡ A 6 2
- ♦ A 9 6 5 4
- ♣ J 8

EAST
- ♠ A Q 2
- ♡ Q 8 7 4
- ♦ 10 7
- ♣ Q 9 4 3

SOUTH
- ♠ 9 5 3
- ♡ K 10 9 5
- ♦ K 8 3
- ♣ 7 6 2

THE AUCTION

NORTH	EAST	SOUTH	WEST
1 ♣	Pass	1 ♡	Pass
1 ♠	Pass	1 NT	Pass
2 NT	Pass	Pass	Pass

THE RESULT

West led the five of diamonds. The defenders made no errors. At the end of play, they had garnered two spade tricks, three diamonds, and a heart.

Down one.

THE ARGUMENT

North stated that he would rather not bid at all than bid twice on the garbage that South held.

For his part, South expressed a complete failure to understand how North, holding a mere 15 points, could raise to two notrump in the face of two minimum responses.

Tempers came to a quick boil, and the hand was submitted for arbitration.

GOREN SETTLES THE ARGUMENT

North's one-spade bid was not forcing.

Since North's bid was not forcing, South showed better than a minimum hand by bidding a second time. Thus, North was justified in looking for a game.

A change of suit by the *responder* is forcing on the opener; but a change of suit by the opener is not forcing on the responder. The responder can pass the opener's simple change of suit, unless it is a reverse bid at a higher level.

However, I do not want to give the impression that a responder should willy-nilly pass the opener's change of suit just because he has a hand that is below average. The opener's range for a simple change of suit can be quite large, and the responder should strive to keep the bidding open.

A responder may pass an opener's second bid suit only if he holds 6 points or a very bad 7 points; with 8 or more points, the responder should bid again.

The common misunderstanding of the "change of suit" principle is even more rife when the opener makes a non-reverse bid at the two-level. For example:

Opener	Responder
1 ◇	1 ♠
2 ♣	?

The opener's bid at the two-level of a suit lower ranking than his first suit is not forcing.

The responder may hold:

♠ Q x x x x
♡ K 10 x
◇ 10 x
♣ J x x

With a weak hand, if responder has a preference for the opener's second suit, he should pass.
A return to the partner's first suit, however, should be made whenever the responder's hand holds better support for the opener's first bid suit.

For example:

[A]	[B]
♠ Q x x x x	♠ K x x
♡ K 10 x	♡ K 10 x x
◇ 10 x x	◇ 10 x x
♣ J x	♣ J 10 x

With *Hand A,* the responder prefers diamonds. He should now bid two diamonds. This is a simple preference. It is not a show of strength, and must not be construed as quality support.

With *Hand B,* although the responder has a mild preference for clubs, he should nevertheless return to his partner's first bid suit because that suit may be longer.

Also see: Argument 82.

ARGUMENT 81

Is the opener's jump rebid of his original suit forcing?

THE HAND

```
                    NORTH
                    ♠ 9 2
                    ♡ A 8
                    ◇ A K Q J 7 2
                    ♣ K 8 5
    WEST                              EAST
    ♠ A Q J 4                         ♠ K 10 6
    ♡ J 9 6 3 2                       ♡ 7 4
    ◇ 6                               ◇ 10 8 5 4
    ♣ 7 6 4                           ♣ A Q 10 3
                    SOUTH
                    ♠ 8 7 5 3
                    ♡ K Q 10 5
                    ◇ 9 3
                    ♣ J 9 2
```

THE AUCTION

NORTH	EAST	SOUTH	WEST
1 ◇	Pass	1 ♡	Pass
3 ◇	Pass	3 NT	Pass
Pass	Pass		

THE RESULT

The contract would have been fine had the defenders led a red suit. Unfortunately for the declarer, West led a spade, and the defenders took the first four tricks in that suit, and followed with two tricks in clubs.

Down two.

THE ARGUMENT

North, incensed at having lost a part score and 100 honors, expressed himself in no uncertain terms about South's second bid.

South complained that he could not see why he was being criticized—after all, hadn't North made a forcing bid?

GOREN SETTLES THE ARGUMENT

The only reason I can think of why South bid again is because it was his turn.

A jump by the opener in his own suit is not forcing. Such a bid shows a hand of about 19 points (adding 1 point for the fifth trump, 2 points for the sixth trump, etc.). The bid invites one's partner to bid again, if he holds better than a minimum for his original one-over-one response.

On this hand, South is just about as minimum as he can be for a response; so to do anything other than pass is to invite lots of trouble.

The principle would not apply, had the opener—with a different hand, of course—jumped in a new suit on his second turn. Such a bid would have been absolutely forcing. Then the responder would have been absolutely obliged to bid again. Had the opener, for example, rebid two spades, South would have had no problem—he would have had an easy raise to three spades.

A jump shift to three clubs, however, would leave South in a difficult position. That bid would offer a choice between a false preference of three diamonds—not an attractive prospect with a doubleton in partner's suit—or a bid of three notrump. While considerably exaggerating the power of his spade stopper, this department would opt for the bid of three notrump, as the least of evils.

ARGUMENT 82

Is the responder's rebid in a new suit forcing?

THE HAND

	NORTH	
	♠ Q 6	
	♡ K 10 7	
	◇ K J 5	
	♣ A 10 9 8 7	

WEST		EAST
♠ A 9 8 2		♠ 5 4
♡ 8 3		♡ J 6 2
◇ Q 8 2		◇ A 10 9 4 3
♣ Q J 6 3		♣ K 4 2

	SOUTH
	♠ K J 10 7 3
	♡ A Q 9 5 4
	◇ 7 6
	♣ 5

THE AUCTION

NORTH	EAST	SOUTH	WEST
1 ♣	Pass	1 ♠	Pass
1 NT	Pass	2 ♡	Pass
Pass	Pass		

THE RESULT

South made eleven tricks in hearts.
He lost one trick each in spades and diamonds.

THE ARGUMENT

Even before the dummy's cards were exposed, South
was shouting. Didn't North know that a change of suit

by the responder was forcing? North simply couldn't pass in this situation!

North kept his cool. He reminded South that blow-ups were bad for the blood pressure. He confidently insisted that South could have bid the same way with a weak hand, in which case, any further bid by North would put the partnership overboard.

GOREN SETTLES THE ARGUMENT

North is right!

A change of suit by the responder is forcing in every case but one. The exception is when the opener has shown limited strength with a rebid of one notrump. When the responder, on his next turn, then bids a suit lower in rank than his original suit, such a bid is not forcing.

There is a sound reason for this. Assume that the responder has a hand such as:

> ♠ J 10 x x x
> ♡ Q 9 x x x
> ◇ x x
> ♣ J

The opener bids one club. The responder replies one spade. Now the opener rebids one notrump. Obviously, notrump cannot be the right place to play the hand —the final contract should be at the two-level in one of the responder's suits.

However, if a change of suit (a two-heart bid) by the responder would now be forcing, there is no way to get the hand into a relatively safe spot.

On the hand submitted, therefore, South should not have bid two hearts; to create a force, he should have jumped to three hearts.

Before leaving the subject, let us look at another bidding sequence:

NORTH	EAST	SOUTH	WEST
1 ♣	Pass	1 ♡	Pass
1 NT	Pass	2 ♠	Pass

South's rebid of two spades is absolutely and unequivocally forcing.

A rebid by responder over the opener's one notrump rebid in a suit higher in rank than his original response is forcing.

Also see: Argument 80.

ARGUMENT 83

When should the opener of a four-card spade suit bid once again over his partner's one notrump response?

THE HAND

```
              NORTH
              ♠ 7 5
              ♡ K 10 9 6 4
              ◇ A 8 6 2
              ♣ 5 4

WEST                          EAST
♠ Q 9 8 2                     ♠ 10 6 4
♡ 8 3                         ♡ 7 2
◇ K Q 10 4                    ◇ J 7 5
♣ A 10 7                      ♣ K Q J 9 3

              SOUTH
              ♠ A K J 3
              ♡ A Q J 5
              ◇ 9 3
              ♣ 8 6 2
```

THE AUCTION

SOUTH	WEST	NORTH	EAST
1 ♠	Pass	1 NT	Pass
Pass	Pass		

THE RESULT

East led a club. The defenders took the first five tricks and the declarer claimed the rest.

Four hearts was impregnable.

In one notrump, North-South made two.

THE ARGUMENT

North was rather dismayed at the result, and quite vocal about South's timid bidding.

South maintained that he had read somewhere that Goren recommended that the opener should pass his partner's one notrump response, if he, the opener, held a balanced minimum.

GOREN SETTLES THE ARGUMENT

It is *usually* correct to pass in this situation. However, *usually* doesn't mean *always*. What is the exception?

When the opener has made a bid of one spade on a four-card suit but also holds a good four-card heart suit, it is prudent to overcall the responder's one notrump with two hearts.

The reason for this should be obvious. By opening one spade, you often force your partner to respond one notrump even when he has a good holding in the heart suit. To blindly pass one notrump in this case might mean missing a superior contract, or even a game in hearts.

Therefore, it is best to check back on the responder's holding by rebidding two hearts. If you strike gold, good enough. If not, at worst you will play a 4-3 fit at the two-level. You might do as well there as in one notrump; perhaps better.

Also see: Argument 70.

ARGUMENT 84

After a jump-shift by the responder, what rebids by the opener do not promise extra values?

THE HAND

NORTH
- ♠ K 6
- ♡ 8 5
- ♢ A Q 8 3
- ♣ A K Q 9 2

SOUTH
- ♠ Q 7 2
- ♡ A K 7 6 3
- ♢ K 10 5 4
- ♣ 8

THE AUCTION

SOUTH	WEST	NORTH	EAST
1 ♡	Pass	3 ♣	Pass
3 NT	Pass	Pass	Pass

THE RESULT

The declarer had no difficulty fulfilling his contract. After a spade lead, he took one spade trick, two heart tricks, four diamond tricks, and three club tricks.

However, twelve tricks could have been made in a diamond contract.

THE ARGUMENT

North faulted South for the failure to reach the good

diamond slam. He criticized South's rebid of three notrump as being misleading. Once South showed a balanced hand with no particular fit or slam aspirations, North concluded that any increase of the contract could be hazardous.

South's vehement view was that his first responsibility was to show that he held a minimum opening bid. Surely there was no valid reason why North had not introduced the diamond suit on his second turn.

GOREN SETTLES THE ARGUMENT

South is confusing a jump shift with a demand opening bid. In the latter case, the responder's initial response must indicate whether he has a positive bid or not, irrespective of his distribution.

In responding to a jump shift, the opener should continue to bid his hand in a natural manner, much as if the responder's bid had not been a jump shift but a simple response.

After a jump shift, a new suit rebid by the opener does not show extra values; such a bid merely continues the description of his hand.

Imagine for a moment that North had responded to his partner's one-heart opening bid with two clubs. There can be no question but that with the cards held by South, his rebid would have been two diamonds. After all, one of the reasons he had opened the hand in the first place was that he was two-suited. Because he held nine cards in the red suits, South added two distributional points when deciding whether to open the bidding and so had brought his point count to 14.

The fact that North responded three clubs rather than two clubs should not have caused South to depart from his normal style. South's correct rebid was three diamonds.

Suppose that South held:

[A]	[B]
♠ Q x x	♠ A J x
♡ A K J x x	♡ K Q x x x
◇ K 10 x	◇ K 10 x
♣ x x	♣ x x

With *Hand A*, South should rebid three hearts, to highlight his good suit. North would continue to three notrump.

Holding *Hand B*, South has a natural three notrump rebid which would show a balanced hand with scattered values. North would pass.

Note that in neither case is a slam a sound venture.

ARGUMENT 85

When should you raise your partner's two-level response, rather than rebid your own suit?

THE HAND

```
                    NORTH
                    ♠ 8 3
                    ♡ Q J 10 6 4
                    ◇ A 10 4
                    ♣ K 10 8
WEST                                    EAST
♠ Q 10 5 4                              ♠ 9 6
♡ 9 2                                   ♡ K 7 3
◇ K 8 2                                 ◇ Q J 9 5
♣ Q 7 4 2                               ♣ A J 6 3
                    SOUTH
                    ♠ A K J 7 2
                    ♡ A 8 5
                    ◇ 7 6 3
                    ♣ 9 5
```

THE AUCTION

SOUTH	WEST	NORTH	EAST
1 ♠	Pass	2 ♡	Pass
3 ♡	Pass	4 ♡	Pass
Pass	Pass		

THE RESULT

North was fortunate that the heart king was favorably situated; but though the trump finesse succeeded, the contract did not. The declarer lost two tricks in each minor suit.

Down one.

236

THE ARGUMENT

South was quick to criticize North for going to game with only 10 high-card points. "If I couldn't bid the four hearts, partner," he averred, "you certainly had no right to bid again on your hand. You are minimum for your first bid. You don't have any further strength for another."

In vain, North tried to point out that he had good intermediates, and a control in each unbid suit. He claimed South might have held 15 or 16 points in support of the heart contract, in which case game was nearly assured.

GOREN SETTLES THE ARGUMENT

With a hand that is a near minimum, your first task is to warn your partner of this fact. You do this by making the rebid that will sound least encouraging to your partner, generally a rebid of your own suit.

South's hand is about as minimum as it could be. Thus, even though he holds relatively good support for what is likely to be a five-card suit bid by partner, he should have chosen to rebid two spades at his first turn to slow down the action. On his next turn—if there was going to be one—he could support his partner. North would then be in a better shape to place the final contract.

Let us consider another opening by South. Suppose he held:

♠ A K Q 7 2
♡ K 8 5
◇ K 6 3
♣ 9 5

This time, though South's spade holding is better than

on the original hand and his heart support is one point weaker, a rebid of three hearts is preferable to a rebid of spades. For, holding the king of diamonds, South's hand is worth 16 points at a heart contract, and game is likely. Now South wants to encourage his partner to go on to game. Heart support is what North is probably looking for. Notice that with this holding by South, four hearts cannot be defeated.

Avoid carrying the bidding to the three-level unless your hand is better than a minimum when revalued in support of your partner's suit.

Also see: Argument 74.

ARGUMENT 86

Which one of the partners should quit when their hands do not fit?

THE HAND

NORTH
- ♠ K J 10 9 6 4 2
- ♡ 4
- ◇ 6
- ♣ K 6 5 2

WEST
- ♠ Q 8 5
- ♡ K 7 2
- ◇ Q 10 9 7
- ♣ A J 10

EAST
- ♠ A 3
- ♡ J 8 6 5
- ◇ K 8 3
- ♣ 8 7 4 3

SOUTH
- ♠ 7
- ♡ A Q 10 9 3
- ◇ A J 5 4 2
- ♣ Q 9

THE AUCTION

SOUTH	WEST	NORTH	EAST
1 ♡	Pass	1 ♠	Pass
2 ◇	Pass	2 ♠	Pass
3 ◇	Pass	3 ♠	Pass
4 ◇	Dbl	4 ♠	Dbl
Pass	Pass	Pass	

THE RESULT

North's contract ended up down two.

THE ARGUMENT

North raged that even a half-wit would have passed two spades with the South hand.

South maintained that, with two five-card suits, he had to show his distribution, hoping to find a better spot to play the hand than two spades.

The discussion became personal, and it was decided to seek an objective tribunal.

GOREN SETTLES THE ARGUMENT

Bridge is a bidder's game, and most people seem to seek the maximum enjoyment by bidding as often as they can. However, one should bear in mind that bridge is a partnership game, and that both players presumably are trying to achieve the best interests of their side.

Just as hands improve when there is a fit, so a holding goes rapidly downhill when it becomes apparent that the partnership hands do not mesh. In that event, it becomes the responsibility of the first bidder to recognize the misfit and to end the auction.

South had offered North the choice of two suits, yet North had persisted in rebidding his own suit, knowing full well that South had at least 9 cards—possibly 10 —in the red suits. Furthermore, North had rebid his suit at the lowest level possible, and therefore he could not be expected to have too good a hand.

With a weak hand and any sort of holding in hearts, North could have made a preference bid of two hearts. He could even have passed two diamonds with only a fragmentary holding in that suit. His actual course of rebidding his own suit should have made it ominously clear that North felt his hand would be of value only in a spade contract.

Accordingly, South's sanest action was to pass two spades, in the hope that his side could garner a part score. To continue after North went to three spades was an indignity for which, unfortunately, North, too, had to pay.

Let me add one word of praise for both partners. Neither bid notrump as a way out on a misfit hand. *Before you try notrump as an escape hatch, ask yourself this: If neither of us can support the other's holding, where are our tricks going to come from?*

ARGUMENT 87

What strength is needed for a non-jump rebid of three in a new suit?

THE HAND

```
                    NORTH
                    ♠ 7 4
                    ♡ A K J 6 2
                    ◇ K 10 5 2
                    ♣ 9 3
WEST                                    EAST
♠ A 10 9 2                              ♠ J 5
♡ 10 8 4 3                              ♡ Q 9 5
◇ 9                                     ◇ J 7 4
♣ K Q 10 4                              ♣ A J 8 7 5
                    SOUTH
                    ♠ K Q 8 6 3
                    ♡ 7
                    ◇ A Q 8 6 3
                    ♣ 6 2
```

THE AUCTION

SOUTH	WEST	NORTH	EAST
1 ♠	Pass	2 ♡	Pass
3 ◇	Pass	5 ◇	Pass
Pass	Pass		

THE RESULT

West had a natural club lead, and the defenders took two tricks in that suit. There was no way to avoid losing the ace of spades.

Instead of making a valuable partscore, North-South went down one in a hopeless game.

THE ARGUMENT

South reminded North that not every hand should be played in game. He suggested that North should have held more than an ace and a couple of kings to contract for eleven tricks.

North countered that some terrible deeds were being perpetrated in these troubled times, but none matched South's three-diamond bid for sheer misrepresentation.

GOREN SETTLES THE ARGUMENT

North was right.

South was so eager to show his distribution that apparently he did not realize that he was considerably overstating his values.

A bid of a new suit at the three-level is made only with a very good hand. It shows values well above a minimum opening bid, generally a hand worth the equivalent of 17 points or better.

There is sound logic to support this principle. The opening bidder must bear in mind that the hand is a possible misfit. By introducing a new suit at the level of three, he might be forcing his partner to show preference with inadequate trump support. If the opener does this with a 13-point hand, even though his partner has shown about 11 points for his two-over-one response, the opener's second action may force the bidding too high.

On the hand submitted, South should have suppressed his diamond suit for the moment and have simply rebid two spades. Should North then have bid two notrump, South would have been free to introduce his diamond suit, without that appearing to be a strong bid.

North could have then raised to four diamonds, but the bidding would have properly ended there, for South already has bid as high as he could, and at this point had no further values to declare.

Note that if North's first response had been two clubs instead of one heart, South's correct rebid would have been two diamonds. It was the quick ascent to the three-level that misrepresented South's strength.

ARGUMENT 88

Does a partner's raise increase the value of the opener's hand?

THE HAND

```
              NORTH
              ♠ 9 5 2
              ♡ K 6 5 4
              ◇ K 7
              ♣ 10 7 5 2

WEST                        EAST
♠ J 8 7 6                   ♠ Q 10 4 3
♡ 8                         ♡ Q 10
◇ A 5 3 2                   ◇ 10 8 6 4
♣ K J 6 3                   ♣ A Q 9

              SOUTH
              ♠ A K
              ♡ A J 9 7 3 2
              ◇ Q J 9
              ♣ 8 4
```

THE AUCTION

SOUTH	WEST	NORTH	EAST
1 ♡	Pass	2 ♡	Pass
3 ♡	Pass	Pass	Pass

THE RESULT

Ten tricks were made in short order.

THE ARGUMENT

South decided that attack was the best means of defense, and led with his right. "A player of your experience ought to know that kings are underrated in

245

the point count," he shouted. "Holding two kings, four trumps, and a ruffing value in diamonds, why on earth didn't you bid on to four hearts?"

North was not the sort of player who is easily cowed. "I really don't think I could have had much less than I did—a mere 7 points. If you could make ten tricks with my 7 points, then obviously you could have bid to game by yourself."

GOREN SETTLES THE ARGUMENT

I cannot stress too often or too long the importance of a fit in evaluating the potential of a hand. The strongest hands can founder on the rocks of a misfit, where there is no suit for the partnership to develop and no adequate trump suit. Conversely, a hand that seems to be only slightly better than minimum improves vastly once a good trump fit has been located.

The opener must revalue his hand once a trump fit has been established. A simple adjustment is in order: Add 1 point for a fifth card in the trump suit. Add 2 points for a sixth card in the trump suit. Add 2 points more for each additional card in the trump suit.

Applying this formula to South's hand, we see that his holding is actually worth 20 points. Even if his partner has a dead minimum of 6 points for his raise, barring unfortunate duplication, the combined holding should offer a play for game. Instead of putting pressure on his partner, it was South's responsibility to leap to game on his second turn.

ARGUMENT 89

How can you decide which high cards are "working"?

THE HAND

```
                  NORTH
                  ♠ A Q 9 6 5
                  ♡ A 6
                  ◇ 8 5
                  ♣ A Q 8 3
WEST                              EAST
♠ J 8 2                           ♠ 3
♡ K 10 9 2                        ♡ J 8 7 4
◇ K Q 6 4                         ◇ A J 9 3
♣ J 5                             ♣ 9 6 4 2
                  SOUTH
                  ♠ K 10 7 4
                  ♡ Q 5 3
                  ◇ 10 7 2
                  ♣ K 10 7
```

THE AUCTION

NORTH	EAST	SOUTH	WEST
1 ♠	Pass	2 ♠	Pass
3 ♣	Pass	3 ♠	Pass
Pass	Pass		

THE RESULT

East led the ace of diamonds, but no lead would have prevailed, and the defenders won only three tricks in the red suits.

The declarer took ten tricks.

THE ARGUMENT

North complained that his partner had no sense of card valuation. South held two key cards, yet signed off with three spades.

South shouted back that, by any standards, he had a near minimum for his raise, and on top of that had the worst possible distribution.

GOREN SETTLES THE ARGUMENT

Although it is wise to master the point count, it is folly to allow the point count to become your master.

The valuation of North's hand depended not so much on the count of his high cards, but where those high cards were.

South should have upped each of his black suit kings to 4 points each. Now his hand counts 10 points.

North's bid of three clubs was an asking bid which meant: "Partner, do you hold any values in the club suit?"

South's return to three spades said, "My hand holds absolutely minimum values—nothing in the club suit."

South should have answered: "My hand holds good club and spade values." His correct rebid should have been four spades.

When a partnership has definitely decided on a trump suit at a low level of bidding, a bid of a new suit by the opener is a type of "asking" bid. The responder should answer within the confines of the second suit, if he has some control in that suit. If the responder does not have any further strength in the second suit, he merely returns to the agreed trump suit. This does not indicate additional values; it is simply a sign-off.

In the instant hand, the bid of three clubs by North asked South whether he held an ace of clubs, a king of clubs, a singleton in clubs, or any other feature in the suit, such as a queen-jack.

ARGUMENT 90

Holding three cards of your partner's suit, how do you choose between a jump rebid and a jump raise?

THE HAND

NORTH
♠ K764
♡ AK32
♢ 763
♣ 95

WEST
♠ 52
♡ QJ854
♢ J108
♣ AJ6

EAST
♠ J1098
♡ 1096
♢ 9
♣ KQ843

SOUTH
♠ AQ3
♡ 7
♢ AKQ542
♣ 1072

THE AUCTION

SOUTH	WEST	NORTH	EAST
1 ♢	Pass	1 ♠	Pass
3 ♠	Pass	4 ♠	Pass
Pass	Pass		

THE RESULT

The defenders started with three rounds of clubs. North ruffed the third round. He then drew three rounds of trumps in the hope that the suit would split evenly. This was not the case.

Down two.

Five diamonds could have been made.

THE ARGUMENT

North went to some pains to inform South that eleven tricks at a diamond contract was a breeze. He criticized his partner for jump-raising the spades with only three trumps.

GOREN SETTLES THE ARGUMENT

It is usually preferable for the opener to jump rebid a good six-card minor suit rather than give a jump raise in the responder's major with only three trumps.

A jump raise of the partner's trump suit promises four-card support.

Where the opener has a good six-card unit in a good hand, it is imperative he inform his partner of this. The future of the hand might lie in a notrump contract, or in the partner's major, or in the opener's minor.

The correct way for South to describe his hand is to jump rebid to three diamonds. On the illustrated hand, North will investigate his options by bidding three hearts, for three notrump might be the right contract.

South pinpoints his club weakness by giving preference to three spades.

North is also aware that the club suit presents a flaw for notrump purposes. Since he holds only a four-card spade suit, his correct bid is to show his diamond support by a bid of four diamonds. Now the opener will carry the contract to five.

Note that had South held four-card spade support, his jump raise to three spades would have been eminently correct. So would the final contract.

It is well to note a seeming exception.

When you hold three excellent trumps (A-K-Q,

A-K-J, for example) a jump raise of your partner's suit should not be ruled out. The lack of
three such honors in your partner's hand greatly
increases the likelihood that he is not bidding on
a four-card suit. Or if he is, that he will choose another call on his rebid in preference to rebidding
a mangy four-carder.

ARGUMENT 91

Holding both major suits, which one do you bid after a Stayman response to your opening notrump?

THE HAND

NORTH
- ♠ Q J 5
- ♡ A 10 8 7
- ◇ 9 6
- ♣ A 7 6 2

WEST
- ♠ K 9
- ♡ 9 5
- ◇ A J 7 4 2
- ♣ 10 8 4 3

EAST
- ♠ 10 4 3 2
- ♡ 6 3 2
- ◇ K 8 3
- ♣ Q 9 5

SOUTH
- ♠ A 8 7 6
- ♡ K Q J 4
- ◇ Q 10 5
- ♣ K J

THE AUCTION

SOUTH	WEST	NORTH	EAST
1 NT	Pass	2 ♣	Pass
2 ♠	Pass	3 NT	Pass
Pass	Pass		

THE RESULT

West led a diamond and the defenders took the first five tricks. Later, the declarer lost the spade finesse. Down two.

THE ARGUMENT

When it was discovered that four hearts could have been made, North and South were at each other's throats. North suggested that, as South's hearts were so much better than his spades, he should have declared that suit first.

South contended that if North had not been in such an all-fired hurry to bid three notrump, they would have had time to arrive at a proper heart contract.

GOREN SETTLES THE ARGUMENT

When the notrump bidder holds four cards in each major suit, he must make sure that both suits are mentioned in the auction.

Following this precept, South should have bid four hearts over his partner's three notrump bid, and the 4-4 fit would have produced an unbeatable contract.

Note that North could not bid anything other than three notrump at his second turn. A bid of two notrump would have ended the forcing situation, and might have been passed out if South held a minimum notrump opening. A bid of three hearts would have promised a five-card suit and would have requested the opener to raise with three-card support.

There is some divergence of opinion about the best way to respond to one's partner's Stayman request when the notrump opener holds two four-card majors. My preference is to bid the suits in their natural order—that is, spades first—and indeed, this is the approach of Stayman himself. Others follow the "up-the-line" approach and bid hearts first; while a third school advocates bidding the stronger major first.

Whichever procedure you follow, be sure your partner understands your methods. And unless your partner has a strong preference, I recommend that you go with the majority and bid spades first.

ARGUMENT 92

How do you show a maximum notrump and a fit?

THE HAND

NORTH
♠ K Q 10 9 3
♡ A 10 8 2
◇ 7 3
♣ K 6

SOUTH
♠ A J 5
♡ K 7
◇ A K 8 5
♣ Q J 5 4

THE AUCTION

SOUTH	WEST	NORTH	EAST
1 NT	Pass	2 ♣	Pass
2 ◇	Pass	3 ♠	Pass
4 ♠	Pass	Pass	Pass

THE RESULT

Twelve tricks were made with routine play.

THE ARGUMENT

For a while, it seemed as if there were going to be a repeat of the Bennett Murder Case. *(In 1931, after John Bennett of Kansas City went down in a four-spade contract that Mrs. Bennett thought he should not have bid but should have made, she shot him.)*

North maintained that South should have done something other than bid a mere four spades.

South protested strongly that it was up to North to take action—North knew they were in the slam zone, and she (North) should have checked on aces, and then bid the slam herself.

GOREN SETTLES THE ARGUMENT

South was at fault.

With a maximum notrump and a good fit for the suit in which the responder has jumped, an opener should cue-bid to show interest in slam.

To illustrate this point, let us look at another hand that the opener might have held that would be consistent with the action he took on the actual hand:

♠ A J x
♥ K Q
♦ Q J x x
♣ Q J 10 x

With this hand, the opener should raise the responder's three-spade bid to four. For the responder to bid on would be to place a game contract in jeopardy.

If this is the case, the opener should not have bid a mere four spades with the hand he actually held, for the two hands are vastly disparate in strength. He should have had a way to show a maximum notrump, good controls, and good support.

South has available an idle bid to get his message across. Over three spades, South should have bid four diamonds. Opposite a partner who has forced in a major suit, this cannot be an attempt to find an alternate contract. Without spade support, the opener would simply rebid three notrump. Therefore, such a bid can only mean: "Partner, I like your bid, and I have a maximum notrump. My outside strength is partly in diamonds, which I control. If you have a very good hand, I would be most interested in a slam!"

With North's diamond weakness plugged, it is relatively simple to get to slam. A bid of four notrump by North would be Blackwood, for the spade suit has been implicitly agreed upon. North could contract for six spades when she learns that only one ace is missing in the partnership.

Suppose that the three-spade bid was not a slam try, but something like:

♠ K Q 10 9 x
♡ Q J x x
◇ x x
♣ K x

The four-diamond cue-bid will have done no harm; North would have simply signed off at four spades.

ARGUMENT 93

Can the notrump opener ignore his partner's sign-off?

THE HAND

                        NORTH
                        ♠ Q 6 3
                        ♡ 10 5 4
                        ◇ K 10 9 5 4 2
                        ♣ 5

    WEST   EAST
    ♠ 8 2   ♠ A 10 9 7 4
    ♡ 7 6   ♡ K 9 8 2
    ◇ Q J 8 6   ◇ 3
    ♣ A J 10 6 3   ♣ Q 7 4

                        SOUTH
                        ♠ K J 5
                        ♡ A Q J 3
                        ◇ A 7
                        ♣ K 9 8 2

THE AUCTION

SOUTH	WEST	NORTH	EAST
1 NT	Pass	2 ◇	Pass
2 NT	Pass	3 NT	Pass
Pass			

THE RESULT

West led the jack of clubs. Though the heart finesse succeeded, the declarer could make only eight tricks. Down one.

THE ARGUMENT

South ranted at North for raising to three notrump on only 5 points.

North retorted that he disliked partners who insisted on playing every hand. He, North, had signed off in two diamonds, and South had no business bidding again.

South shot back with the retort that the only real sign-off was "pass"; and as far as he was concerned, he intended passing up his next opportunity to play with North.

Before the gendarmes were called in, it was suggested that outside adjudication was required.

GOREN SETTLES THE ARGUMENT

It is a common misconception that a bid of two in a suit in response to an opening bid of one notrump compels the opener to pass. A bid of two in a suit (other than clubs) might be made on a hand that is completely devoid of any high-card strength, and in practically all cases, the opener should pass such a bid. However, the opener may bid again if he holds both strong trump support and a maximum notrump.

On the hand submitted, South's holding fulfills only one of these two conditions: He does have a maximum opening notrump, but his support for responder's suit is anything but strong. Therefore, he should have passed.

Let us consider an alternative hand that South might have held:

♠ K J x
♡ Q J 9 x
♢ A Q x
♣ K Q 10

This time, South has both a maximum point count and excellent trump support. If North has little more than six diamonds headed by the king, three notrump should be a perfectly playable contract. Now South would be perfectly correct to carry on—but his rebid should be three diamonds—not two notrump.

With a good diamond suit and an outside queen, North would be expected to go on to three notrump. For in such a situation, the opener is saying to the responder, "Look, friend, I know your holdings are paltry. I know you're signing off. I know you hold no hope for our side. But I see a glimmer, nevertheless. I have an 18-point notrump and a good fit with your long suit which I think we can establish."

So the rule is:

If the responder to an opening notrump signs off in a trump suit, and the opener nevertheless carries on by raising the responder's suit, the responder is forced to game if he holds a six-card suit headed by a high honor and has as much as a guarded queen on the side.

What if North's hand is something like this:

♠ Q x x
♡ x x x
♢ J x x x x x
♣ x

He simply passes three diamonds. At notrump, his hand might be completely trickless for, unless South's diamond holding is something like A-K-x-x, the diamond suit might be shut out of the play altogether.

Note that the only way the notrump opener can show a maximum opening and excellent trump support is by raising the responder's suit. A rebid of two notrump has no meaning whatsoever. Except, perhaps, that the responder should seek a different partner.

ARGUMENT 94

Is there any reason for a jump rebid by the opening two-bidder?

THE HAND

```
                    NORTH
                    ♠ Q 6 3
                    ♡ 5 2
                    ♢ 9 7 6 5 2
                    ♣ 10 8 3
WEST                                        EAST
♠ 10 9 7 5 4                                ♠ 8 2
♡ 9 3                                       ♡ A 8 4
♢ A 8 3                                     ♢ J 10 4
♣ J 7 6                                     ♣ K 9 5 4 2
                    SOUTH
                    ♠ A K J
                    ♡ K Q J 10 7 6
                    ♢ K Q
                    ♣ A Q
```

THE AUCTION

SOUTH	WEST	NORTH	EAST
2 ♡	Pass	2 NT	Pass
3 ♡	Pass	Pass	Pass

THE RESULT

West led a spade. With the help of a finesse in clubs, the declarer made eleven tricks.

THE ARGUMENT

North insisted that South, with his exceptionally

strong hand, should have bid three notrump, a contract that would have made as the cards lie.

South faulted North for passing three hearts. True, he was permitted to take that action if he had a valueless hand, but North held the queen of spades. On the strength of that card alone, South claimed, North should have raised to four hearts.

Each questioned the other's sense of card valuation, and I was elected to be judge of the Court of Appeals.

GOREN SETTLES THE ARGUMENT

When an opener begins with a two-bid, that bid is absolutely forcing for one round only. After a two-notrump response, a rebid of three in the same suit can be passed out by a responder who is dead broke. Therefore, a rebidder who holds game in his hand is compelled to jump to game (or bid another suit) on his second turn. This jump bid says that the opener has game in his own hand—it is not a shutout bid. The responder can still move forward if his hand warrants.

In the given hand, looking at the question from South's point of view, there are just too many circumstances that would allow game to be made even if North held a yarborough. A lead into declarer's tenaces in either black suit would provide a tenth trick. There were many chances for endplays. The queen of spades might drop.

Taking all these factors into consideration, South was an overwhelming favorite to make four hearts. He should have taken the strain off his partner by jumping to four hearts.

It was difficult for North to assess the value of the queen of spades. In this hand, it happened to be a key card. But on many hands, that card would turn out to be valueless. Though I would not chide a partner who raised to game, I do not consider it a dereliction of duty on North's part to have passed on his holding.

ARGUMENT 95

Should a pre-emptive bidder ever rebid?

THE HAND

	NORTH	
	♠ A J 10 8	
	♡ Q 10 9 5 3	
	◇ 10 4	
	♣ A J	

WEST		EAST
♠ K 9 5 2		♠ Q 7 6 4
♡ A K J 4		♡ 7 6
◇ 3		◇ K Q 9
♣ K 8 5 2		♣ Q 7 6 4

	SOUTH	
	♠ 3	
	♡ 8 2	
	◇ A J 8 7 6 5 2	
	♣ 10 9 3	

THE AUCTION

SOUTH	WEST	NORTH	EAST
3 ◇	Dbl	4 ◇	4 ♠
5 ◇	Dbl	Pass	Pass
Pass			

THE RESULT

The defense was reasonably accurate, and the declarer ended up with a loss of 500 points.

Down three.

THE ARGUMENT

North was almost incoherent, but just about found breath to run through a long list of bridge crimes he claimed South had been guilty of in the past. None, he raged, could equal this latest effort in stupidity.

South was convinced that the only idiotic action during the bidding was North's raise to four diamonds. Who ever heard of anyone going to that level with two low trumps?

GOREN SETTLES THE ARGUMENT

Even though bridge is a bidder's game, there comes a time in the life of every player when he must learn to say pass.

A pre-emptive bidder has described his hand accurately with his opening bid. Unless forced to bid by his partner, he should, for the rest of the auction, remain silent—with the possible exception of punishing the opponents for an indiscretion.

When the pre-emptor's partner raises the opening bid, it may be for any of a variety of motives. He may be making it a bit more difficult for the opponents to enter the auction. He may be trying to buy the hand. He may be preparing to sacrifice. Or, as was the case on this deal, he may be enticing the opponents into the auction so that he can wield the axe.

Only the responder knows what he is up to. It is the business of his partner to keep quiet and out of his way.

Had South passed and not bid five diamonds, North would have doubled four spades. Instead of losing 500 points, North-South would have made a substantial profit, for East would have been defeated by at least two tricks.

CHAPTER 14

Secondary Responses

ARGUMENT 96

*When should the responder show a prefer-
ence rather than rebid his own suit?*

THE HAND

```
                    NORTH
                    ♠ A K 6 2
                    ♡ 10 7
                    ◇ 9 3
                    ♣ A K J 9 3

    WEST                               EAST
    ♠ J 7                              ♠ Q 10 8 4 3
    ♡ K Q J 5                          ♡ A 9 6 4
    ◇ Q 8 6 2                          ◇ J 7
    ♣ 6 5 2                            ♣ 8 4

                    SOUTH
                    ♠ 9 5
                    ♡ 8 3 2
                    ◇ A K 10 5 4
                    ♣ Q 10 7
```

THE AUCTION

NORTH	EAST	SOUTH	WEST
1 ♣	Pass	1 ◇	Pass
1 ♠	Pass	2 ◇	Pass
Pass	Pass		

THE RESULT

The defenders took two heart tricks and two trump tricks.

North-South, as the cards lie, would have made five clubs against any defense.

THE ARGUMENT

South was rather proud of having made an overtrick.

North was most upset at having missed a reasonable game at five clubs.

South contended that he had done all he could—indeed, he had stretched his values to make a second forward-going bid.

North said that only a half-wit would consider two diamonds a forward-going bid. Had South never heard about supporting his partner's call?

GOREN SETTLES THE ARGUMENT

When the opener has bid two suits, it is more important for the responder to give preference to the opener's first-bid suit than to rebid a five-card minor suit of his own.

This rule conforms to the often-reiterated principle of looking for a fit. Had South simply bid two clubs on his second turn, North would have revalued his hand to 18 points and then bid three clubs. South might then have rebid his diamonds, and this in all likelihood would have resulted in North-South reaching the five-club game.

The way South bid the hand, North feared a misfit. Despite his relatively good hand, game did not seem likely. There was a glaring weakness in the heart suit that ruled out a notrump contract; and ten tricks at a spade contract, or eleven in clubs seemed fanciful.

After South's dogged repetition of his diamonds, North correctly elected to pass at what might be his side's last opportunity for a plus score.

ARGUMENT 97

When should the responder quit bidding?

THE HAND

                  NORTH
                  ♠ A 9 5
                  ♡ Q 7
                  ◇ A Q J 7 4
                  ♣ J 6 5

WEST   **EAST**
♠ Q 10 6 2   ♠ K J 4
♡ 8 4   ♡ K J 10 3
◇ K 8 3 2   ◇ 9 6
♣ 10 9 3   ♣ K Q 4 2

                  SOUTH
                  ♠ 8 7 3
                  ♡ A 9 6 5 2
                  ◇ 10 5
                  ♣ A 8 7

THE AUCTION

NORTH	EAST	SOUTH	WEST
1 ◇	Pass	1 ♡	Pass
2 ◇	Pass	2 ♡	Pass
3 ♡	Pass	Pass	Pass

THE RESULT

West led a spade, and the outcome was most unfortunate. Though the declarer obtained one discard on the diamond suit (East did not want to ruff), he lost two spades, three hearts, and a club.

Down two.

THE ARGUMENT

North claimed that South did not have the values for two bids, and that he should have passed two diamonds.

South insisted that, with a doubleton diamond and a five-card major, he was duty bound to fully describe his hand. What reason was there for North to raise with only a doubleton heart and a scant 14 points?

GOREN SETTLES THE ARGUMENT

When an opener makes a minimum rebid, the responder should not act again unless he holds a hand that is clearly better than average. Since an average hand holds 10 points in high cards, a "better than average" hand contains at least 11 points in high cards.

It is obvious that South did not hold 11 points. Therefore, he should have passed North's rebid of two diamonds.

One thing is certain. Once North could do no better than repeat his diamonds at the lowest level possible, thereby showing a hand limited to some 15 points at best, any hope for game should have been abandoned. Under these circumstances, for South to bid again simply because he held five hearts was a futile act— to put it kindly.

From North's point of view, when South rebid two hearts he was making a forward-going move, showing good hearts and a hand which counted at least 11 points. This put North-South in the game zone. Treating South's bid in this way, North's Q-x in hearts became important. Not to have bid three hearts could easily have cost a game.

ARGUMENT 98

Does support by the opener improve the responder's hand?

THE HAND

```
                NORTH
                ♠ A J 6 3
                ♡ 7 2
                ♦ A Q J 7 2
                ♣ 9 5

WEST                            EAST
♠ 10 9                          ♠ 8 4
♡ K Q 8 6 5                     ♡ A J 10 4 3
♦ 6 3                           ♦ 10 8 5
♣ A J 8 4                       ♣ K Q 10

                SOUTH
                ♠ K Q 7 5 2
                ♡ 9
                ♦ K 9 4
                ♣ 7 6 3 2
```

THE AUCTION

NORTH	EAST	SOUTH	WEST
1 ♦	1 ♡	1 ♠	2 ♡
2 ♠	Pass	Pass	Pass

THE RESULT

Ten tricks were there without even the need for a finesse.

THE ARGUMENT

North upbraided South for not making another try when his spades had been supported.

South pointed out that he held only 10 points, and that the combined North-South assets were but 24 points, including distribution. In theory, that was not enough for a game.

North muttered something about South's addition being right but his figuring being wrong. Couldn't South have thought for a moment and have put the picture together?

GOREN SETTLES THE ARGUMENT

It is all too easy for a workman to blame his failure on his tools. Here the fault lies with the workman not having a complete grasp of the sophisticated tool he is employing.

When a responder's suit has been raised by the opening bidder, the responder should revalue his hand in the same way that the opener does when his suit has been supported.

If we apply this principle to South's hand, we find that the re-evaluation increases South's hand from 10 points to almost 12. We have to add a point for the fifth spade. The fact that South holds the king of his partner's suit gives that particular card added value.

These factors, in themselves, were not sufficient cause for South to bid game, but he should have made a try for game, in case his partner had opened with somewhat better than a bare minimum. The recommended bid with South's holding is three spades.

There is no guarantee that North-South will end in four spades, despite the fact that the hands mesh perfectly. However, South will have made an effort in the right direction. North is up against a close decision whether to pass or to continue on to four spades. If he is the aggressive type, and he is imaginative, he well might bid to game. No one could fault him too much either way, though I would say that in rubber bridge, the scoring odds in his favor should propel him to go all the way.

ARGUMENT 99

In bidding notrump, how can the partners check for stoppers?

THE HAND

```
                    NORTH
                    ♠ 9 2
                    ♡ K 9 5
                    ◇ 8 5
                    ♣ A K J 7 6 2
WEST                                    EAST
♠ J 10 8 5                              ♠ Q 6 4 3
♡ Q 10 2                                ♡ 8 4
◇ K Q 10                                ◇ A J 9 6 4
♣ 10 4 3                                ♣ 9 5
                    SOUTH
                    ♠ A K 7
                    ♡ A J 7 6 3
                    ◇ 7 3 2
                    ♣ Q 8
```

THE AUCTION

NORTH	EAST	SOUTH	WEST
1 ♣	Pass	1 ♡	Pass
2 ♣	Pass	3 NT	Pass
Pass	Pass		

THE RESULT

Ten tricks were there for North-South, except for one problem. They were off the whole diamond suit, and West was inspired to lead the king of diamonds. As a result, the defenders took the first five tricks.

Down one.

THE ARGUMENT

North informed everyone at the table, as well as the neighbors down the hall, that in his opinion, South should be nominated as Masochist of the Year. As supporting evidence, he would produce South's leap to three notrump with one suit totally and glaringly unguarded.

South charged that North's correct rebid was two hearts—everyone knew how important it was to establish a fit as soon as possible.

GOREN SETTLES THE ARGUMENT

There is no pardoning South's jump to three notrump. He should have made use of a basic axiom:

A change of suit by the responder is forcing.

South's first rebid should have been two spades. No peril attaches to this bid. Since it is forcing, North cannot pass it out. This tactic would have enabled South to pinpoint his strength, and so give his partner a chance to clarify his holding. These is little danger that North will raise spades, for he did not rebid one spade when he had the opportunity—after South's bid of one heart—thereby denying he held four cards in that suit. With only three-card support, North would be most unlikely to raise a spade suit which has been bid secondarily.

What the bid would accomplish is to smoke out the presence or reveal the absence of a diamond stopper in the North hand. If North bids two notrump over two spades, South can now safely go on to game, knowing that North has a diamond stopper and that the lead will come up to the North hand.

On the actual hand, North would rebid three hearts. South can then go on to four hearts in the firm conviction that he is in the best contract—as indeed he would be.

ARGUMENT 100

Is notrump a good alternative when you have no fit?

THE HAND

```
                    NORTH
                    ♠ 9
                    ♡ A K 8 7 3 2
                    ◇ Q J 7 6
                    ♣ Q 8

    WEST                            EAST
    ♠ K 10 6 3                      ♠ Q 7 4
    ♡ 9 6                           ♡ Q J 5
    ◇ A 9 2                         ◇ K 10 8 4 3
    ♣ J 7 6 4                       ♣ 5 2

                    SOUTH
                    ♠ A J 8 5 2
                    ♡ 10 4
                    ◇ 5
                    ♣ A K 10 9 3
```

THE AUCTION

NORTH	EAST	SOUTH	WEST
1 ♡	Pass	1 ♠	Pass
2 ♡	Pass	3 ♣	Pass
3 ◇	Pass	3 NT	Pass
Pass	Pass		

THE RESULT

West led a low diamond, and dummy's jack brought the king. East continued with a diamond to West's ace. A third diamond brought out dummy's queen.

The declarer could make only eight tricks. There was no way for him to develop a ninth before the defenders collected the setting tricks.

273

An examination of the full deal at the completion of play revealed that, with careful play, North can make four hearts against any defense.

THE ARGUMENT

South took North to task for failing to bid his good six-card suit a third time.

North ranted that South's bid of three notrump was close to the worst bid of the year.

GOREN SETTLES THE ARGUMENT

On hands that are a partial misfit, notrump is generally the worst contract to play in, unless either the declarer or the dummy has a long, running suit to provide a source of tricks.

South's decision to bid three notrump was unilateral. North's bid of three diamonds on the third round of the auction should have alerted South to the probability that the hands did not fit well, and that, therefore, tricks might be hard to come by in a notrump contract. Instead of just barging into game, South should have offered his partner a choice of contracts.

Far better than a bid of three notrump would have been a bid of three hearts. North bid the hand in such a way that he was marked with six hearts and only four diamonds. South had no reason to fear that North would expect anything more substantial from him than a doubleton heart from his delayed support, for North was cognizant of the fact that South had already bid two suits and was quite likely to have ten cards in those suits—thus not leaving room in his hand for many hearts.

North's queen of clubs is an important card. He would go on to four hearts, realizing that, in all probability, making his contract would depend on no more than a finesse.

ARGUMENT 101

Does a preference after a two-over-one response show a good hand?

THE HAND

NORTH
- ♠ A K 10 7 2
- ♡ 8 6
- ◇ A J 8 2
- ♣ 7 3

WEST
- ♠ 9 5
- ♡ A K 9 7 2
- ◇ Q 9 5 4
- ♣ J 6

EAST
- ♠ 8 6 4
- ♡ Q 10 3
- ◇ K 10 6
- ♣ Q 10 5 4

SOUTH
- ♠ Q J 3
- ♡ J 5 4
- ◇ 7 3
- ♣ A K 9 8 2

THE AUCTION

NORTH	EAST	SOUTH	WEST
1 ♠	Pass	2 ♣	Pass
2 ◇	Pass	2 ♠	Pass
Pass	Pass		

THE RESULT

The defenders started with three rounds of hearts, the declarer ruffing the third round. The declarer then lost a diamond trick to East's king. A club return was taken by the declarer. After cashing the ace of diamonds, the declarer was able to ruff two diamonds in dummy.

The declarer thus made ten tricks.

THE ARGUMENT

A disconsolate North felt he had been misled by his partner. South, on his second bid, he insisted, should have given him a jump raise to three spades, so he would know that South had a fairly substantial trump holding, and was not just giving him a preference bid on something like three small spades.

South staunchly asserted he had left no values unbid.

GOREN SETTLES THE ARGUMENT

I can understand North's being upset at missing a game, but he really has no one to blame but himself. South's bidding was constructive, and there was no reason for North, who had a sound opening bid, not to bid again.

Let us examine the auction in the cold light of reason. South started off by responding at the two-level, thereby guaranteeing at least 10 points. On his next turn, he supported his partner's first-bid suit.

Had South held any less, he was not compelled to first introduce the club suit before returning to the opener's initial declaration. He could simply have raised one spade to two.

North should have realized that South's hand was worth 11-12 points at a spade contract, not quite enough to insist on game opposite a minimum opening bid. A bid of three spades by South would have been 100% forcing.

North should not pass out a hand worth 15 points. After a raise by his partner, North's hand revalues to exactly that.

When the responder has bid a new suit at the two-level and later shows support for the opener's trump suit, the opener, if he holds five trumps instead of his possible four, should revalue his hand upwards.

CHAPTER 15

Competitive Bidding

ARGUMENT 102

*Do you need the same values to reopen
as to overcall?*

THE HAND

```
              NORTH
              ♠ J 10 8
              ♡ Q 3
              ◇ K J 8 3
              ♣ A K 7 3

WEST                        EAST
♠ A K 9 6 3                 ♠ Q 5 4
♡ K 9                       ♡ 10 7 6
◇ A 10 2                    ◇ Q 7 6 4
♣ 10 9 5                    ♣ 8 6 4

              SOUTH
              ♠ 7 2
              ♡ A J 8 5 4 2
              ◇ 9 5
              ♣ Q J 2
```

THE AUCTION

WEST	NORTH	EAST	SOUTH
1 ♠	Pass	Pass	Pass

THE RESULT

The declarer made eight tricks—five trumps, one
heart and two diamonds.

North-South could have made nine tricks at a heart contract.

THE ARGUMENT

North contended that it could not have been right to allow the opponents to buy the hand at the one-level without any competition. Since South held a six-card suit, South could afford to show it at the two-level.

South was aghast at the thought of entering the auction at the two-level with only 8 points. He argued that North held a full opening bid, and that he should have doubled at the first opportunity.

GOREN SETTLES THE ARGUMENT

North would have liked to show his strength with a takeout double on his first turn. However, his shortness in hearts correctly made him decide that discretion was wiser than competition, for a double of a major implies that the doubler can furnish good support for the other major.

If anyone is to blame for allowing the opponents to play the hand, it is South. The auction should have told him that there was a distinct possibility that the hand belonged to his side. It is he who should have entered the auction.

When an opponent opens the bidding and two passes follow, fourth hand may take some liberties in deciding to compete for the part score. There is a margin of safety provided by the fact that the player at his right does not hold the 6 points required to respond, and the player at his left could not open with a demand bid.

Logically, then, his partner must have a fair hand. Why, then, didn't he make a takeout double? Usually because, as was the case here, he has some length in the opponents' suit and a weakness elsewhere, though on occasion it might be because his hand is a touch too weak for that action.

A word of caution. This premise doesn't give you carte blanche to reopen the bidding on a smattering of points whenever an opening bid to your left has been followed by two passes.

Consider this hand:

♠ K 10 8 2
♡ A J 9 8 3
◇ 7 2
♣ K 9

Though you have only five hearts this time, your hand is considerably stronger than before. Again, your left-hand opponent's one-spade opening bid is passed around to you. Should you reopen?

The answer is no. The key is your length in opener's suit, which makes it likely that partner is short. Therefore, he is more likely to have length in the other suits, or a long suit of his own. Why then did he not make an overcall or a takeout double when he had the opportunity to do so? Probably because he did not have the necessary values.

It is extremely likely that the opener has a very good hand, perhaps even close to a demand bid. If you reopen the bidding, you might be running into a penalty double, or giving the opener an opportunity to show a strong, two-suited hand, thus enabling your opponents to get to a better contract, possibly even to a game.

Also see: Arguments 103, 129.

ARGUMENT 103

How strong must you be to overcall?

THE HAND

```
                    NORTH
                    ♠ J 8 7 4
                    ♡ Q 10 5 4
                    ◇ 7 6
                    ♣ J 9 5

WEST                                    EAST
♠ A 10 5 2                              ♠ Q 6 3
♡ 9                                     ♡ A K 6 3 2
◇ K J 8 3                               ◇ 10 2
♣ 7 6 4 2                               ♣ K Q 10

                    SOUTH
                    ♠ K 9
                    ♡ J 8 7
                    ◇ A Q 9 5 4
                    ♣ A 8 3
```

THE AUCTION   [*North-South are vulnerable*]

EAST	SOUTH	WEST	NORTH
1 ♡	2 ◇	Dbl	Pass
Pass	Pass		

THE RESULT

West led a heart. East won the king and ace, and continued with a third heart for West to ruff. A defense of pinpoint accuracy followed.

A penalty of 1,100 points was the result since North-South were vulnerable. But even if North-South were not vulnerable, a 700-point shellacking would have ensued.

When leading a heart for his partner to ruff, East chose the two, asking for the return of the lower side suit—clubs in this case. This line of play assured East of two entries. When East got in, he led trumps, permitting West to score both his king and his jack. Eventually, South had to lead spades from his own hand, losing two tricks in that suit as well.

THE ARGUMENT

South bemoaned his bad luck. He thought the penalty rather excessive for a perfectly normal action; after all, he held a full opening bid.

North didn't feel inclined to sympathize. He was especially upset at the size of the penalty, since the opponents couldn't have made game. He accused South of making a "lunatic bid."

GOREN SETTLES THE ARGUMENT

It never ceases to astonish me how often, after an overcall has been punished, the overcaller wails: "But partner, I had 14 points!" It all stems from a failure to understand the underlying principles of overcalling.

A player who opens the bidding does so completely in the dark. He has about a king more than his equal share of the high cards, and he hopes to find his partner with values that will enable his side to reach game.

The overcaller knows that the opening bidder has a third or more of the high cards in the deck. Game for his side, therefore, is less than likely. Since he may be trapped between two good hands, safety becomes a prime consideration.

The old rule of 2 and 3 is a good yardstick to go by. An overcaller should be within two tricks of his overcall if vulnerable; within three tricks, if not vulnerable. This rule limits the penalty to 500 points should partner prove to be trickless.

Such a penalty should not be too serious, for in many cases, the opponents may have made game.

Here are some of the considerations that might induce you to enter the auction: (1) *Lead direction:* Getting your side off to a good start, should your partner have the opening lead against an opposing contract. (2) *Nuisance value:* Robbing the opponents of bidding space. (3) *Competition:* Enabling your side to buy the hand, or forcing the opponents to a level where you might defeat them.

Be wary of broken suits when you overcall—a bad trump break could result in a bloodbath if your suit is full of holes.

Consider these holdings:

> (A) A Q 4 3 2
> (B) K J 4 3 2
> (C) K Q J 10 2
> (D) Q J 10 9 2

Hand A is a potential death-trap. So is *Hand B*. With a bad break, you might be able to make just one trick in the trump suit.

However, *Hand C* is shockproof against most bad distributions. The same is true of *Hand D*.

Never overcall at the level of two in a suit in which you might lose more than two tricks with a bad break.

Assume that your right-hand opponent opens the bidding with one club, and you hold:

> ♠ x x
> ♡ A x x
> ◇ K Q x x x
> ♣ x x x

There is really not much point to an overcall of one diamond. You have little margin of safety. Moreover, you have not created much of a nuisance, for the responder can still bid one heart, or one spade.

However, let's switch the suits around. Let's make your hand:

♠ K Q x x x
♡ A x x
♢ x x x
♣ x x

The hand has exactly the same strength, but now there's a point to overcalling one spade. You hold the master suit, and you may be able to compete effectively for a part score. If your partner holds excellent support, you might even make game. In addition, your overcall consumes the whole of the one-level. If your left-hand opponent wants to enter the bidding, he now has to do so at the two-level.

Also see: Argument 102.

ARGUMENT 104

How many points do you need to raise an overcall?

THE HAND

```
                NORTH
                ♠ A 7 6
                ♡ A K 8 5 4 2
                ◇ 8 3
                ♣ Q 7
WEST                              EAST
♠ K Q 3 2                        ♠ J 10 8 4
♡ 7                              ♡ Q 9 6
◇ A K J 5 4                      ◇ Q 10 7
♣ J 8 3                          ♣ 6 5 4
                SOUTH
                ♠ 9 5
                ♡ J 10 3
                ◇ 9 6 2
                ♣ A K 10 9 2
```

THE AUCTION   [*North-South are vulnerable*]

WEST	NORTH	EAST	SOUTH
1 ◇	1 ♡	Pass	2 ♣
Pass	Pass	Pass	

THE RESULT

West led the king of diamonds and shifted to a trump. The declarer won, drew a third trump, and ran the jack of hearts. East won, and the defenders took their diamond trick.

The declarer made just three clubs. But *four* hearts would have been a lead-pipe cinch.

THE ARGUMENT

South accused North of passing a forcing bid.

North responded that he had no objection to playing South's own private version of bridge, but he should have been told of all departures from standard practice. As far as he was concerned, it looked as if the hand was a misfit, and he was getting out while the going was good.

South replied that he would never dream of passing a minor suit takeout if he held a six-card major suit.

While the acrimony mounted, East suggested the hand be submitted to higher authority.

GOREN SETTLES THE ARGUMENT

In responding to an overcall, the responder should consider the number of tricks he is bringing his partner rather than the number of points he holds.

An overcall usually shows a good suit of at least five cards. Therefore, you need less trump support to raise a partner's overcall than you do to raise an opening bid, where the bidder might be opening with only a four-card trump suit. Three trumps are adequate support for an overcaller's suit.

A simple change of suit by the overcaller's partner is not forcing.

There are two ways to compel an overcaller to bid again: (1) Make a cue-bid of the enemy suit; or (2) jump shift.

Obviously, it is easier to make game in a major suit than in a minor. Therefore, there was little or no point here in South's introducing his minor suit, when South knew that the partnership held a fit in a major. To have properly evaluated what his bid should have been, South should have merely added his probable

tricks—three, if you consider the possible spade ruff—
to his partner's announced minimum.

Since North must have at least five playing tricks for
his vulnerable overcall, South knew by a process of
addition that his side should be good for eight tricks.
We would favor on this hand a raise to two hearts,
which North would have raised to game.

However, note that when your partner's overcall has
been in a minor suit, it might be worthwhile to introduce a major suit. Let's assume the auction has gone.

1 ♠	2 ♣	Pass	2 ♡

South holds:

> ♠ x x
> ♡ A K 10 9 x
> ◇ x x x
> ♣ Q x x

Here the best shot for game is in a heart contract.
South should bid two hearts. If North has some support, game can be reached and possibly made.

North must share some of the responsibility for missing game. He had the values for a second bid—either
three clubs or two hearts—and that might have gotten
the auction back on the track.

ARGUMENT 105

After an overcall of one's partner's notrump opening, does the responder's free bid show strength?

THE HAND

```
                    NORTH
                    ♠ A 9 3
                    ♡ K 9 8
                    ♦ A J 4
                    ♣ K J 6 3

WEST                                    EAST
♠ Q 10 6 4 2                            ♠ J 7
♡ J 5 4 3 2                             ♡ A 6
♦ 9 5                                   ♦ K Q 10 7 6 2
♣ 10                                    ♣ A 8 7

                    SOUTH
                    ♠ K 8 5
                    ♡ Q 10 7
                    ♦ 8 3
                    ♣ Q 9 5 4 2
```

THE AUCTION

NORTH	EAST	SOUTH	WEST
1 NT	2 ♦	Pass	Pass
Pass			

THE RESULT

South led a low club, and the declarer came to eight tricks simply by ruffing two clubs in dummy.

THE ARGUMENT

South realized that, as the cards lie, he and his partner could have made two notrump. He blamed North for not reopening the bidding with a double.

North's defense was that he had shown everything he had with his first bid, and he could take no further action with his balanced hand.

GOREN SETTLES THE ARGUMENT

After an opponent overcalls one's partner's one notrump opening, all of the responder's bids take on a natural meaning except for a cue-bid in the enemy's suit. A bid of two notrump is no longer an invitation to your partner to go on to game if he holds a maximum hand; instead, the bid is an attempt to compete for a part score, and it does not promise a stopper in the overcaller's suit.

If your partner has opened one notrump, and you hold a smattering of points, the odds are that the hand belongs to your side. Assume you have some 5 or 6 points; if your partner's opening bid promised 16 to 18, you have somewhere between 21 and 24 points between you—or a majority of the strength. That could be enough to make a two-level contract. You are practically guaranteed that you will not come to too much harm.

Unless you have some way to enter the auction, the opponents will be able to steal you blind. Anytime they have a good suit, they can enter the auction at the two-level. If they catch the responding hand with not enough strength to go to game, and with the wrong distribution for a penalty double, they will get away with buying the contract at the two-level.

To prevent this, the responder's bid of two notrump assumes a natural meaning. It tells the opener that the responder has some strength, though not enough to bid game. The bid more or less promises a balanced hand, but the responder does *not* promise a stopper in the enemy's suit. He is bidding on his strength, and on the presumed strength of his partner's hand.

Also see: Argument 106.

ARGUMENT 106

After an opening notrump, when an opponent intervenes, what bids are forcing?

THE HAND

NORTH
- ♠ K J 4
- ♡ A Q 5
- ♢ Q J 5 4 3
- ♣ K J

WEST
- ♠ 9 3 2
- ♡ 10 8 6 2
- ♢ K 7
- ♣ 9 7 6 3

EAST
- ♠ A Q 8 7 6 5
- ♡ 3
- ♢ 9 8 6
- ♣ A 10 2

SOUTH
- ♠ 10
- ♡ K J 9 7 4
- ♢ A 10 2
- ♣ Q 8 5 4

THE AUCTION

NORTH	EAST	SOUTH	WEST
1 NT	2 ♠	3 ♠	Pass
3 NT	Pass	Pass	Pass

THE RESULT

East led a spade. The resulting carnage did little to improve partnership confidence, especially when it was realized that four hearts could not be defeated.

THE ARGUMENT

South asserted that North's three notrump bid was ill-advised. He had asked for a suit and North should

289

have bid his diamonds. South would then have shown his hearts, and North-South would have arrived at the right contract.

North insisted that the only bid South could reasonably have made was three hearts. In response to South's statement that this would not be forcing, his reply was unprintable.

GOREN SETTLES THE ARGUMENT

You have hit on a hand that is troublesome even for experts. By overcalling the notrump opening bid with two spades, East has made it extremely difficult for North-South to conduct a logical auction. The only forcing bid available is three spades, and it is odds on that North will bid three notrump.

This is a judgment situation. Notrump could prove an uncomfortable contract with a singleton in the opponents' suit. Since North most likely has three hearts for his opening notrump, I favor a bid of four hearts with the South hand.

Even should North have only a doubleton honor in hearts, the 5-2 fit should prove quite playable.

Some players have tried to overcome this problem by playing that in this sequence, *and in this sequence only,* a bid of three hearts is considered forcing. The theory is that the opener can now bid three notrump with good stoppers in the enemy suit, and bid to four in the major with only two-card support in the responder's suit.

However, this treatment is contrary to standard practice. Don't spring it on your partner as a surprise and expect him to understand what you intend.

When your partner opens with a notrump bid, and your opponent interferes with an opposing bid, no bid in another suit by the responder is forcing. The only absolute force is a cue-bid in the overcaller's suit.

Also see: Argument 105.

ARGUMENT 107

May you raise an overcall with only two trumps?

THE HAND

	NORTH	
	♠ 9	
	♡ A K J 8 4	
	◇ 10 3	
	♣ A J 6 4 3	

WEST		EAST
♠ A K Q 7 2		♠ J 10 6 3
♡ 9 6		♡ 7 5 3 2
◇ A 9 8		◇ Q 5 4
♣ 10 7 2		♣ 9 8

	SOUTH	
	♠ 8 5 4	
	♡ Q 10	
	◇ K J 7 6 2	
	♣ K Q 5	

THE AUCTION

WEST	NORTH	EAST	SOUTH
1 ♠	2 ♡	Pass	Pass
Pass			

THE RESULT

North made five club tricks and five heart tricks.

THE ARGUMENT

South was deeply incensed at missing the game, and blamed it all on his partner. He insisted that North's hand was too strong for an overcall—North should have doubled at his first turn. How could he, South, think that an aceless hand could produce game opposite a mere overcall? And with only two hearts!

GOREN SETTLES THE ARGUMENT

An overcall is based on trick-taking ability—not on points. The overcaller's partner should bear this in mind when considering what action to take.

Normal trump support for an overcall is less than that required for an opening bid. This is because an overcall is almost never made on a four-card suit. At the two-level, an overcall guarantees a good five-card suit. Thus, three low trumps, or Q-x, are adequate support for an overcaller.

A vulnerable overcall at the two-level promises about six playing tricks. South's hand could be counted on to produce at least three tricks, for the queen of trumps is worth a full trick. Thus South should have realized that his side's combined holding is in the game zone. The least South could have done was to have advised his partner of this fact by raising to three hearts, an invitation North would have been delighted to accept with his excellent distribution.

We discount South's remark that North should have made a takeout double. A two-suited hand is generally better suited to an overcall than to a takeout double.

ARGUMENT 108

Is a jump raise of an overcall forcing?

THE HAND

```
              NORTH
              ♠ A 8 5 2
              ♡ A Q J 6 3
              ◇ J 5
              ♣ 7 2
WEST                              EAST
♠ K J 7                          ♠ Q 9 6 4 3
♡ 10 5                           ♡ 8 4
◇ A K 6                          ◇ 8 7 4 2
♣ K J 10 8 4                     ♣ Q 5
              SOUTH
              ♠ 10
              ♡ K 9 7 2
              ◇ Q 10 9 3
              ♣ A 9 6 3
```

THE AUCTION   [*North-South are vulnerable*]

WEST	NORTH	EAST	SOUTH
1 ♣	1 ♡	Pass	2 ♡
Pass	Pass	Pass	

THE RESULT

After a club lead, the declarer had no trouble
making ten tricks.

His only losers were two diamonds and a club.

THE ARGUMENT

North and South entered the fray hot and heavy.
Holding only one ace and one king, South claimed he,
on his part, had done all he could by keeping the

bidding open for one round after his partner's minimum overcall.

North pointed out that South had completely ignored his distributional assets. South had ample values to jump to game, thundered his partner.

South just couldn't see North's point of view.

GOREN SETTLES THE ARGUMENT

Yes, South should have taken more vigorous action. But North was wrong about what that action should have been. South's hand was worth four tricks in support of hearts. The king of trumps and ace of clubs were each a full trick. Even if the defenders lead trumps, South has two ruffing tricks because of his singleton spade and his four trumps. He definitely should have shown these values with a jump raise to three hearts.

Unlike a jump raise of an opening bid, the jump raise of an overcall is not forcing to game. Rather, it expresses the trick-taking ability of the hand. In effect, it says: Partner, even if you are minimum for your overcall, I believe our side can take nine tricks. If you have no extra values, you are free to pass. However, if you have better than minimum values and you think we can make game, I would be delighted to hear you bid on.

North would then value his hand at six tricks because of his fourth spade, and would go on to game.

However, change his hand to:

♠ A x x
♡ A Q J x x
♢ J x
♣ x x x

Now the hand is worth only five tricks, and North should pass. Note that with this hand, nine tricks are all that North-South can make against a proper defense.

ARGUMENT 109

What does an overcall of one notrump show?

THE HAND

                    NORTH
                    ♠ 8 5 4
                    ♡ 7 6
                    ◇ Q 7 3
                    ♣ A Q 8 7 2

WEST   EAST
♠ 10 6 3 2   ♠ Q 9 7
♡ 5 4   ♡ A K 10 9 2
◇ J 10 4 2   ◇ A 8 6
♣ J 6 4   ♣ 9 3

                    SOUTH
                    ♠ A K J
                    ♡ Q J 8 3
                    ◇ K 9 5
                    ♣ K 10 5

THE AUCTION

EAST	SOUTH	WEST	NORTH
1 ♡	Dbl	Pass	2 ♣
Pass	3 ♣	Pass	5 ♣
Pass	Pass	Pass	

THE RESULT

The defenders took the ace-king of hearts and the ace of diamonds.

Down one.

In the post-mortem, it was discovered that three notrump would have been a relatively simple contract.

THE ARGUMENT

In South's opinion, North's leap to five clubs was rather precipitate. He suggested that North might have tried three diamonds to show a stopper, in which case three notrump would have been the next bid.

North retorted that South, with his balanced hand, should have been the one to bid notrump, and at his first turn.

South found it laughable that anyone should think that he should merely overcall at his first opportunity, holding such a fine hand.

GOREN SETTLES THE ARGUMENT

The notion that a one notrump overcall shows a weak hand is an old wives' tale.

An overcall of one notrump is the equivalent of an opening bid of one notrump, showing a balanced hand. The overcaller would have opened the bidding with one notrump had he been afforded the opportunity.

Indeed, many players tend to make the upper limit of the bid even higher than that for an opening notrump, giving the bid a range of 16-19 points. Of course the hand must also contain a sound stopper in the opponents' suit—more often two stoppers.

Such a hand will usually meet the technical requirements for a takeout double, for it will have support for all the unbid suits. However, to make a takeout double with the hand could lead to complications if your partner, with a weak hand, were to respond at the two-level. At this point, to describe the hand properly, the doubler would have to rebid in notrump at a still higher level, risking a substantial penalty if the opponents hold the balance of power.

There is an additional advantage to overcalling with one notrump with this type of hand. In a single bid, you have delineated both the strength and shape of your hand, placing your partner in an excellent position to judge the final contract.

On the hand in question, had South overcalled with one notrump instead of doubling, North held sufficient values to raise to three notrump, since the club suit rates to produce four, or possibly five, tricks.

There is one further advantage to a one notrump overcall of opponents' bid in a major.

Since a notrump overcall does not urge partner to bid the other major, as would a takeout double, if partner *does* show that major he indicates at least a five-card suit.

ARGUMENT 110

What constitutes a jump overcall?

THE HAND

```
                    NORTH
                    ♠ J 10 6
                    ♡ A
                    ◇ K J 7 2
                    ♣ J 8 4 3 2
    WEST                            EAST
    ♠ 5                             ♠ 8 4 3
    ♡ K 8 6 4                       ♡ Q J 10 9 3
    ◇ Q 10 8 5 4                    ◇ A 9
    ♣ A 10 7                        ♣ K Q 5
                    SOUTH
                    ♠ A K Q 9 7 2
                    ♡ 7 5 2
                    ◇ 6 3
                    ♣ 9 6
```

THE AUCTION

EAST	SOUTH	WEST	NORTH
1 ♡	1 ♠	4 ♡	Pass
Pass	Pass		

THE RESULT

The declarer needed only a modicum of care to hold his losers to one spade, one diamond, and the ace of trumps.

Making four.

North-South had a fine sacrifice in four spades, which would go down only one provided the declarer correctly guessed the diamond situation—not unlikely in view of the bidding.

Given a heart opening, South leads a club from

dummy. Regardless of the line of defense, South can lose only two clubs, one diamond, and one heart. Any error on the part of the defenders will permit South to make the contract.

THE ARGUMENT

South accused North of being chicken for not sacrificing at four spades.

North retorted that he thought there was a good chance to defeat four hearts, in view of his partner's overcall and his own defensive values. He wanted to know why South hadn't overcalled *two* spades.

"Don't you know that two spades would be a forcing bid showing a strong hand?" inquired South.

GOREN SETTLES THE ARGUMENT

In the good old days of yore, a jump overcall did show an extremely strong hand; it asked one's partner to bid unless he did not have a trick.

This use of the bid had just one thing against it— lack of frequency. The type of hand on which it could be employed seldom came up. In modern play, therefore, the meaning of the bid has changed.

A jump overcall is considered to be a preemptive bid. Its requirements are:
1. **A good suit at least six cards long;**
2. **A high-card range of 6-9 points, concentrated in the long suit;**
3. **Minimal defensive values;**
4. **The jump overcaller should reasonably expect to take within three tricks of his bid in his own hand if not vulnerable, and within two tricks of his bid, if vulnerable.**

Apart from the fact that jumping the bidding makes it awkward for the opposing side to exchange information, the overcaller often suggests a profitable sacrifice. Thus, on this hand, North would know that his side has little defensive prospect against four hearts, especially as his three spades make it more likely that his side has, at best, one defensive trick in the suit.

Offensively, however, North holds three or four tricks, if you take into account his potential heart ruffs. Therefore, a save at four spades cannot be expensive.

Let us change the South hand slightly to:

♠ A J 10 x x x
♥ x x
♦ x x
♣ K J x

South still has 9 high-card points and a six-card spade suit. This time, however, he should overcall one diamond with one spade. The fact that almost half his strength is outside his long suit makes the hand too good defensively for a jump overcall of two spades, action which could lead his partner to take a needless save against a four-heart contract.

Exception:

Not vulnerable, some players use a jump overcall as a desperate measure on much weaker hands than South's. I do not recommend this tactic, for the opponents are seldom in the dark, but my partner may be. But, of course, I do not mind this arrangement as long as my partner warns me in advance.

ARGUMENT 111

After your partner's overcall, should you show stoppers in the enemy suit?

THE HAND

```
                    NORTH
                    ♠ A K 10 7 2
                    ♡ 6
                    ◇ 7 5 4
                    ♣ A 9 8 3
    WEST                                EAST
    ♠ 8 3                               ♠ Q J 6 4
    ♡ K J 10 7 2                        ♡ 9 8 5 3
    ◇ A J 9                             ◇ K 10 2
    ♣ K Q 2                             ♣ J 7
                    SOUTH
                    ♠ 9 5
                    ♡ A Q 4
                    ◇ Q 8 6 3
                    ♣ 10 6 5 4
```

THE AUCTION

WEST	NORTH	EAST	SOUTH
1 ♡	1 ♠	Pass	1 NT
Pass	Pass	Dbl	Pass
Pass	Pass		

THE RESULT

Declarer won West's spade lead with the ace, played the ace and another club. West won and returned a spade which was won by the dummy's king. A third club was led from the dummy and, again, was won by West. West made the perfect return of the nine of

301

diamonds which was won by East's king. East played the nine of hearts which was won by South's ace. South cashed his high club, giving him two spade tricks, two club tricks, and one heart trick.

The hand went down two, doubled.

THE ARGUMENT

South blamed North for passing one notrump doubled with an unbalanced hand. He thought North should have run to two clubs.

North pointed out that two clubs would not have fared much better after a trump lead. Besides, North remarked, he saw no reason for making a bid that was predicated upon the assumption that he was playing with a lunatic who bid without regard to safety.

GOREN SETTLES THE ARGUMENT

North is quite right.

The purpose of bidding after your partner has overcalled is to advance your side towards game. Should you be convinced there is no game, there is little point in entering the auction simply to hear the sound of your voice.

South let the fact that he held values in the opponents' suit blind him to the reality that he held scant values overall. The overcall had promised four or five tricks. South's collection of garbage could add one trick of his own, with no solid suit to develop.

There was no reason to suspect that notrump would be a better contract than spades. By his overcall, North had, at least, promised a reasonable suit. However, at a notrump contract there might not be the time to develop the suit if the defenders attacked the entries in North's hand. Clearly, South would have been much wiser to pass.

Let us assume that South held the king of diamonds along with the queen of diamonds. Now there is a chance for game in notrump. With such a hand, it would be in order for South to bid one notrump after his partner's overcall. Further movement toward game would now be up to his partner.

ARGUMENT 112

What are the requirements for an "Unusual Notrump" overcall?

THE HAND

```
                    NORTH
                    ♠ K 7 6 5
                    ♡ 6 5
                    ◇ 7 3 2
                    ♣ J 7 6 3
    WEST                                    EAST
    ♠ J 10 8 2                              ♠ Q 9 4
    ♡ K J 9 8 3                             ♡ A Q 10 7 4
    ◇ K 4                                   ◇ J 8 6
    ♣ 9 5                                   ♣ A 4
                    SOUTH
                    ♠ A 3
                    ♡ 2
                    ◇ A Q 10 9 5
                    ♣ K Q 10 8 2
```

THE AUCTION   [*East-West are vulnerable*]

EAST	SOUTH	WEST	NORTH
1 ♡	2 NT	4 ♡	6 ♣
Dbl	Pass	Pass	Pass

THE RESULT

The defenders took one heart trick, one diamond, and one club.

Down two.

There were several ways to defeat an East-West contract of four hearts.

THE ARGUMENT

South challenged North about the trick-taking power of his hand.

North suggested that someone ought to explain to South what the "Unusual Notrump" overcall was all about. From where North sat, after South's bid, it was possible that the opponents could make a grand slam. He was taking an advance sacrifice in the hope that the opponents would settle for a penalty substantially less than the value of their slam.

South retorted that such sacrifices could advance a partnership to insolvency.

GOREN SETTLES THE ARGUMENT

For many years, when a prospective partner asked me whether I played the "Unusual Notrump," I replied in the negative. This hand presents a typical case explaining why I have, for the most part, declined to play the convention; for most players simply do not understand the basic idea behind the convention.

The Unusual Notrump is not a bid designed to get you to game. The primary purpose of the bid is to suggest a possible sacrifice to your partner in the event that your opponents reach game, or to so crowd the auction by stealing bidding space that your opponents do not find their best spot.

It is not enough for the overcaller to hold ten or eleven cards in the minor suits for his bid; the overcaller should have less than an opening bid when making the bid.

There is no minimum point count for an Unusual Notrump bid. The more distributional the hand, the weaker it is likely to be in high-card content.

Here are some typical Unusual Notrump overcalls of an opening bid of one heart:

♠ x	♠ xx	♠ x
♡ x	♡ x	♡ —
◇ Q J 10 x x	◇ A J 10 x x	◇ Q J x x x x
♣ K J 10 x x x	♣ K J x x x	♣ K x x x x x

How then should South have handled the auction with the hand he actually held? He should have simply overcalled with two diamonds, intending to bid clubs on his next turn.

For one thing, South's hand was too good defensively to have suggested to his partner that it might be more profitable to sacrifice should the opponents reach game. Moreover, there was no reason for South to insist on a minor suit contract. Depending upon North's holding, either four spades or three notrump might have turned out to be a more viable contract than either of the minors. The Unusual Notrump almost always shuts out such alternatives.

ARGUMENT 113

How do you respond to your partner's "Unusual Notrump" overcall?

THE HAND

```
                    NORTH
                    ♠ —
                    ♡ 6
                    ◇ K J 10 5 4 2
                    ♣ A 10 7 5 4 2

WEST                                    EAST
♠ A K 10 7 2                            ♠ 9 8 6
♡ J 9 5 4                               ♡ Q 10 8
◇ A 7                                   ◇ Q 9 6 3
♣ K 8                                   ♣ Q J 9

                    SOUTH
                    ♠ Q J 5 4 3
                    ♡ A K 7 3 2
                    ◇ 8
                    ♣ 6 3
```

THE AUCTION

[*North-South are vulnerable*]

WEST	NORTH	EAST	SOUTH
1 ♠	2 NT	Pass	Pass
Pass			

THE RESULT

East led the nine of spades. Dummy's jack forced the king. West returned the spade deuce, and South won with the queen. The declarer made only one spade trick, two heart tricks, and one trick in each of the minor suits.

Down three.

307

THE ARGUMENT

North accused South of gross dereliction of duty. His unusual two notrump was a bid that requested a minor suit takeout, and South had failed to show his better minor. Three clubs would just barely have been made.

South stoutly maintained he was quite justified in passing two notrump. North's bid had announced a minor-suit hand, it's true, but South had the majors well stopped. The whole trouble stemmed, he claimed, from the fact that North did not have the values for a vulnerable Unusual Notrump overcall.

GOREN SETTLES THE ARGUMENT

South's argument is slightly fatuous. He should, instead, have acted like the chap in days gone by who said: "I seen my duty and I done it!" His partner asked him to name his better minor, and since he had a distinct preference he should have bid three clubs.

By employing the Unusual Notrump, the over-caller has described a hand with great offensive strength in the minor suits but little defensive potential. With a hand of little help to his partner, the responder should bid his better minor at the lowest level possible.

Having all your strength in the major suits is no reason to pass your partner's Unusual Notrump. To make a notrump contract, there must be a source of tricks. Misfits play better in suit contracts than in notrump.

With strength in the majors and some fit for one of your partner's suits, it is a good tactic to raise your partner pre-emptively to the four-level. You hope the opponents will compete further in the majors, allowing you to double. A jump to either game or slam in either minor is a two-way action. It might be made with a good fit for partner's suits, in the expectation of making your contract, or it might be an advance sacrifice made with a weak hand, in the hope of shutting the opponents out of the auction.

CHAPTER 16

Slam Bidding

ARGUMENT 114

When is a hand unsuitable for Blackwood?

THE HAND

```
          NORTH
          ♠ K J 8 3
          ♡ A 10 8 5
          ◇ J 7
          ♣ K 8 3

          SOUTH
          ♠ A Q 10 9 5 2
          ♡ K Q J
          ◇ 9 5
          ♣ A Q
```

THE AUCTION

SOUTH	WEST	NORTH	EAST
1 ♠	Pass	3 ♠	Pass
4 NT	Pass	5 ◇	Pass
6 ♠	Pass	Pass	Pass

THE RESULT

West led the ace and king of diamonds, both of which held. With any other lead, the hand would have made.

THE ARGUMENT

North thought it rather ignominious to have bid a slam that was beaten by the time two tricks had been played. Since he had done nothing but jump raise his partner's suit, he felt he was innocent of any wrong, and therefore considerably aggrieved.

South was voluble in his own defense. "My hand revalued to 23 points. My partner had shown an opening bid, so we had to be in the slam zone. How could I know that the ace and king we were missing were both in the same suit? Rather than bawl me out, you should be commiserating with me on our bad luck."

North still found himself short on sympathy.

GOREN SETTLES THE ARGUMENT

Like many conventions, Blackwood is more often abused than used correctly. Its originator, Easley Blackwood, always said that if he had a penny for every time his convention was misused, he would be a mighty rich man. Certain key conditions must be met before launching into ace-asking.

There is no point employing Blackwood if, after receiving the desired response, three suits in the combined hands will have first-round control, but the fourth suit may lack even second-round control. If that condition exists, the information obtained by asking for aces will be useless.

Consider South's hand. After North's response to Blackwood, he knew that his side was off an ace, but he did not know whether or not he could make twelve tricks. In other words, the suit in which the ace was missing—diamonds—might also lack second-round control.

Even if North held two aces, the hand might not play well in slam.

The right way to approach this hand is by using cue-bids. This method would soon elicit the information that the diamond suit was not controlled. Then South would play the hand in five spades, or perhaps in four spades.

The cue-bid sequence might go:

South	North
1 ♠	3 ♠
4 ♣	4 ♡
5 ♡	5 ♠
Pass	

Also see: Arguments 124, 125.

ARGUMENT 115

How do you respond to Blackwood with a void?

THE HAND

NORTH
- ♠ K 8
- ♡ A Q 8 6 5 2
- ◇ K Q 8
- ♣ A 7

SOUTH
- ♠ Q J 5 4
- ♡ K J 10 7
- ◇ A J 9 3 2
- ♣ —

THE AUCTION

NORTH	EAST	SOUTH	WEST
1 ♡	Pass	3 ♡	Pass
4 NT	Pass	5 ♡	Pass
7 ♡	Pass	Pass	Pass

THE RESULT

The play was soon over. East, on opening lead, laid down the ace of spades. Dummy came down and simultaneously, North hit the ceiling. It was obvious to all concerned that he held a spade loser.

THE ARGUMENT

North was apoplectic as he inquired where South had ever learned the responses to Blackwood. He thought that one ace was shown via five diamonds.

South observed that North wouldn't have been so vituperative had the ace been in spades rather than in clubs.

"If you don't count a void as an ace," argued South, "how can you ever show it?"

GOREN SETTLES THE ARGUMENT

When responding to Blackwood, never count a void as an ace. Duplication of values can exist with the responder's void duplicating one of partner's aces, rather than an unprotected suit.

There are several methods of showing a void in response to Blackwood. Easley Blackwood suggests the following way:

Respond in the suit that normally would show the number of aces you hold, but *jump* the bidding one level.

Thus with one ace and a void, you respond six diamonds; with two aces and a void, you respond six hearts, etc.

There is a slight drawback to this method, in that it is not always possible to locate the void. Thus, on the hand in question, it would not help North to know that South has a void, for he has no way of knowing whether that void is in spades or in clubs. Obviously, a club void is not worth much, while a spade void gives a grand slam a reasonable chance.

An alternative method allows the responder to pinpoint his void:

With one ace and a void, the responder bids six in his void suit, provided that suit is lower-ranking than the agreed trump suit. If the void is in a suit ranking higher than the trump suit, the responder jumps to six of the agreed suit. With two aces and a void, the responder bids five no-trump.

Had North-South been employing this method, North would have been able to stay in six hearts, knowing his side was missing an ace that would cash. In response to North's Blackwood inquiry, South would bid six clubs. That shows one ace and a void in clubs, so North knows he must lose the ace of diamonds or the ace of spades. Had South's void been in spades, he would respond six hearts. Now North can take a chance on the grand slam.

Some words of caution. Before employing either of these methods, make sure that your partner knows which method you are playing. And always be cautious about showing a void. Bear in mind that you are committing your side to six, and also be aware that if the void is not useful to your partner, you may be forcing him to an unmanageable level.

ARGUMENT 116

What are the implications of a Blackwood five notrump bid?

THE HAND

```
                    NORTH
                    ♠ A Q J 9 5 3
                    ♡ K
                    ◇ A 8
                    ♣ A 6 5 2
    WEST                                EAST
    ♠ 7 6                               ♠ 4
    ♡ Q J 10 8 6 2                      ♡ 9 5 4 3
    ♡ 7 2                               ◇ Q 6 3
    ♣ Q 9 8                             ♣ K J 10 4 3
                    SOUTH
                    ♠ K 10 8 2
                    ♡ A 7
                    ◇ K J 10 9 5 4
                    ♣ 7
```

THE AUCTION

NORTH	EAST	SOUTH	WEST
1 ♠	Pass	3 ♠	Pass
4 NT	Pass	5 ◇	Pass
5 NT	Pass	6 ♡	Pass
6 ♠	Pass	Pass	Pass

THE RESULT

North made all the tricks with no difficulty.

THE ARGUMENT

No one was quite sure where the bidding went wrong. North bemoaned the fact that a grand slam had been missed, and declared that South should have bid three diamonds on his first turn. Certainly, South's original pass had been timid. Only a jump shift could fully assert the strength of his holding.

South contended that the one who initiates Blackwood becomes the captain of the hand. South had abided by his partner's decision; for that he deserved commendation, not complaint.

GOREN SETTLES THE ARGUMENT

The subject of captaincy of a hand is vastly overdone, particularly when it applies to the Blackwood convention.

The four notrump bidder is captain of the hand if, over his partner's response, he either stops short of slam or bids a slam directly. However, the moment he bids five notrump, he waives his captaincy, and now either player can place the final contract.

A second Blackwood inquiry of five notrump is more than just a request for partner to announce how many kings he possesses. That bid also guarantees that there is no ace missing—that the Blackwood bidder and his partner hold all four.

In most cases, the responder will dutifully show his kings when asked to, for on most hands the final contract cannot be determined by the responder. However, some hands are not limited by the number of kings that are held. The hand under discussion is a typical case.

The moment North confirmed possession of all four aces, South should have realized that the only likely loser on the hand could be a heart. Even in the event that North holds three diamonds to the ace, North-South will have nine cards in the suit, and there is an excellent chance it can be brought in without a loser. With any lesser number of diamonds in the North hand, South's diamonds can be set up for discards of North's hearts.

Thus, the number of kings North-South hold becomes immaterial. South should have bid the grand slam in spades directly over North's inquiry for kings.

WARNING: Unless the previous bidding has virtually guaranteed that partner holds both the ace and king of trumps (e.g., you respond two hearts to partner's one spade opening; he then rebids three spades while you hold Q-J-10-8 in spades) beware of bidding seven if you hold neither the ace nor the king of trumps.

ARGUMENT 117

How do you respond to Blackwood after a cue-bid of the enemy suit?

THE HAND

```
              NORTH
              ♠ 8
              ♡ A K J 10
              ◇ K Q J 5 3
              ♣ A K J

              SOUTH
              ♠ A 9 3
              ♡ Q 9 8 5 2
              ◇ 7 4 2
              ♣ 5 3
```

THE AUCTION

WEST	NORTH	EAST	SOUTH
1 ♠	2 ♣	Pass	4 ♡
Pass	4 NT	Pass	5 ♣
Pass	5 ♡	Pass	Pass
Pass			

THE RESULT

West led the king of spades, and North greeted the sight of South's ace with a yell that was enough to awaken the dead.

Twelve tricks were duly made.

THE ARGUMENT

North remarked that he was quite used to partners who couldn't count up to thirteen, but this was the first time he had met one who couldn't get beyond zero.

319

South reminded his partner that, having cue-bid spades, the ace of spades was not to be counted when responding to Blackwood.

GOREN SETTLES THE ARGUMENT

Twenty years ago, I would have thrown my support to South. But bridge, like most things in life, has not stood still.

In the good old days, a cue-bid of the opponents' suit guaranteed either the ace or a void in the suit. Today, that no longer holds true. A cue-bid is used as a strong takeout or a forcing bid; therefore, the responder to Blackwood must count every ace for his response.

The old method did have its advantages. When his partner cue-bid and the responder was looking at the ace of that suit, he knew this card was worthless, for his partner had to be void in the suit, so the responder did not show that ace in the Blackwood sequence. Today's methods make it more difficult to evaluate the worth of that ace.

However, there are sound reasons why the change in the cue-bid came about. The most convincing one is frequency. The occasions when a player held a very strong hand, support for the other suits *and* the ace or a void in the opener's suit were so rare that the bid was in virtual disuse. By permitting a cue-bid with a singleton in the suit, the frequency of occurrence was greatly increased.

This situation, where the cue-bid of the opposing suit is meant as a takeout double, is not to be confused with the following:

NORTH	EAST	SOUTH	WEST
1 ♡	2 ♢	3 ♡	Pass
4 ♢	Pass	4 ♡	Pass
4 NT			

Here, North has gone out of his way to cue-bid the enemy suit *before* bidding four notrump to ask for aces. This clearly shows first-round control in the over-caller's suit, and South should not count the ace of diamonds when responding to show the number of aces he holds.

ARGUMENT 118

How do you respond to Blackwood after interference?

THE HAND

```
                    NORTH
                    ♠ K Q 7 2
                    ♡ A Q 6 5 2
                    ♢ 9
                    ♣ A 8 7
WEST                                    EAST
♠ J 10 6 5 4                            ♠ 9
♡ 4                                     ♡ 7 3
♢ K 6 5 4 2                             ♢ A Q J 10 8 3
♣ 5 3                                   ♣ 10 9 6 4
                    SOUTH
                    ♠ A 8 3
                    ♡ K J 10 9 8
                    ♢ 7
                    ♣ K Q J 2
```

THE AUCTION

NORTH	EAST	SOUTH	WEST
1 ♡	2 ♢	3 ♡	4 ♢
4 NT	5 ♢	Dbl	Pass
Pass	Pass		

THE RESULT

East lost one spade, one heart, and two clubs, but his 100 honors cut his deficit to 200 points.

The loss was paltry in view of the fact that North-South could have made six hearts.

THE ARGUMENT

South claimed that since East had "stolen" his bid by bidding five diamonds he couldn't respond in Blackwood. A double, he claimed, eloquently resolved his dilemma. North should have realized that East's bid was, in reality, *his* bid.

North retorted that he had never studied divination. Not being a mind reader, he couldn't figure out *that* kind of a holding. Surely, South could have discerned that their partnership held all the outside strength. The only question, beside a losing trick in diamonds, was whether a trump trick would be lost. Since South held the king and the jack of hearts, he should have gone on to six hearts.

GOREN SETTLES THE ARGUMENT

Experience has shown that in a situation of this sort it is better to agree upon a convention than to rely on logic. Here are two ways to handle Blackwood after interference.

The oldest method of handling Blackwood after interference by an opponent is to pass with no ace, bid the next suit over the interference bid with one ace, and so on, in steps.

Using this method, South should have shown his one ace with a bid of five hearts. Then North would have gone on to six hearts. A double merely suggested that this was the surest way to collect a big penalty.

The alternate method can be remembered by the acronymic DOPI, which stands for: Double = 0 aces, Pass = 1 ace. Two aces are shown by bidding the next suit up the line.

If North-South had been playing DOPI, South would have passed five diamonds to show one ace. North would then have bid six hearts.

My preference is for the DOPI method, and not just because it is easier to remember. DOPI offers more chance of doubling the opponents for a substantial penalty, on hands where the partnership is not prepared to contract for slam. When you do not hold an ace, there is a greater likelihood that your side cannot make a slam, and that it will be more profitable to play the hand for penalties.

Incidentally, don't feel too bad about getting signals crossed in Blackwood situations. On at least two occasions in world championship play, expert partnerships of long duration found that they hadn't agreed on how to play Blackwood after an interference bid.

Some players use a method acronymically designated as DIPO: double = 1 ace; pass = 0 aces. I prefer DOPI for reasons expressed above.

ARGUMENT 119

When does a four-club bid call for aces?
(Gerber Convention)

THE HAND

```
          NORTH
          ♠ A Q 10 7 3
          ♡ A 8
          ◇ 7
          ♣ A Q J 9 2

          SOUTH
          ♠ K J 5 4
          ♡ 10 7 3 2
          ◇ 9 5 2
          ♣ K 8
```

THE AUCTION

NORTH	EAST	SOUTH	WEST
1 ♠	Pass	2 ♠	Pass
4 ♣	Pass	4 ◇	Pass
4 ♠	Pass	Pass	Pass

THE RESULT

As soon as dummy came down, the declarer began to look unhappy.

A small slam had obviously been missed.

THE ARGUMENT

Clearly, there had been a misunderstanding. North had intended his four-club bid to show a strong two-suiter.

South had understood the bid to be the Gerber Convention, asking for aces, and had responded with four diamonds to show no ace.

The partnership was using the convention, but there was some disagreement as to whether, in this sequence, four clubs was Gerber.

GOREN SETTLES THE ARGUMENT

Before discussing the argument, perhaps we should recapitulate the Gerber convention.

A bid of four clubs asks for aces. Partner responds in steps as in Blackwood: 4 ◇ = 0 aces or four aces; 4 ♡ = one ace; 4 ♠ = two aces, etc. The 4 ♣ bidder can then ask for kings with a subsequent bid of 5 ♣, and responder shows his kings in the same manner. But . . . see below.

The advantage of the convention is that it keeps the bidding at a lower level than does Blackwood. Some people even play that you can ask for queens with 6 ♣.

However, Gerber can have a drawback in suit play. Quite often, as was the case in this particular hand, the bid of four clubs is more useful in its natural sense. For example, if the four-club bid by North had to be Gerber, there would be no sensible way to probe for a slam. North would have to content himself with a bid of three clubs. Now even if South jumped to four spades North could not be sure that twelve tricks were there.

When first introduced by John Gerber back in 1938, *any* four-club bid was treated as ace-asking. However, because many experts found that a natural bid of four clubs was needed in many situations, most players today limit the use of the convention to the times when it is wheeled into action directly over the notrump bid.

Consider these two auctions:

	[A]			[B]	
NORTH		SOUTH	NORTH		SOUTH
1 NT		4 ♣	1 NT		3 ♣
			4 ♣		

South's bid of four clubs in *Hand A* is Gerber, asking for aces. However, North's four-club bid in *Hand B* is natural, showing support for South's suit. Either player can ask for aces by using the Blackwood convention.

It is not necessary that the bidding be opened with one or two notrump for a four-club bid to be Gerber. For example:

NORTH	SOUTH
1 ♡	2 ◇
2 NT	4 ♣

The simplest way to play the rule is:

Any time a jump to four clubs immediately follows a notrump bid by partner, it is a Gerber call for aces.

There's even an exception to this general rule. If your partner's notrump bid has been doubled, you can still retreat to four clubs for safety without having partner begin ace-showing.

ARGUMENT 120

When should you jump to five of the agreed major?

THE HAND

           NORTH
           ♠ 7 5
           ♡ A Q J 9 5 4
           ◇ K Q 7
           ♣ A J 3

           SOUTH
           ♠ 9
           ♡ K 10 8 7
           ◇ A 10 9 2
           ♣ K 9 6 4

THE AUCTION

NORTH	EAST	SOUTH	WEST
1 ♡	1 ♠	3 ♡	Pass
4 NT	Pass	5 ◇	Pass
5 ♡	Pass	Pass	Pass

THE RESULT

Six hearts, an excellent contract that had many chances, was made.

THE ARGUMENT

North berated South for missing the slam. South was the one with the singleton spade. In view of the auction, she should have realized the importance of that holding.

From South's point of view, two aces could have been missing, so she didn't see how she could bid

328

again. North was captain of the hand. She maintained that North's hand was unsuited to Blackwood. Some form of cue-bidding should probably have been used, though she wasn't sure just how the auction should go.

GOREN SETTLES THE ARGUMENT

The partnership in this hand missed its optimum spot because Blackwood was used on a hand that was not suited to that convention; the opener held one suit with no controls—spades.

Whether or not to contract for slam depends on South's holding in the "pointed" suits, to use the jargon of today's players when referring to spades and diamonds.

North should have used cue-bidding to determine where South's strength lay. Unless his partner holds the ace of diamonds, North can forget all about slam, for he will surely lose a spade trick as well as the diamond ace, even should South hold the ace of spades.

Thus, a cue-bid of four clubs is indicated on the North cards; that would bring the welcome response of four diamonds. Now all that remains is to check on the spade situation.

An opener can ask his partner about control of the unbid suit by bidding over game in the agreed suit.

Thus, on hearing the diamond cue-bid from his partner, the opener should jump to five hearts. Logically, the bid says: "Partner, we have checked over everything but the spade situation. I have two losers there, and so cannot venture six on my own. How are you fixed in that department?"

The responder has several options. With a singleton spade, he can bid six hearts. With the ace or a void in the opponents' suit, the responder can cue-bid that ace (if it is in a suit lower-ranking than the agreed trump suit; therefore not in this instance) to give his partner the option of bidding seven if he so desires.

ARGUMENT 121

What is the Grand Slam Force?

THE HAND

NORTH
♠ Q J 10 9 5 2
♡ A K 5 3
♢ K Q 5
♣ —

SOUTH
♠ A K 8 3
♡ 7
♢ A 9 4 2
♣ Q J 6 2

THE AUCTION

NORTH	EAST	SOUTH	WEST
1 ♠	Pass	3 ♠	Pass
4 ♣	Pass	4 ♢	Pass
5 NT	Pass	6 ♢	Pass
6 ♠	Pass	Pass	Pass

THE RESULT

Thirteen tricks were made in short order.

THE ARGUMENT

North wanted to know why South, holding both the ace and the king of trumps, had not bid seven spades.

South wanted to know what sort of new-fangled response North was trying to introduce. A Blackwood bid of five notrump asked for kings, and South showed one king with his response of six diamonds. North should have checked for aces and then gambled on the

330

grand slam, for even if South's king were in clubs, the contract would depend on no worse than a finesse.

GOREN SETTLES THE ARGUMENT

A five-notrump bid is *never* Blackwood unless it is preceded by a four notrump bid. Even if the asker holds all four aces in his own hand, he must first bid four notrump. A follow-up bid of five notrump then announces possession by the partnership of all four aces, and asks the responder to show his kings.

When not preceded by four notrump, a bid of five notrump is the Grand Slam Force. It requests the responder to bid seven of the agreed suit, if he holds two of the three top trump honors.

This bid is not new. It was invented by Ely Culbertson, and described in a "Bridge World" article in 1936 under the byline of Josephine Culbertson, Ely's wife. As a result, it is known in many European countries as "Josephine."

Since South held both the ace and the king of spades, his correct bid was seven spades.

Also see: Arguments 122, 123.

ARGUMENT 122

Can you show different holdings in response to the Grand Slam Force?

THE HAND

NORTH
♠ K Q 5 4
♡ A 10 9 6 3 2
◇ A K 3
♣ —

SOUTH
♠ A 10 7
♡ K 8 7 5
◇ 10 2
♣ J 10 9 5

THE AUCTION

NORTH	EAST	SOUTH	WEST
1 ♡	Pass	2 ♡	Pass
3 ♣	Pass	3 ♠	Pass
5 NT	Pass	6 ♡	Pass
Pass	Pass		

THE RESULT

The declarer raked in all the tricks.

THE ARGUMENT

South, something of a perfectionist, was rather upset at not getting to seven hearts, and upbraided his partner in rather intemperate terms. He thought that, as North held six trumps, he should have gambled on South for the king or the queen-jack, in the latter case relying on a finesse for the grand slam.

North contended he had tried to get there by using the Grand Slam Force. Since South might have raised him to two hearts with four low trumps or with three to the queen, South should have been the one to go on.

GOREN SETTLES THE ARGUMENT

You play in a tough game. In most games, getting to six hearts would have earned plaudits.

No one is very much to blame. It is not easy to reach a grand slam when you start with a bid of one in a suit and partner makes the relatively weak response of a single raise. However, a refinement of your methods in responding to the Grand Slam Force would have gotten you there.

There is a method whereby you can show specific holdings in response to the Grand Slam Force.

Over five notrump, a bid of six clubs denies holding any of the three top honors; a bid of six diamonds shows the queen of trump; a bid of six hearts shows the king of trump; a bid of six spades shows the ace of trump.

If the partnership's agreed trump suit is diamonds, a bid of six hearts over five notrump can commit the partnership to a grand slam contract. So the Grand Slam Force, used this way, must be exercised with extreme caution.

Also see: Arguments 121, 123.

ARGUMENT 123

How can you check on trump quality?

THE HAND

```
            NORTH
            ♠ 10 9 6 5
            ♡ A 8
            ◇ K Q 5 4 2
            ♣ K 2

            SOUTH
            ♠ A Q 8 7 4 3
            ♡ K Q 9 7
            ◇ A
            ♣ A 3
```

THE AUCTION

SOUTH	WEST	NORTH	EAST
1 ♠	Pass	3 ♠	Pass
4 NT	Pass	5 ◇	Pass
5 NT	Pass	6 ♡	Pass
7 ♠	Pass	Pass	Pass

THE RESULT

The contract depended on losing no trump tricks.
The spade finesse failed, and so did the grand slam.

THE ARGUMENT

North accused South of wanton waste of a vulnerable small slam in an overambitious venture. Since South could not be sure that the king of spades was not missing, North continued his diatribe, he should have been content to bid a small slam.

South said he was sure that one of North's two kings

had to be in spades—after all, North had jump-raised the spade suit. Why hadn't he simply bid two diamonds, then raised spades at his next turn?

GOREN SETTLES THE ARGUMENT

I am sure that, on calm reflection, South will absolve North of any guilt. He is a good enough bridge player to know that the delayed game raise (first bidding a new suit, then jumping to game in partner's suit) is usually made when holding only three trumps. North's choice of a spade jump raise was impeccable.

The bidding went off the track because the Blackwood Convention didn't provide the information that South was searching for. What he needed was a form of the Grand Slam Force.

The bid of five notrump is not available for a Grand Slam Force when that bid has been preceded by four notrump—it is then a request for kings. However, on the hand in dispute South is not really interested in how many kings North holds, unless perchance he has all three he is missing. South is interested specifically in whether North has the king of spades.

If North has that card, the grand slam is an odds-on chance, for North's other values should take care of the club loser. Without the king of spades, the grand slam depends at very least on a trump finesse, and therefore the bid is no bargain.

There is a bid available that might clarify the situation for South.

A bid of a new suit at the six-level can have no natural meaning. Therefore, it can be assigned the function of a trump-suit asking bid, similar to the Grand Slam Force. After a Blackwood inquiry, a bid at the six-level of a new suit _lower-ranking_ than the trump suit asks responder to assess the quality of his trumps.

If responder's trumps are not any better than the least that might be expected for his bidding up to that point, the responder signs off in the agreed trump suit. If they are better than the least promised, he bids the grand slam.

Thus, with his actual holding, North would veto a grand slam try of, say, six clubs, for his trump support could not be worse. However, had his trumps been K-x-x-x, he would have been strong enough to go all out for seven.

Also see: Arguments 121, 122.

ARGUMENT 124

Is there a "correct" cue-bid?

THE HAND

```
                    NORTH
                    ♠ K J 8 3
                    ♡ A 10 8 5
                    ◇ J 7
                    ♣ K J 7

                    SOUTH
                    ♠ A Q 10 9 5 2
                    ♡ K Q J
                    ◇ 9 5
                    ♣ A Q
```

THE AUCTION

SOUTH	WEST	NORTH	EAST
1 ♠	Pass	3 ♠	Pass
4 NT	Pass	5 ◇	Pass
6 ♠	Pass	Pass	Pass

THE RESULT

The defenders cashed two high diamonds.
Down one.

THE ARGUMENT

Incensed at losing a game, North called South a bridge idiot for bidding Blackwood with two quick losers in diamonds.

South wanted to know how he could go on to slam if he couldn't check on aces.

North agreed that it was vital to check on controls,

337

but that cue-bids should have been the method employed.

GOREN SETTLES THE ARGUMENT

Let us first of all define a cue-bid.

A cue-bid is a forcing bid in a suit in which the bidder obviously does not want to play.

When employed at a high level after a trump suit has specifically or implicitly been agreed upon, the cue-bid shows control of the suit that has been bid.

There are two types of controls: (1) First-round, either the ace or a void; (2) Second-round, either the king or a singleton.

Here are some general principles of cue-bidding that should be observed.

First-round controls are shown before second-round controls.

Suits are cue-bid "up the line," thus showing the lowest (cheapest) control first.

If either player bypasses a suit, it denies first-round control of that suit.

Let us apply these principles to the hand in question. A possible auction could have been:

SOUTH	NORTH
1 ♠	3 ♠
4 ♣	4 ♡
4 ♠	5 ♣
5 ♡	5 ♠
Pass	

In a strong auction, once the trump suit has been agreed on, a bid in any new suit is a cue-bid. The four-club and four-heart bids each show first-round control of the bid suit. The five-level bids show second-round control of those suits, for first-round controls had already been shown. The auction makes it abundantly clear that both first- and second-round diamond controls are missing, and that five spades is the limit of the hand.

Now, let's change the North hand to:

> ♠ K J x x
> ♡ A 10 x x
> ◇ K Q
> ♣ x x x

This time, the auction might be:

SOUTH	NORTH
1 ♠	3 ♠
4 ♣	4 ♡
4 ♠	5 ◇
6 ♠	Pass

Note that North's five-diamond cue-bid cannot be other than second-round control. With first-round diamond control, he would have shown it over four clubs in preference to showing first-round control of hearts— in accordance with the principle of bidding the cheapest control first.

Also see: Arguments 114, 125.

ARGUMENT 125

Does the opponents' intervention change cue-bidding practices?

THE HAND

```
                NORTH
                ♠ A Q 10 7 6 2
                ♡ A 7 2
                ♢ A 6 4
                ♣ K
   WEST                          EAST
   ♠ 5 4                         ♠ 9
   ♡ 10 8 6 5 4 3                ♡ K Q J
   ♢ Q 10                        ♢ J 8 7 5
   ♣ Q 7 4                       ♣ J 9 8 6 3
                SOUTH
                ♠ K J 8 3
                ♡ 9
                ♢ K 9 3 2
                ♣ A 10 5 2
```

THE AUCTION

NORTH	EAST	SOUTH	WEST
1 ♠	Pass	3 ♠	Pass
4 ♢	Pass	5 ♣	Pass
5 ♡	Dbl	6 ♠	Pass
Pass	Pass		

THE RESULT

The defense was immaterial.
The declarer made all thirteen tricks.

THE ARGUMENT

North blamed South completely for missing the grand slam, claiming that South's leap to six spades was premature. Any other bid would have been better.

South insisted that North's judgment was as poor as his logic. If South could jump to a small slam in the face of East's announcement of heart strength, obviously he, South, had to be short in the heart suit. North should have gone on to seven spades.

North countered that he was not sure whether South was shorter in hearts or sense.

GOREN SETTLES THE ARGUMENT

A butt-in by the opponents can often provide the bidders with an opportunity they might not otherwise obtain.

East's double of the heart cue-bid now permitted South two extra opportunities to convey information without increasing the level of the bidding: The two calls were "Pass" and "Redouble."

A pass after a cue-bid has been doubled denies any control in the doubled suit. The pass indicates at least two losers in the suit.

A redouble of a doubled cue-bid shows second-round control of the suit, generally in the form of a singleton.

A redouble here would have allowed North to contract for seven spades with a degree of certainty. Since South had no values in hearts, he was a strong favorite to hold the king of spades for his eager cooperation in the search for slam. The ace of clubs would provide a haven for a losing diamond and two hearts could be ruffed in dummy.

East's double of the heart cue-bid to show strength in hearts was an exercise in futility, for it served no lead-directing purpose. East had forgotten that he, himself, would be on lead against a spade slam.

A third opportunity was conveyed by East's double.

A raise of the cue-bid announces the ace or a void in the cued suit.

Also see: Arguments 114, 124.

CHAPTER 17

Doubles

ARGUMENT 126

When should you raise your partner rather than double?

THE HAND

                    NORTH
                    ♠ A 7 6 2
                    ♡ A J 10 5 4
                    ◇ K J 5
                    ♣ 6

    WEST   EAST
    ♠ Q J 10 3   ♠ K 8 5
    ♡ 7 6 3 2   ♡ 9
    ◇ Q 4 2   ◇ A 8 7
    ♣ 9 4   ♣ K Q 10 8 3 2

                    SOUTH
                    ♠ 9 4
                    ♡ K Q 8
                    ◇ 10 9 6 3
                    ♣ A J 7 5

THE AUCTION

NORTH	EAST	SOUTH	WEST
1 ♡	2 ♣	Dbl	Pass
Pass	Pass		

THE RESULT

The defense was accurate. The defenders scored a

spade ruff in addition to the ace of spades. Also, the ace of hearts, and two tricks in each minor suit.

The declarer was down two.

However, the compensation was inadequate, for four hearts could have been made with a successful finesse against the queen of diamonds.

THE ARGUMENT

North blamed the poor result on South's double of two clubs. He maintained that the proper action was to bid two notrump, which he would not have left in.

South felt that his double was strictly called for. With only 10 high-card points, a game seemed unlikely. It was obvious that his side had the majority of the points. South maintained that, if North didn't like the double, he could have taken it out.

GOREN SETTLES THE ARGUMENT

A double of two of a minor suit is usually the safest type of penalty double, provided you don't think your side has a game available. Even if the opponents should happen to make the contract, you haven't doubled them into game.

However, though a double of a low-level minor suit contract can be made fairly freely, there are certain conditions that must be met before you try to punish the opponents.

A key feature of a double of two of a minor is shortness in your partner's suit. Hands where your side has a fit are better suited to offense than defense.

Despite the fact that South's club holding was attractive, his hand was unsuited to a low-level penalty double because too much of his strength was concentrated in his partner's suit. He should have contented himself with a normal raise to two hearts. That would have allowed North to revalue his hand, and would probably have led to the heart game.

But suppose we switch the spade and heart suits in South's hand, making his holding:

♠ K Q x
♡ x x
♢ x x x x
♣ A J x x

The point count remains exactly the same, but now there is no fit. A game is most unlikely, and the penalty could be fairly substantial. By all means, with such a hand, double for penalties, and expect a reasonable return.

ARGUMENT 127

Can a subsequent double by the overcaller be for takeout?

THE HAND

            NORTH
            ♠ Q 9 5 2
            ♡ Q 8 4
            ◇ 9 7 4 2
            ♣ K 3

            SOUTH
            ♠ 7 4 3
            ♡ A K J 9 5
            ◇ 6
            ♣ A Q 5 4

THE AUCTION

EAST	SOUTH	WEST	NORTH
1 ◇	Dbl	3 ◇	3 ♠
Pass	Pass	Pass	

THE RESULT

The carnage was relatively mild. East led the ace of diamonds and shifted to a trump. The defenders scored four trumps and two diamonds.

The hand was down three.

THE ARGUMENT

South averred that North bid rather more than his values when he ventured to the three-level with just a king, and two queens, and only a four-card suit into the bargain.

346

North claimed that he was, in effect, simply supporting one of South's suits. Of course, he couldn't really characterize 7-4-3 as a suit. In fact, that's where the trouble started!

GOREN SETTLES THE ARGUMENT

Hands with one very strong major and relative weakness in the other suits are better suited to an overcall than a takeout double. Such hands, if circumstances permit, can best be described by a takeout double on the second round of bidding.

Since the hand should play well if the overcaller can find a 5-3 fit in his strong suit, it is best tactics to declare that suit immediately, rather than ask your partner to show a suit. There is a distinct danger that you might end up playing in a weak 4-3 suit rather than in a strong 5-3 fit.

Let us see what would have happened had South simply overcalled one heart. West would compete with two diamonds, and that would get passed round to South. Now, South can reopen with a double, and thus describe his hand adequately. North can compete to the three-level in hearts.

Let us change the South hand somewhat, so that we have either of these two holdings:

[A]	[B]
♠ A J x x	♠ A J x
♡ A K Q x x	♡ A K Q x x
◇ x	◇ x
♣ x x x	♣ x x x x

With either of these hands, South should make a takeout double of a one-diamond opening bid. On the first hand, to overcall in hearts might mean missing a 4-4 spade fit. On the second, South has three *good* spades and so need not unduly fear a 4-3 fit.

Where the opening bid is in a major suit, other considerations come to bear. Consider these two hands:

	[A]		[B]
♠	x x	♠	x x
♡	A Q x x	♡	A Q x x
◇	K Q 10 x x x	◇	x
♣	x	♣	K Q 10 x x x

Assume that your right-hand opponent opens the bidding with one spade. Should you double or bid your long suit? Strange as it may seem, there are two different answers to this question. With *Hand A*, you should not give up too soon on a possible heart fit: Make a takeout double. On *Hand B*, a takeout double is too risky: Overcall with two clubs.

Can you see the difference in the two hands? In *Hand A*, you hold the two higher-ranking of the missing suits. No great harm can ensue if your partner responds two clubs to your double. You can correct to two diamonds.

In *Hand B*, however, you are in trouble if your partner responds two diamonds. You are forced to the three-level on a minimum holding that is imperilled by a possible misfit.

TIP: Be wary of making a takeout double on a hand that has no tolerance for the middle-ranked unbid suit.

ARGUMENT 128

Is a repeated double still for takeout?

THE HAND

```
                    NORTH
                    ♠ A K Q 7
                    ♡ 6
                    ♢ K J 10 5
                    ♣ K Q 8 4
WEST                                    EAST
♠ J 2                                   ♠ 10 9 6 5
♡ A K 10 8 4                            ♡ Q 7 3
♢ A 9 7 4                               ♢ 6 2
♣ J 5                                   ♣ A 10 9 7
                    SOUTH
                    ♠ 8 4 3
                    ♡ J 9 5 2
                    ♢ Q 8 3
                    ♣ 6 3 2
```

THE AUCTION

WEST	NORTH	EAST	SOUTH
1 ♡	Dbl	2 ♡	Pass
Pass	Dbl	Pass	Pass
Pass			

THE RESULT

West made eight tricks without too much difficulty.

THE ARGUMENT

South came in for considerable criticism—and that's putting it mildly—because of his pass of two hearts doubled. North insisted that his second double was still for takeout—that South could pass only if he wanted

349

to convert the double to one for penalties. To do that, South would have to hold good trumps.

South insisted that he had announced a bust by passing when two hearts was bid. He just had nothing to show and North should have realized that his partner would interpret a second double as a penalty double.

GOREN SETTLES THE ARGUMENT

A responder's bid over a takeout double removes the obligation for the doubler's partner. However, this waiver does not carry over to subsequent rounds of the auction.

If no suit has been declared by the doubler, a second double is still a takeout double, unless the bidding has passed the level of three spades.

North's first double announced shortness in hearts, an ability to support the unbid suits, and at least an opening bid. The second double reinforced this, saying that North held much better than a minimum opening bid.

Once a player has made a takeout double, all subsequent doubles of that suit by the original doubler remain for takeout and request his partner to respond. This obligation on the doubler's partner remains until such time as that partner has bid a suit or notrump, or has doubled the opponents for penalties, or until the doubler has removed the obligation by bidding a suit of his own.

On the hand submitted, South's hearts were not strong enough to convert his partner's double to one for penalties. Therefore, he was obliged to bid, no matter how distasteful this might have seemed.

A bid of two spades would not have come to any serious harm. South can scramble up six or seven tricks, depending on how the play goes. It is unlikely that either opponent would be able to double two spades for penalties, so the declarer would escape relatively lightly. But even a set at two spades doubled would be preferable to allowing the opponents to score a game in two hearts doubled.

The sequence that occurred above differs from the following:

WEST	NORTH	EAST	SOUTH
1 ♡	Pass	1 NT	Pass
2 ♡	Dbl		

In this sequence, North's double is for penalties. Had North wanted to hear from his partner, he could have doubled the one heart bid for takeout. Instead, after East had limited his hand, North doubled West's rebid of his suit. Clearly, North holds a bunch of hearts and a good hand, and expects to defeat two hearts on his own.

ARGUMENT 129

How strong a hand is needed for a reopening double?

THE HAND

```
                    NORTH
                    ♠ Q 7 6 5 2
                    ♡ A 7
                    ◇ J 9
                    ♣ K 7 6 2
WEST                                    EAST
♠ K 8                                   ♠ 10 9 3
♡ J 4 2                                 ♡ Q 10 8 3
◇ A 10 3                                ◇ Q 6 5 4
♣ A Q J 9 4                             ♣ 10 5
                    SOUTH
                    ♠ A J 4
                    ♡ K 9 6 5
                    ◇ K 8 7 2
                    ♣ 8 3
```

THE AUCTION

WEST	NORTH	EAST	SOUTH
1 ♣	Pass	Pass	Pass

THE RESULT

North led the ace of hearts, followed by the seven. South won his king and gave his partner a heart ruff. A spade was led to the ace and a fourth heart was played. The declarer ruffed with the queen and North overruffed. A spade was led to the declarer's king, and the dummy was entered with the ten of clubs. The queen of diamonds was covered by South's king and won by the declarer's ace. When trumps were drawn, the declarer led a low diamond, fetching the jack and establishing his ten.

The declarer made his contract.

North-South could have made a spade partial.

THE ARGUMENT

South charged North with dereliction of duty for not overcalling one spade when he had the chance.

North counter-charged that, after East's pass, South should have reopened the auction with a double.

GOREN SETTLES THE ARGUMENT

South was asking himself the wrong question. It is not a case of: "The opponents don't stand to gain much in one club, so why fight?" Rather, South should have asked himself: "Is there some reason why the opponents have gotten no higher than one club? Should I sell out so cheaply, and let them have an uncontested part score?"

From the auction, it was obvious that East was pitifully weak—most players strain to keep a one-club bid open for at least one round.

Though South is not over-endowed with high cards, since West did not start out with a forcing two-bid, it should have been clear to South that North must have a fair hand—quite likely just a shade short of an overcall or a takeout double.

In the passout seat, South is entitled to contest the auction with slightly fewer points than he might otherwise. Since he does not have a suit of his own to bid, he should request his partner to show his suit with a takeout double.

In the passout position, the requirements for a takeout double can be shaded to about 11 points.

South must bear in mind that North will allow for the

fact that the double may be sub-standard, and will bid accordingly. Thus, if South does hold 15 points, he should bid once again over his partner's response.

Also see: Arguments 102, 130.

ARGUMENT 130

How strong must your hand be to reopen with a double when an opponent's one notrump opening is passed to you?

THE HAND

```
                    NORTH
                    ♠ 109752
                    ♥ J6
                    ◇ K74
                    ♣ AQ3

      WEST                          EAST
      ♠ KQ8                         ♠ J64
      ♥ Q954                        ♥ 1073
      ◇ AJ3                         ◇ 852
      ♣ KJ4                         ♣ 10985

                    SOUTH
                    ♠ A3
                    ♥ AK82
                    ◇ Q1096
                    ♣ 762
```

THE AUCTION

WEST	NORTH	EAST	SOUTH
1 NT	Pass	Pass	Pass

THE RESULT

North led a low spade to the ace, and the declarer unblocked by playing his queen. The spade return was taken by the dummy's jack and the ten of clubs was run to North's queen. A spade return forced out the declarer's remaining stopper. The king of clubs was allowed to win, but the declarer's only other trick was the ace of diamonds.

Down three.

THE ARGUMENT

Since East-West were vulnerable, North-South missed an extra 500 points by failing to double. North accused his partner of napping at the helm.

South countered by asserting that anyone knew that to double an opposing notrump, you needed the equivalent of a notrump opening yourself; it was obvious that his hand was almost a trick short of such strength.

GOREN SETTLES THE ARGUMENT

While it is true that in the direct seat, a double of a notrump opening bid shows a hand of 16-18 points, in the balancing seat, the emphasis of the bid shifts: In the passout position, it is no longer the prime intention to punish the opponents. The objective now is to get your side into the auction on a hand where you have no clear-cut action.

Accordingly, the reopening double in the passout seat can be made on a hand that is about a trick weaker than is required for a double in the direct position, or on about 12 to 15 points.

If your partner has the balance of the power, as was the case in the hand submitted, he can convert to penalties by passing. However, if the balance of power is more or less evenly divided, he should take out in his best suit.

What, then, do you do with a hand of 16-18 points in the balancing seat? Experience has shown that the wisest course is simply to pass, and take your shot at defeating the contract undoubled. You and the opener hold a combined count of somewhere between 32 to 36 points, which does not leave much for the two other players at the table. When you double in the direct seat, your cards are placed to best advantage—over the strong hand. In the balancing seat, you are under the gun, and so your hand decreases in value.

Should your partner turn out to be broke, and your right-hand opponent comes up with all the rest of the points, you are putting yourself in a position you are unlikely to relish.

In the hand in dispute, had South elected to reopen with a double, North would have been happy to pass and collect adequate reward.

Also see: Argument 129.

ARGUMENT 131

Should a passed hand reopen the bidding after an opponent opens one notrump?

THE HAND

```
                    NORTH
                    ♠ A 5 4
                    ♡ Q 9 3
                    ◇ A Q 7
                    ♣ K 6 4 3
WEST                                    EAST
♠ K 8 3                                 ♠ 10
♡ A J 10 2                              ♡ 7 6 4
◇ K J 6                                 ◇ 10 8 5 2
♣ A J 8                                 ♣ Q 10 9 7 2
                    SOUTH
                    ♠ Q J 9 7 6 2
                    ♡ K 8 5
                    ◇ 9 4 3
                    ♣ 5
```

THE AUCTION

EAST	SOUTH	WEST	NORTH
Pass	Pass	1 NT	Pass
Pass	Pass		

THE RESULT

North led a low club, won by dummy's nine. A heart to the ten lost to North's queen, and the defender made a fatal error when he led the ace and another spade.

The declarer made exactly seven tricks.

As the cards lie, North-South can make four spades.

THE ARGUMENT

North charged South with deserting the field in the face of the enemy.

"With my 6 points?" demanded South. "If *anyone* must take action, it is you. You hold close to a no-trump opening bid, and you accuse *me* of cowardice?"

GOREN SETTLES THE ARGUMENT

Whether or not South had previously passed has no bearing on this situation. The same reasoning would apply if West had opened the bidding in first seat with one notrump, and that had been passed around to South.

South's weakness is not the point of issue. The less he has, the more he can expect his partner to hold, and the better he can expect the hand to play since the majority of missing high cards will be behind the no-trump bidder. Therefore, it is up to South to see that the opponents do not steal the hand.

Let us analyze the logic of the situation. West has shown a hand of 16-18 points, and East could not act. Ergo, he has fewer than 8 points. If we give East-West a combined holding of 22 or 23 points, that leaves 17 or 18 for North-South. Since South has only 6 of them, he can expect his partner to have a fair hand and to be ideally placed behind the strong hand.

A passed hand should reopen the bidding any time he holds a respectable six-card suit and a smattering of points.

The reopener need not fear precipitate action by his partner, who is presumed to be aware of the mathematics of the situation.

ARGUMENT 132

When should you overcall rather than double?

THE HAND

```
                    NORTH
                    ♠ A J 7 6 3
                    ♡ 8 2
                    ◇ 9 3
                    ♣ K J 7 2

WEST                                    EAST
♠ Q 8                                   ♠ K 10 4 2
♡ J 9 5 3                               ♡ Q 6
◇ Q J 8 6 2                             ◇ A K 10 7 5
♣ 10 6                                  ♣ 9 3

                    SOUTH
                    ♠ 9 5
                    ♡ A K 10 7 4
                    ◇ 4
                    ♣ A Q 8 5 4
```

THE AUCTION

EAST	SOUTH	WEST	NORTH
1 ◇	Dbl	2 ◇	3 ♠
Pass	4 ♡	Pass	4 ♠
Pass	Pass	Pass	

THE RESULT

The defense was impeccable.
North ended up down two.
His side could have made five clubs.

THE ARGUMENT

North treated his partner with deep contempt from the moment dummy came down. "Your takeout double promised spades," he thundered.

"Your fault entirely," countered South. "You had two suits but persisted in bidding only one. Why didn't you bid clubs the second time round? You must admit that my hand is too strong for an overcall!"

Was it?

GOREN SETTLES THE ARGUMENT

First, let us once and for all bury a misconception. An overcall is not necessarily an admission of weakness, nor does an overcall announce a hand of limited strength. Many hands that are quite good are not suited to a takeout double. Such hands can range in strength up to 16 points.

Let us look at the requirements of a takeout double.

A takeout double shows a hand about the equivalent of an opening bid—a strength of 13 points. The doubler promises support for all the unbid suits, or a self-sufficient suit of his own.

Ideally, the takeout doubler should have at least four cards in each unbid suit, but one cannot always come up with perfection.

In cases where the doubler does not have an extremely good hand or a very strong suit, he should hold at least three cards in each unbid suit. The corollary to this is: Do not double for takeout if one of your suits is a doubleton.

Experience shows that two-suited hands are generally difficult to bid if a takeout double is employed. They are generally easier to handle through an overcall. One must try to bid both suits.

Notice how effective this procedure would have been

on the hand in question. Even if North did not bid after West raised to two diamonds over South's one-heart overcall, South would have been able to reopen the bidding with a call of three clubs, showing strong distribution values. A final contract of five clubs would now become fairly simple to reach.

ARGUMENT 133

What are the requirements for a low-level penalty double?

THE HAND

```
                    NORTH
                    ♠ 6 3
                    ♡ A K 9 5 4
                    ◇ K 7 3
                    ♣ A J 6
    WEST                            EAST
    ♠ 5                             ♠ A Q 10 8 7 4
    ♡ Q 10 6 2                      ♡ J 8
    ◇ Q 10 5                        ◇ 8 6 4
    ♣ Q 10 9 8 2                    ♣ K 7
                    SOUTH
                    ♠ K J 9 2
                    ♡ 7 3
                    ◇ A J 9 2
                    ♣ 5 4 3
```

THE AUCTION   [*Both sides are vulnerable*]

NORTH	EAST	SOUTH	WEST
1 ♡	1 ♠	1 NT	Pass
2 NT	Pass	3 NT	Pass
Pass	Pass		

THE RESULT

West led the ten of clubs. In the course of play, the declarer lost a trick to the queen of diamonds.

He ended up down two.

THE ARGUMENT

South regarded the result as merely unlucky.

North was violently incensed by his partner's final bid of three notrump. He argued that, holding only 9 points in high cards, South had told all of his story with his original bid of one notrump. South simply had no further values with which to go to game.

GOREN SETTLES THE ARGUMENT

I can't find fault with South's final raise to three notrump. The king-jack of spades behind the overcaller must be worth more than 4 points. Besides, a game that depends on guessing a queen is not bad.

However, I do not agree with the whole auction. North-South lost a bushel of points on the deal, for East wound up with a small profit instead of suffering, as he should have, a major loss. South's correct action at his first turn was a penalty double of the one-spade overcall.

The amount of money lost annually by failure to double low-level contracts must be unbelievable.

How can you decide when to double for penalties? Here is a simple guideline.

After your partner has shown strength either by doubling for takeout or by opening the bidding, if your right-hand opponent makes the bid that *you* wanted to make, double for penalties.

Note that the operative word in the previous statement is *wanted*. Had East passed, South would gladly have made a response of one spade.

However, let us change South's holding to:

♠ K J 9 2
♡ x x
♢ Q x x
♣ x x x x

Now if North opens the bidding with one heart, and East passes, South owes North the courtesy of keeping the bidding open with a one-spade response. However, he does so with no particular joy in his heart, for any rebid by North could work the bidding to too high a level. Therefore, had East overcalled one spade, South should pass with pleasure. He did not *want* to bid one spade: he would have been *forced* to. He can therefore leave all subsequent action to his partner.

Note for those who play Negative Doubles (in which a double of one spade would show strength in the unbid suits): South would pass over one spade. North would be expected to reopen with a double, which South would then pass for penalties.

ARGUMENT 134

*Is holding the balance of power a good
enough reason to double a high-level
minor suit contract?*

THE HAND

NORTH
- ♠ A Q J 7 6
- ♡ K 10 6 2
- ◇ 7
- ♣ K 9 8

WEST
- ♠ 3
- ♡ 7
- ◇ K Q J 9 8 3 2
- ♣ A Q 6 3

EAST
- ♠ 10 9 8 4
- ♡ A 8 5 4 3
- ◇ 10
- ♣ J 7 5

SOUTH
- ♠ K 5 2
- ♡ Q J 9
- ◇ A 6 5 4
- ♣ 10 4 2

THE AUCTION [*Both sides are vulnerable*]

NORTH	EAST	SOUTH	WEST
1 ♠	Pass	2 ♠	3 ◇
3 ♠	Pass	Pass	4 ◇
Pass	Pass	Dbl	Pass
Pass	Pass		

THE RESULT

North led the ace of spades and continued the suit.
The declarer ruffed, and then led the king of trumps.
South won the ace, and forced the declarer to trump
another spade. The declarer ruffed again, and then

drew the outstanding trumps. He conceded a trick to
the king of clubs.

He made four diamonds, doubled.

THE ARGUMENT

North remarked that not even a certificate from a
reputable clinic would convince him of his partner's
sanity. What North objected to most strongly was the
implicit contempt of the opponents conveyed by
South's double.

South parried that his side, by the bidding, guaranteed to hold at least 23 points. With his ace-fourth in
the trump suit, the double was clear-cut. There was no
authority in the world who would hold him liable.

GOREN SETTLES THE ARGUMENT

Well, South has just found one person who will disagree with him—and in the strongest terms.

**Distribution can offset point count. When an
opponent who is vulnerable bids up to the four-
level in the face of oppositional bidding, he may
have a freak hand. He might come close to making
his contract, even if his partner brings him no help.
To double soundly in this situation requires that
the doubler hold some sort of surprise for the
declarer. The doubler should hold a heavy, un-
expected concentration of unimpeachable tricks in
the trump suit.**

From a mathematical point of view, South's double
was foolhardy. With a fit for his partner's suit, he
should realize that a substantial part of the partnership's assets were likely to be wasted in defense. Assume for the moment that South does succeed in
defeating West's contract by one trick. He will have
gained an extra 100 points for his courage. But should
West make his contract, South has doubled his opponents into rubber—a game which will cost 630 points

—since the opponents will score 710 points, instead of 80. Thus South is betting almost 13 to 2 that he can defeat the contract. If he considers those good odds, and he is sufficiently rich, I would like to play against him for a living.

Low-level doubles can provide a rich reward. However, there must be a margin of safety. It is relatively cheap to double a contract of one of a major or two of a minor, for even if the declarer makes his contract, you are unlikely to have presented him with more than 100 additional points, since you have not doubled him into game. If you should happen to beat him two or three tricks, you pick up a handsome penalty. In such a situation, the odds are greatly in your favor.

South should have realized that his partner was marked with diamond shortness by the auction; the hands were likely to fit well. Thus, South would have done better to have bid four spades, both because the contract might be makable, and because the opponents would be likely to make a part score of 80. Down one would be a cheap price to pay to stop the part score.

A final word of caution on doubles:

There is no such thing as a "free" double. Whether the contract is made or is defeated, a "free" double is going to cost points. It is only a question of how many.

Also see: Argument 142.

CHAPTER 18

Responding to Doubles

ARGUMENT 135

In responding to a takeout double, should you prefer a major?

THE HAND

```
                NORTH
                ♠ A J 8 5
                ♡ K Q 7 2
                ♢ 9 5 2
                ♣ A J

                SOUTH
                ♠ Q 10 9 2
                ♡ 8 3
                ♢ 7 6
                ♣ K 9 8 5 4
```

THE AUCTION

WEST	NORTH	EAST	SOUTH
1 ♢	Dbl	Pass	2 ♣
Pass	Pass	Pass	

THE RESULT

South had little difficulty fulfilling his contract. What upset North was that, with a successful spade finesse, ten tricks could have been made in spades.

THE ARGUMENT

South charged North with making a takeout double with an unsuitable hand. How was South to know his partner held only a doubleton club? What if South had been forced to respond with four low clubs?

North countered that a takeout double generally probes for a fit in a major. Why hadn't South shown his spades?

GOREN SETTLES THE ARGUMENT

North is right.

If your response can be made at the level of one, respond to a double with a four-card major rather than with a five-card minor, provided that your major suit is headed by a face card.

There are several reasons for this. If game is likely with your weak responding hand, the odds are that it is in the major rather than in the minor. And even if the hand is to be played in a partial, chances are that your partner has the major suits covered, and you are guaranteed at least a good 4-3, if not a 4-4, fit.

However, on some hands, the safety factor may dictate that you bid your long minor. Consider this hand in response to your partner's takeout double of one club:

♠ J x x x
♡ x x
◇ J x x x x
♣ x x

Your hand is so weak that you do not want to do anything that might excite your partner in the slightest. Here your best course is to slow your partner down with a response of one diamond.

Problems may arise when you have a responding

hand good enough to make two forward-going bids. Consider this example:

♠ A 9 8 3
♡ x x
♢ x x
♣ K 10 x x x

Your partner doubles one diamond. The ideal way to show this hand is first to bid clubs and then spades. This would show a hand of about 9 points with longer clubs than spades.

There is one drawback. Your first response of two clubs might discourage your partner, for he could think that you do not have a major suit. A bid of one spade is more likely to elicit a second sign of life from him, thus giving you a chance to show your clubs.

ARGUMENT 136

When do you respond to a takeout double with a jump bid?

THE HAND

```
              NORTH
              ♠ K Q 8 3
              ♡ A 9 7 6
              ◇ 7 2
              ♣ K 7 4


              SOUTH
              ♠ A 10 5
              ♡ Q J 10
              ◇ 8
              ♣ A Q J 9 3 2
```

THE AUCTION

WEST	NORTH	EAST	SOUTH
1 ◇	Dbl	Pass	3 ♣
Pass	Pass	Pass	

THE RESULT

Needless to say, the king of hearts was in the hand of the opening bidder.

Twelve tricks came rolling home with the help of a finesse in that suit.

THE ARGUMENT

North felt it was shameful to be playing in a partial on a hand that should have presented no problem in at least getting to game. However, before he could say anything, South jumped in with: "Partner, I never expected you to pass me in a forcing bid!"

North remarked that he had heard the skip-bid; nevertheless, in standard methods, the bid was not forcing. As North held a minimum, he was within his rights—nay, obliged—to pass.

GOREN SETTLES THE ARGUMENT

South was confusing a jump response to a takeout double with a jump response to an opening bid. The latter is forcing; the former is not.

A jump response to a takeout double is a strictly limited bid. It shows a hand worth some 11-12 points. Such a bid is not forcing.

Since the doubler's partner might be forced to respond with little or no strength, the jump response assures the doubler that this is not the case. The jump response is encouraging; it assures his partner that it is safe to go further if his double is better than a minimum.

The negative inference the doubler can draw when his partner fails to make a skip response will often keep the doubler from rebidding when it is hopeless to look for game, and when it may be dangerous to bid even once more.

Assume that the doubler holds a minimum 13 points. Even if the jump bidder's suit is a major, the combined assets of his side come to a maximum of 25 points, slightly fewer than are generally required to make game. Where the jump response has been in a minor, the combined values are considerably below those needed for game; 29 points are usually required to undertake an eleven-trick contract.

The responder's hand, in the case cited, would be worth a jump response of three clubs, with no honor in the heart suit, and with a doubleton diamond, and only five clubs. Getting higher than three clubs would assume a risk with no possibility of game. With some other hand, however, North might be encouraged to bid three notrump. For example:

♠ K 8 7 6　　　♡ Q J 4 2　　　◇ A Q　　　♣ K 7 4

A jump response in a major suit does not promise more than four-card length in the trump suit. In a minor, the jump response promises a better suit or a much stronger hand.

South's correct response to his partner's takeout double was a cue-bid of the enemy suit. That is the only forcing bid available to him.

Also see: Argument 137.

ARGUMENT 137

When do you respond to a takeout double with a cue-bid?

THE HAND

```
              NORTH
              ♠ A 9 7 6
              ♡ K Q 9 4 2
              ◇ K 6
              ♣ 4 3

WEST                          EAST
♠ K 2                         ♠ 10 8 5 3
♡ J 3                         ♡ 8 6 5
◇ J 9 7 4                     ◇ 5 3
♣ A K J 9 8                   ♣ Q 10 6 5

              SOUTH
              ♠ Q J 4
              ♡ A 10 7
              ◇ A Q 10 8 2
              ♣ 7 2
```

THE AUCTION

WEST	NORTH	EAST	SOUTH
1 ♣	Dbl	Pass	5 ◇
Pass	Pass	Pass	

THE RESULT

South was unfortunate to find trumps breaking 4-2, with the long trumps behind him. What was doubly unfortunate was that four hearts is a cinch, and that five hearts can be made with careful play.

South went down one.

THE ARGUMENT

North made no secret of the fact that he thought South was both injudicious and hasty in leaping to five diamonds. He thought three diamonds described South's hand adequately.

South maintained that would not be forcing: he jumped to five diamonds because he wanted to be in game opposite a takeout double. He further insisted that North's takeout double was, at best, dubious: had he simply overcalled one heart, the correct contract would have been reached.

GOREN SETTLES THE ARGUMENT

North was absolutely wrong when he wanted South to bid only three diamonds. However, South's bid of five diamonds was considerably off course.

There is only one forcing bid in response to your partner's takeout double: a cue-bid of the opponent's suit. The bid does not guarantee either first- or second-round control of the enemy suit —it simply promises a hand of at least 13 points and creates a forcing situation.

A cue-bid of two clubs by South would have allowed North to bid first hearts and then spades, thereby showing longer hearts. Reaching four hearts would then have become routine.

Incidentally, I endorse North's takeout double. To overcall in hearts might have meant losing a possible spade fit.

Also see: Argument 136.

ARGUMENT 138

When do you respond with one notrump to your partner's takeout double?

THE HAND

```
                NORTH
                ♠ A Q J 2
                ♡ 8
                ◇ K Q J 7
                ♣ A J 10 4

  WEST                          EAST
  ♠ 6                           ♠ K 10 8 7 5
  ♡ A Q J 9 4                   ♡ 7 5 3
  ◇ A 10 6 3                    ◇ 8 2
  ♣ K Q 3                       ♣ 9 8 7

                SOUTH
                ♠ 9 4 3
                ♡ K 10 6 2
                ◇ 9 5 4
                ♣ 6 5 2
```

THE AUCTION   [*East-West are vulnerable*]

WEST	NORTH	EAST	SOUTH
1 ♡	Dbl	Pass	1 NT
Pass	3 NT	Pass	Pass
Dbl	Pass	Pass	Pass

THE RESULT

Down three.

The contract was manhandled. The defenders took
four heart tricks, and one in each other suit for a total
of 500 points.

THE ARGUMENT

South adamantly maintained that North had no right to jump to three notrump with a singleton on the opponent's suit opposite a partner who had made a weakness response.

North countered that South's bid of one notrump must rank among the worst bids ever dredged up. He suggested a pass as the right course of action.

But South was quick at mathematics. If North could add, he would realize that one heart doubled and made with two overtricks would let West chalk up 510 points, plus the advantage of a 60 part-score for the next deal.

GOREN SETTLES THE ARGUMENT

When your partner makes a takeout double, it is your duty to respond irrespective of the weakness of your hand. The only reason for passing is to convert his takeout double to profitable penalties. To do this, you must have a powerful trump suit.

On occasion, you might have to respond to the takeout double in a three-card suit. Do not worry about this. Remember, you are not really bidding a suit of your own—you are, in effect, supporting a suit that your partner has announced that he possesses.

After a takeout double, the weakest possible response is a bid of a suit at the lowest level available. Any other bid, including the cheapest notrump bid, shows values, if only distributional values. The usual meaning of a bid of one notrump in response to the takeout double is a hand of some 8-9 points and stoppers in the enemy suit.

This barred South from bidding one notrump on the hand submitted. His correct response was one spade; since he held no four-card suit other than the one bid by the opponents, he must bid his cheapest three-card suit.

Note that South would have to take the same action with this holding:

♠ x x x
♡ x x x x x
◇ x x x
♣ x x

Despite the fact that he holds five hearts, South cannot convert the double to penalties. To do that, his holding in the trump suit should be no worse than Q J 10 9 2 —a suit that can stand—and indeed requests—an opening trump lead.

With his takeout double, North has assumed full responsibility for low-level contracts. Make your correct response, and then you can blame any mishap on him.

The raise to three notrump by North has my support. Had partner held 8-9 points and a stopper in hearts, the only place to look for a game contract was in no-trump, and that bid would have made in more cases than not.

ARGUMENT 139

How do you rebid after making a takeout double?

THE HAND

```
                    NORTH
                    ♠ J 10 6 2
                    ♡ 7 3 2
                    ◇ 8 6 3
                    ♣ Q 6 5
    WEST                            EAST
    ♠ 9 5                           ♠ 7 4
    ♡ Q 10 6 4                      ♡ A J 5
    ◇ K 9 7 2                       ◇ Q 10 4
    ♣ J 8 4                         ♣ A K 10 9 2
                    SOUTH
                    ♠ A K Q 8 3
                    ♡ K 9 8
                    ◇ A J 5
                    ♣ 7 3
```

THE AUCTION

EAST	SOUTH	WEST	NORTH
1 ♣	Dbl	Pass	1 ♠
Pass	4 ♠	Dbl	Pass
Pass	Pass		

THE RESULT

The result was painful, except for East and West and their families and friends.

The declarer was rather lucky to scrape together seven tricks. Then the fur began to fly.

THE ARGUMENT

South said North should never have encouraged him with a one-spade response—he should have bid one diamond.

North maintained it would be insane to bid a three-card suit when holding a perfectly good four-card suit. South, he hissed, had no conception of card valuation.

GOREN SETTLES THE ARGUMENT

In selecting a rebid, the takeout doubler should bear in mind that he has forced his partner to bid on what might be a bust.

A doubler should never leap to any contract that he cannot reasonably expect to fulfill in his own hand.

Unless the responder to a double has taken some action showing strength, the doubler need not bid again with a hand that ranges from 13 to 15 points. He has shown this much with his initial takeout double. To take further action is to bid the same values twice.

Further action by the doubler after a minimum forced response confirms a very sound double and suggests game-going possibilities.

A raise of the response to the two-level shows at least 16 points.

A raise of the response to the three-level shows at least 19 points.

A raise of the response to the four-level shows at least 22 points.

On the hand before the bar, South has 18 points. He is, therefore, entitled to raise North to two spades and no more. And North would probably go down one trick undoubled. To bid more than that is to look at life not merely through rose-colored spectacles, but while running through red light signals.

South's contention that North should have responded with one diamond as a discouraging tactic is pure Grade A applesauce.

ARGUMENT 140

Is the double of an opening pre-empt for penalty or takeout?

THE HAND

```
                    NORTH
                    ♠ A K 8 3
                    ♡ Q J 8 5 2
                    ◇ 6
                    ♣ A J 6
   WEST                                EAST
   ♠ 7                                 ♠ J 10 6
   ♡ 10 3                              ♡ A 9 7 6
   ◇ K Q J 10 7 4 3                    ◇ A 8 2
   ♣ 9 8 3                             ♣ Q 10 4
                    SOUTH
                    ♠ Q 9 5 4 2
                    ♡ K 4
                    ◇ 9 5
                    ♣ K 7 5 2
```

THE AUCTION

WEST	NORTH	EAST	SOUTH
3 ◇	Dbl	Pass	Pass
Pass			

THE RESULT

The declarer just made his contract, chalking up an undeserved game.

North led the king of spades, followed by the ace. West ruffed and drew trumps in two rounds. The nine of clubs was run to South's king. The heart return was won by the dummy's ace, and the declarer returned to his hand with a spade ruff. The finesse for the jack

383

of clubs was repeated, and the declarer lost only one trick in each major suit and two club tricks.

North-South can make four spades with ease.

THE ARGUMENT

South wanted to know where North expected to get his setting tricks in three diamonds doubled.

North protested indignantly that, since South had not yet spoken, his double was for takeout and not for penalty.

South claimed that takeout doubles were made at the one-level or at the two-level but not at the three-level. A double of three was definitely a business double. What else? South insisted that North, with his blockbuster, should have bid his five-card suit.

"I suppose *that* would have got you to bid four spades?" was North's ice-laden query.

It was a while before the next hand could be dealt.

GOREN SETTLES THE ARGUMENT

Unless there is prior agreement, a double of a pre-emptive bid, like the double of an opening one-bid, is intended for takeout. One's partner is expected to respond in his longest suit but, with some strength in the opponent's suit, may leave the double in.

The general requirements for the double are similar to those for a takeout double at the one-level—support for the three unbid suits, or for at least two of them, provided it includes support for the highest ranking of the unbid suits.

When the bidding is at the three-level, one is required to hold greater strength to double a pre-empt than to double a normal opening bid—about a king more.

As a rough guide to whether your hand is good enough to double an opening pre-empt, mentally replace one of your kings with a low card in the same suit. If you still have enough to double an opening one-bid, then you have a sound double of the pre-empt.

Applying this rule to the hand in question, substitute a low spade for the king. Had West opened the bidding with one diamond, North would still make a takeout double. Therefore, his action was eminently correct.

It is not easy to lay down hard and fast rules for responding to a double of a pre-empt. A good rule of thumb is to presume that your partner expects to find 6-8 points in your hand; if this is all you hold, you should make a minimum response. If you have better than that, you should jump the level one round, unless a lower response puts you in game.

Thus, on the actual hand, South should have bid four spades in response to his partner's takeout double. However, change the king of hearts to a low heart, and South can do no more than bid three spades.

Let us take a look at some other North hands:

[A]	[B]	[C]
♠ A K x x	♠ A K Q x x x	♠ A K Q J x x x
♡ J x x x x	♡ K x x	♡ A x x
◇ x	◇ x	◇ x
♣ A J x	♣ x x x	♣ Q x

With *Hand A*, North is not strong enough to take any immediate action over West's pre-empt.

With *Hand B*, North should bid three spades. Though this action is fraught with some danger, he cannot allow West's bid to exclude him from the auction.

With *Hand C*, North should jump to four spades, since he does not need much from South to make game, and South might not have enough strength to raise if North simply overcalls with three spades.

ARGUMENT 141

When should you convert your partner's takeout double to a penalty double?

THE HAND

```
                    NORTH
                    ♠ 8
                    ♡ A J 8 3
                    ◇ A Q 9 2
                    ♣ K 8 5 4

WEST                                    EAST
♠ A K 6 5 4                             ♠ 3 2
♡ K 9 5                                 ♡ 10 7 6 4
◇ 8 5                                   ◇ K J 10 7
♣ A J 3                                 ♣ Q 10 2

                    SOUTH
                    ♠ Q J 10 9 7
                    ♡ Q 2
                    ◇ 6 4 3
                    ♣ 9 7 6
```

THE AUCTION

WEST	NORTH	EAST	SOUTH
1 ♠	Dbl	Pass	1 NT
Pass	Pass	Pass	

THE RESULT

Since he was not short of entries, West elected to lead the king of spades. After seeing the dummy, he shifted to a diamond. The declarer had no entry to his own hand and had to keep leading from the dummy, with the result that he could not make one notrump.

If one spade doubled had been passed, accurate defense (including the spade lead the pass demanded) would have limited West to six tricks.

THE ARGUMENT

South blamed his partner for leaving in one notrump with his unbalanced hand. He claimed North should have bid two clubs.

North retorted that he expected South to hold more for his bid. How was he to know that his partner's hand was useless at anything but a spade contract?

GOREN SETTLES THE ARGUMENT

When your best source of tricks is in the opponent's suit, convert your partner's takeout double to a penalty double by passing. Such a pass asks your partner to lead a trump.

A response of one notrump to your partner's takeout double is not a weak bid; it is a constructive bid showing as a minimum some 8 or 9 scattered points.

On the bidding, South's hand rated to produce at least three tricks, against a spade contract. As an offensive weapon, his hand was almost worthless; even if South could establish spade tricks, it was most unlikely he would ever be able to get back to his hand to enjoy them.

The danger of responding one notrump with an unsuitable hand is not that you might convert a small profit into a small loss. The menace is that you might convert a potentially huge profit into a disaster.

If North had a slightly better hand than the one he actually held, despite his singleton spade, he would have been correct to jump to three notrump, exposing his side to a crushing penalty double.

ARGUMENT 142

What do you need to double the opponents at a high level?

THE HAND

```
                    NORTH
                    ♠ J 7 6 3
                    ♡ 6 3
                    ◇ Q 5
                    ♣ J 8 7 6 3

    WEST                                EAST
    ♠ 8 2                               ♠ K Q 10
    ♡ 9 5 4                             ♡ Q J 10 8 2
    ◇ A K J 3 2                         ◇ 10 9
    ♣ K 10 2                            ♣ A Q 4

                    SOUTH
                    ♠ A 9 5 4
                    ♡ A K 7
                    ◇ 8 7 6 4
                    ♣ 9 5
```

THE AUCTION   [*Both sides are vulnerable.*]

EAST	SOUTH	WEST	NORTH
1 ♡	Pass	2 ◇	Pass
2 ♡	Pass	3 ♡	Pass
4 ♡	Dbl	Pass	Pass
Rdbl	Pass	Pass	Pass

THE RESULT

There was little to the play. South made his ace of spades and his ace-king of trumps, and the opponents wrapped up a big rubber.

THE ARGUMENT

North, with fine sarcasm, politely offered to buy South a hearing aid, adding that no one who had heard the auction would have doubled with the South hand.

South claimed to be a victim of misfortune. He held three sure tricks, and didn't need much from North to defeat the contract. Besides, since East-West were already in game, the double was a "free double."

GOREN SETTLES THE ARGUMENT

There is no such thing as a "free double." In this case, the double cost 410 points, and even at low stakes that can mount up over a period of time. South had nothing remotely resembling a double.

When the opponents bid strongly to game and your hand contains no unpleasant surprise for the declarer, don't double unless you are sure to defeat the contract in your own hand.

Moreover, it rarely pays to double if the outlook is for a set of one trick. Unless you believe you can set your opponents two tricks, don't double.

For the small amount of points to be gained in a one-trick set—50 if opponents are not vulnerable; 100, if they are—the risks far outweigh the gains. A freak holding, a not altogether culpable misplay, and the declarer collects far more than you can gain. It just isn't worth it.

Here East opened the bidding and West made a two-over-one response. On the bidding, South should realize that East could be better than minimum; therefore, North might hold a complete bust. Also, when East went on to four hearts, he did so in full realization that he didn't have the two top trumps; he realized they could turn up in the opponents' hands. Nevertheless, he felt his side had the values to play for ten tricks.

Note how this case differs from this one below:
South holds:

♠ x
♡ Q J 10 9
◇ K 10 x x
♣ A 10 x x

WEST	NORTH	EAST	SOUTH
1 ♡	Pass	2 ♡	Pass
3 ♡	Pass	4 ♡	?

This time, South's trump holding is going to come as a nasty surprise. On this auction, the declarer certainly does not expect to lose two trump tricks. In addition, East-West climbed uncertainly into four hearts, so they almost surely will have no strength to spare. North must hold some useful values, so here the double is clear-cut. South has at least three tricks in his own hand. If the cards lie badly for the declarer, the penalty could be substantial.

Also see: Argument 134.

ARGUMENT 143

Should you ever run from your partner's penalty double?

THE HAND

```
              NORTH
              ♠ 9 5
              ♡ K Q 9 2
              ◇ 7 5 2
              ♣ A J 8 3

              SOUTH
              ♠ K Q J 7 6 3
              ♡ 8 7
              ◇ A 10 8 3
              ♣ 7
```

THE AUCTION

SOUTH	WEST	NORTH	EAST
1 ♠	2 ♣	Dbl	Pass
Pass	Pass		

THE RESULT

West just made his contract.
North-South had a laydown for three spades.

THE ARGUMENT

South accused North of being trigger-happy. He felt there was no hurry to double two clubs. Had North simply passed, South would have competed once more in spades.

North, cut to the quick, maintained that his double was perfectly sound. The fault lay, he exclaimed, in

South's decision to open the bidding with a hand that was more like a weak two-bid than a one-bid.

GOREN SETTLES THE ARGUMENT

Penalty doubles by the responder are not sacrosanct. They are a strong suggestion that the overcaller might have overreached himself. At low levels, the double is largely optional with the second partner; he can leave it in, if he deems it will be productive, or override it, if he sniffs disaster ahead or greater profit possibilities ahead elsewhere. Such a double is also called a "cooperative double."

What does a "cooperative double" mean? Simply this: The doubler thinks that the contract can be defeated *with the help of his partner*. If, for any reason, the opener's hand does not measure up to what the responder has a right to expect, the opener may—indeed, he should—remove the double.

Normally, an opening bid promises two-and-a-half defensive tricks. By these standards, South's hand was bound to prove a disappointment to his partner. The hand may develop only one defensive trick, and the possible lack of entries is bound to be a defensive liability. The hand is far better suited to offense. South should have warned his partner of this fact by removing the double of two clubs and bidding two spades.

Also see: Argument 144.

ARGUMENT 144

Must the opener, with a good hand, respect his partner's penalty double?

THE HAND

```
                NORTH
                ♠ 8
                ♡ K 9 5 2
                ◇ K 9 8 3
                ♣ A J 7 4

                SOUTH
                ♠ A K J 9 4 3
                ♡ 7
                ◇ A Q J 10 2
                ♣ 5
```

THE AUCTION

SOUTH	WEST	NORTH	EAST
1 ♠	2 ♣	Dbl	Pass
Pass	Pass		

THE RESULT

North-South had little difficulty collecting 300 for the penalty double.

The trouble with this result was that six diamonds was a laydown. Playing in diamonds, the declarer could have ruffed spades with dummy's high trumps to establish his suit.

THE ARGUMENT

North felt that South should have opened with a

393

forcing two-bid despite his relatively low count. He had only four losers, North pointed out. A proper opening bid would have gotten North-South to slam in quick time.

South countered that he never fooled with the high-card values needed for a forcing two-bid—everyone knew he was a sound bidder. The error was North's decision to double rather than bid two notrump.

North retorted that a bid of two notrump with a singleton spade would have been foolhardy.

GOREN SETTLES THE ARGUMENT

A low-level business double is not an irrevocable covenant; it is rather a two-way street that permits partner to move in the opposite direction.

A partner may remove the double whenever his defensive strength is below what the doubler might expect. He should also remove the double when his offensive power is so great that the amount of the penalty might not compensate for the value of a probable game or slam.

There is nothing wrong with the auction up to the point of South's pass. Despite its great distributional strength, South's hand does not quite measure up to a demand bid. North's double of two clubs is unquestionably correct.

However, even though South has all the defensive values promised by his opening bid, he should realize that his prospects for game—or even slam—are bright. North's values cannot be limited entirely to the opponent's suit.

South could have conveyed his message not merely by his refusing to stand for the double. He should have shown the power of his hand with a jump to three diamonds.

North would then raise to four diamonds, and South could check on aces with Blackwood. When North announces one ace, South can contract for slam, for he knows he can set up his spades by ruffing them in the North hand.

Also see: Argument 143.

ARGUMENT 145

Should you rescue if your partner's overcall is doubled?

THE HAND

```
                    NORTH
                    ♠ K Q J 9 8 3
                    ♡ A 5 4
                    ◇ 9 6 3
                    ♣ 2
WEST                                    EAST
♠ 6 4                                   ♠ A 10 5 2
♡ K 10                                  ♡ Q 9 7 6 3
◇ A K J 5 4                             ◇ 10 8
♣ A Q 8 7                               ♣ J 6
                    SOUTH
                    ♠ 7
                    ♡ J 8 2
                    ◇ Q 7 2
                    ♣ K 10 9 5 4 3
```

THE AUCTION

WEST	NORTH	EAST	SOUTH
1 ◇	1 ♠	Pass	2 ♣
Pass	2 ♠	Dbl	3 ♣
Dbl	Pass	Pass	Pass

THE RESULT

In all, the defenders scored nine tricks: two diamonds and a ruff; a heart and a ruff; one spade trick; and three trumps after South overruffed the jack of clubs.

The declarer was down five.

THE ARGUMENT

North bitterly inquired if South had heard of a game called "nullos," where the object was to win as few tricks as possible. At that game, South rated to be a star.

South argued that he never left his partner in with a singleton in the trump suit. Why on earth did North have to rebid his suit, when he knew that South couldn't stand it?

North retorted that he had been taught that there was one sure way to show a bad hand: Pass! And there was no question about the quality of South's hand.

GOREN SETTLES THE ARGUMENT

Do not rescue a partner who hasn't been doubled. There is no guarantee that you will be improving the contract.

North did not invite South into the bidding with a takeout double. Quite the contrary—his overcall suggested that his hand might be useful only in spades.

There was no reason for South to start to play St. George before a dragon had appeared on the scene. If anyone had doubled North's one-spade bid, South could have then decided whether he might dare try to "improve" the contract by bidding two clubs.

Consider these two South hands. In each case, West has opened the bidding with one diamond. North has overcalled one spade, and East has doubled.

[A]	[B]
♠ x	♠ x
♡ x x x	♡ x x x
◇ x x x	◇ x x x
♣ A K 10 x x x	♣ Q J 10 9 x x

Should South rescue with either of these holdings? You grasp the fundamentals of overcalling, if you elected to pass with *Hand A,* and rescue with *Hand B.*

With *Hand A,* you are bringing your partner a pleasant surprise—two tricks. There is no reason to suppose that your club suit will play any better than your partner's spade suit and you will have to play at one level higher.

Hand B is a different matter entirely. Here, your hand will produce four tricks playing in clubs, but none at any other contract. If you can scramble a few tricks from your partner's hand, you might not be too badly off in a club rescue. If the ace and king are divided in the opponents' hands, it is even possible you can get away undoubled, so, with your otherwise hopeless hand, you should certainly run to two clubs.

ARGUMENT 146

When should you double an overcall of a strong two-bid?

THE HAND

```
                    NORTH
                    ♠ 4
                    ♡ A K 10 9 6 3
                    ◇ A K J
                    ♣ A K 5

    WEST                            EAST
    ♠ 5 3                           ♠ A K J 9 8 6
    ♡ J 8 4                         ♡ 5 2
    ◇ 10 7 6 3                      ◇ 9
    ♣ J 8 6 4                       ♣ Q 10 7 3

                    SOUTH
                    ♠ Q 10 7 2
                    ♡ Q 7
                    ◇ Q 8 5 4 2
                    ♣ 9 2
```

THE AUCTION

NORTH	EAST	SOUTH	WEST
2 ♡	2 ♠	Dbl	Pass
Pass	Pass		

THE RESULT

South was quite right in his assessment that East would be unable to make his contract.

As a matter of fact, East went down two tricks.

This was little balm to North, as six hearts was unbeatable.

THE ARGUMENT

North accused South of taking unilateral action.

South said there was no reason for North to pass the double. North's hand was so good that he, North, could make game almost alone.

North rebutted that his hand contained four or five losers, and that he had a fistful of tricks on defense. He couldn't be blamed, he claimed, for abiding by his partner's judgment.

GOREN SETTLES THE ARGUMENT

Whenever one's partner opens the bidding with a strong two-bid and the responder holds a smattering of points, the chance for a slam should always be in the responder's mind. Therefore, the responder should avoid, if possible, any action that might cause the opener to fear that the hand is a possible misfit.

It is not a simple matter to lay down guidelines for the double of an overcall after one's partner has opened with a strong two-bid. However, as a rule of thumb, *the responder should have virtually no strength other than in the suit bid by the overcaller*. The reason for this is that high cards in other suits might be key cards in the opener's quest for slam.

Here, the responder has two queens outside of the overcaller's suit, one of them in the opener's trump suit. Both queens are key cards, filling in gaps in the declarer's hand.

South's correct action is either to pass and await further developments, or to bid two notrump. In either case, the opener is likely to rebid four hearts. South can then raise to five, and North will surely bid the slam.

Here is an exception to the stated rule:

If the responder has so much strength that he

suspects that the overcall was psychic, he should double to expose the bluff.

When the overcaller runs to his real suit, the responder can then bid his hand naturally. However, to act in this manner, his strength must be such that the penalty may offer the biggest chance for profit should the overcaller decide to stand for the double.

CHAPTER 19

Proprieties

ARGUMENT 147

Must you have the book requirements for your bid?

THE HAND

                    NORTH
                    ♠ Q 9 5 4 3
                    ♡ 7
                    ◇ K 5 4
                    ♣ K 10 3 2

WEST   **EAST**
♠ A J 10 2   ♠ K 8 6
♡ 4   ♡ J 10 6 5
◇ Q J 9 6   ◇ 10 7 2
♣ A 9 7 4   ♣ Q J 8

                    SOUTH
                    ♠ 7
                    ♡ A K Q 9 8 3 2
                    ◇ A 8 3
                    ♣ 6 5

THE AUCTION

NORTH	EAST	SOUTH	WEST
Pass	Pass	3 ♡	Dbl
Pass	Pass	Pass	

THE RESULT

With the ace of clubs in the West hand, the declarer had no difficulty in fulfilling his doubled contract.

He lost one trick in each suit.

THE ARGUMENT

East and West were rather unhappy at the result. When it was revealed that South had opened a preemptive bid with 16 points including 13 in high cards, East suggested that the action was illegal.

GOREN SETTLES THE ARGUMENT

A player is not bound to abide by book recommendations for a particular bid. A player may bid what he likes, when he likes.

Naturally, this presupposes that North and South did not have any agreement that opening three-bids in third seat would be made on good hands. In that case, their opponents should have been so informed

This does not mean that I am in agreement with South's bid of three hearts. Opposite a partner who has passed, you can take certain liberties with a preemptive opening bid, but South's hand is far too strong for that. There are too many hands presenting a good play for game which one's partner would pass out after a pre-empt. Notice that in this hand South would have made four hearts, had the suit divided 3-2 instead of 4-1.

ARGUMENT 148

In rubber bridge, should you explain a bidding convention to your opponents before using it?

THE HAND

                    NORTH
                    ♠ 8
                    ♡ J 6 5 3
                    ♦ A 8 3
                    ♣ A 10 6 5 4

WEST   EAST
♠ K Q J   ♠ 10 9 7 6 3 2
♡ A 4   ♡ 8
♦ K 10 7 2   ♦ 9 5 4
♣ K J 8 2   ♣ Q 7 3

                    SOUTH
                    ♠ A 5 4
                    ♡ K Q 10 9 7 2
                    ♦ Q J 6
                    ♣ 9

THE AUCTION

WEST	NORTH	EAST	SOUTH
1 NT	Pass	2 ♡	Pass
2 ♠	Pass	Pass	Pass

THE RESULT

North led the ace of clubs and continued with the four. South ruffed and shifted to the queen of diamonds, which was ducked in dummy. South continued with a low diamond, and West's ten was captured with the ace. North gave his partner another club ruff, and the ace of trumps spelled down one.

As the cards lie, North-South can make twelve tricks at a heart contract.

THE ARGUMENT

South remarked that the auction seemed rather strange in view of East's heart singleton. East replied that he and his partner were employing transfer bids* over notrump openings, and that it should have been obvious to South from his heart holding that something was going on. The Laws of Contract Bridge entitled him (South) to ask if there was anything in the bidding he did not understand. South felt that East-West's use of a convention with which they were unfamiliar had put his side at a disadvantage. He felt it was unfair to employ exotic methods in a rubber bridge game.

GOREN SETTLES THE ARGUMENT

I can do no better than quote from the Proprieties section of the Laws of Contract Bridge:

"It is improper to use, in calling or playing, any convention the meaning of which may not be understood by the opponents. Conventional calls or plays should be explained to the opponents before any player has looked at his cards."

Personally, I am not greatly in favor of using rubber bridge conventions with which the opponents might not be familiar. I feel the least one can do is tell the opponents what you would like to play, and ask them if they have any objection to your employing those methods. If they do object, I would abide by their decision, especially in a case where you could play equally good bridge without such a gadget.

* Using transfer bids, a response of two diamonds to one notrump asks opener to bid two hearts; a response of two hearts calls for opener to bid two spades.

In rubber bridge, it is not fair to profit from your opponents' unfamiliarity with your bidding methods. They might need time to develop a defensive structure to cope with your bids. If, for any reason, they are unwilling or unable to do so, it is not very sporting to insist on having your way.

I do not for a moment doubt that North-South were injured by the fact that they did not know that East-West were employing a convention in their bidding. Had he been aware of that fact, South could have doubled two hearts to announce a heart suit. In that case North, with a fit for his partner, two aces and a singleton, might certainly have bid either three or four hearts after opener had transferred to two spades.

No penalties are provided for breaches of that portion of the rubber bridge laws which comes under the heading of proprieties. If this incident had occurred in a tournament, a tournament director might be asked to rule on awarding an adjusted score and either side could then carry the tournament director's ruling to a committee for decision on whether the ruling had been correct. Some bridge clubs have an authority in attendance to rule on such cases. But the average home game must decide for itself whether damage has been done and how restitution should be made.

Obviously, in this case, East-West were at fault in not having explained their convention. But it might be argued that South should have been suspicious enough to ask West (the partner of the player who had made the conventional bid) what he understood by it. West would be obligated to explain, whereupon South's double would be a clear indication that he had a good heart suit. The rules give South this privilege; yet not every player is aware that this is so.

East-West could claim that ignorance of the law is no excuse and that South's hand calls for a double whether East's bid is real or conventional.

South might then argue that he feared his partner might read a double as calling for a takeout.

I cite all these possibilities to show how difficult it is

to come to a clear conclusion and to reinforce my suggestion that conventions of this kind should be used only with the consent of the opponents and, of course, should be explained if consent is given.

ARGUMENT 149

Are players bound by their conventions?

THE HAND

```
              NORTH
              ♠ K 8
              ♡ A Q 3
              ◇ K Q 10 2
              ♣ K 9 8 3

  WEST                          EAST
  ♠ A 10 9 6 2                  ♠ Q 4 3
  ♡ J 8 5 4                     ♡ K 9
  ◇ A                           ◇ J 7 6
  ♣ A Q 6                       ♣ J 10 5 4 2

              SOUTH
              ♠ J 7 5
              ♡ 10 7 6 2
              ◇ 9 8 5 4 3
              ♣ 7
```

THE AUCTION

NORTH	EAST	SOUTH	WEST
1 NT	Pass	2 ♣	Pass
2 ◇	Pass	Pass	Pass

THE RESULT

Though the declarer took a losing heart finesse, he took eight tricks. His losers were one spade, two hearts, and a trick in each minor suit.

East-West could have made at least nine tricks at a spade contract.

THE ARGUMENT

North-South had announced that they were playing

forcing Stayman—that is, a two-club response promised 7-8 points and meant that the bidding could not die before either two notrump or three of a major suit had been reached.

West declared that South's tactics had been improper; he said that he, West, would have entered the auction had he realized that South was broke. Since South had employed a conventional bid, he expected to find South with certain values and to find East with a near bust.

GOREN SETTLES THE ARGUMENT

A convention is an agreement between partners as to how a certain bid should be treated—it is not a binding contract. Either partner may depart from their announced standards without penalty. Such action is not improper; it certainly is not illegal.

In some cases this could be dangerous action, for one's partner might play the conventional bidder for values that he does not hold.

On this particular hand, South made a good bid when he elected to bid Stayman over his partner's notrump opening. Obviously, his hand was useless at notrump, but would produce some tricks in the form of ruffs at any suit contract other than clubs. South intended passing any rebid by opener.

West should not have been taken in by South's tactics. Had he held 7-8 points, he would not have passed two diamonds. Thus, West could have reopened the bidding, knowing that South was broke and that East must have some points.

It might have been more difficult to combat South's ploy if the East-West hands had been transposed, or if West had held one less ace. However, even in the latter case West should double to get East to name his best suit, on the theory that the fewer points in the West hand, the more he would find in East's hand.

ARGUMENT 150

May you "read" your partner's hesitation?

THE HAND

NORTH
♠ A 9 8 5
♡ K 8 5 2
◇ K J 3
♣ 9 2

SOUTH
♠ K Q 4
♡ A Q J 7 6 3
◇ 9
♣ A K 3

THE AUCTION

SOUTH	WEST	NORTH	EAST
1 ♡	Pass	3 ♡	Pass
4 NT	Pass	5 ♣	Pass
6 ♡	Pass	Pass	Pass

THE RESULT

The ace of diamonds was the only trick for the defense.

The declarer made his contract.

THE ARGUMENT

North had hesitated for quite a while before responding with five clubs to his partner's Blackwood inquiry for aces.

East congratulated South on his brave bid. Not everyone would contract for six hearts when the auction showed that the partnership was missing two aces.

410

South murmured that North was bound to have had an ace for his jump raise in hearts even though his five-club bid specifically denied holding an ace.

When West suggested that North's hesitation might have influenced South's unusual action, South was insulted, and unpleasant words followed.

GOREN SETTLES THE ARGUMENT

It is easy to understand why North hesitated before showing no ace in response to South's Blackwood. He deemed that his initial jump raise was rather shaded, so he decided to "correct" his first overbid by lying about the number of aces he held.

It seems to me that South was influenced by this hesitation. South knew that North could count to zero in far less time than he had taken to respond, and South decided he knew why it had taken North so long to bid. Accordingly, South jumped to six—despite the fact that he was apparently missing two aces.

I would like to quote from the Proprieties.

A player should carefully avoid taking any advantage which might accrue from an impropriety committed by his side.

And from the section on "Violations of Ethical Conduct."

The following acts should be carefully avoided ... A call made with undue delay.

There are many aceless hands North could hold that would qualify for a jump raise to three hearts.
For example:

♠ x
♡ K 10 x x
◇ K Q J
♣ Q J 10 x

It would need a very powerful argument to convince

me that had North responded in tempo to Blackwood with five clubs, South would still have had the courage to bid six hearts.

I am in agreement with West's criticism.

A player whose partner has taken unduly long to bid should lean over backwards not to take any advantage of the information gleaned from the hesitation.

South might argue, for example, that perhaps North had paused because he held a void suit, not an ace. In that event, South's bid of six would have been an outright gamble that North was void in spades rather than in clubs, and it could have been a losing gamble.

Such an argument, even if borne out by North's hand, could not justify South's action. South was not entitled to build any surmise on the information conveyed by the length of time his partner took to respond.

Is there a penalty for South's action? In a tournament, there might be. In rubber bridge, one can only insist that such conduct is not proper. If the same sort of thing happens again, the sole recourse is to seek other company.

I recommend the method followed when a high-society English whist club found one member's conduct intolerable. They did not ask him to resign. Instead, they all resigned and formed a new club, which the offending player was not invited to join.

ARGUMENT 151

Can you open the bidding when your partner has hesitated?

THE HAND

NORTH
- ♠ K 9 5 3 2
- ♡ A 7
- ◇ Q J 3 2
- ♣ 5 2

SOUTH
- ♠ Q 10 7 4
- ♡ K 9 5
- ◇ K 10 7
- ♣ K 6 3

THE AUCTION

NORTH	EAST	SOUTH	WEST
Pass	Pass	1 ♠	Pass
4 ♠	Pass	Pass	Pass

THE RESULT

South lost one spade, one diamond, and one club. He made his game.

THE ARGUMENT

East took great exception to South's opening the bidding after his partner, the dealer, had hesitated perceptibly before passing. South saw nothing reprehensible about his action; he was in third seat, and it was his practice to open light in that position. South was merely doing what he always did.

West quoted the "unwritten law": that North's hesitation barred South from opening. He also said that after hesitating for so long, North should have made some bid.

GOREN SETTLES THE ARGUMENT

There seems to be considerable misunderstanding about what can or should be done by the partner of a player who has hesitated. So let's try to get the facts straight.

A hesitation by your partner does not bar you from taking any clear-cut action. However, you should lean over backwards to make sure that any action you do take after your partner has hesitated cannot be faulted, and that such action stands on its own merits.

On the hand in question, had North not hesitated South *might or might not* have decided to open light in the third seat. It is a matter of style. On the hand South held I would not have opened.

Since the action is doubtful in the first place, South should have gone out of his way to avoid a questionable bid after North had hesitated. He should have passed with a doubtful hand, *even though he might normally have opened*.

However, South is not automatically barred by his partner's hesitation. Suppose he had held:

♠ A Q x x x
♡ K x x
♢ K x x
♣ J x

Now South has a perfectly sound opening bid in any position. The fact that North hesitated before passing does not prevent South from bidding.

As to North's being "compelled" to bid after an undue hesitation, no such understanding exists. A player should try to avoid such an action, but when it occurs the only obligation falls upon his partner.

ARGUMENT 152

Is it improper to vary your bidding tempo?

THE HAND

```
                    NORTH
                    ♠ A J 10 3 2
                    ♡ 10
                    ◇ 9 5 2
                    ♣ A Q 8 7
WEST                                    EAST
♠ 9 7                                   ♠ K 8 6 4
♡ A K J 7 2                             ♡ Q 9 6
◇ K Q 6                                 ◇ J 10 8 4 3
♣ 10 9 6                                ♣ 3
                    SOUTH
                    ♠ Q 5
                    ♡ 8 5 4 3
                    ◇ A 7
                    ♣ K J 5 4 2
```

THE AUCTION

WEST	NORTH	EAST	SOUTH
1 ♡	1 ♠	2 ♡	2 ♠
3 ♡	4 ♣	Pass	Pass
Pass			

THE RESULT

The declarer lost one trick in each side suit.
He made his contract.

THE ARGUMENT

South, normally a rapid bidder, had a problem over
East's raise to two hearts, and it took him a while to
bid two spades. However, he had no problem over his
partner's four-club bid, and passed in a flash.

East and West both felt that the action at the table was rather unusual. Most players would presume that four clubs was forcing, yet South had no difficulty in passing. North, having apparently found a major suit fit, trotted out a minor suit at the four-level on a hand that was not all that good. Moreover, he didn't seem to be upset when partner passed.

East-West called the director and claimed unethical behavior.

GOREN SETTLES THE ARGUMENT

In a vacuum, North's bid of four clubs is unusual, but no one should be blamed for making an occasional bad bid. South had a problem, and so he took some time before raising his partner's spades.

However, taken in conjunction with South's known habits of machine-gun bidding, it could be argued that North took advantage of South's hesitation. The Proprieties state: *Calls should be made in a uniform tone, without special emphasis or inflection, and without undue haste or hesitation.*

We are not robots, and cannot make every bid and play at exactly the same tempo. Once in a while, one will be faced with a difficult situation that takes time to solve. There is nothing wrong with taking time, if you have to.

If you do convey to your partner that you have a problem by taking undue time before making a bid, it is his responsibility to see that his later action is not predicated on your hesitation.

On the hand given, a bid of three spades by North would not have been questioned by anyone—though the contract might have foundered with repeated forces in hearts. A bid of four clubs, though, might be open to suspicion. North should, therefore, have avoided the possibility of an unpleasant situation; he should have refrained from bidding his club suit.

ARGUMENT 153

Are you allowed to bid what you do not have?

THE HAND

```
                    NORTH
                    ♠ A Q 7 2
                    ♡ 6
                    ◇ K 10 5
                    ♣ A J 8 3 2
    WEST                                EAST
    ♠ 10 6 3                            ♠ J
    ♡ A K J 5 4                         ♡ 10 9 8 3 2
    ◇ A J 9 2                           ◇ 8 7 6 3
    ♣ 5                                 ♣ K 6 4
                    SOUTH
                    ♠ K 9 8 5 4
                    ♡ Q 7
                    ◇ Q 4
                    ♣ Q 10 9 7
```

THE AUCTION

WEST	NORTH	EAST	SOUTH
1 ♡	Dbl	1 ♠	1 NT
Pass	Pass	Pass	

THE RESULT

The defenders started off by taking five hearts after West led the king and ace. West shifted to a club, and the defenders also cashed the king of clubs and ace of diamonds.

The hand was down one.

THE ARGUMENT

When it was discovered that North-South could have made four spades, North took South to task for bidding one notrump with his unbalanced hand.

But both strongly objected to East's bid of one spade, calling it sharp practice, and inquired why West hadn't raised to two spades.

GOREN SETTLES THE ARGUMENT

There is nothing illegal or unethical about bidding a suit you don't have.

In days gone by, it was a common practice. Such a bid is known in the trade as a "psychic." Used sparingly, a psychic can still be a potent weapon; but psychics frequently backfire, and are therefore dangerous to their users. Nowadays, they are losing popularity.

East's bluff bid of one spade is the simplest form of psychic bidding. There is no good reason why it should have been effective. South should have been alert to the possibility that East was trying to put one over on him. North's double of one heart had marked that bidder with spades, and South was looking at five cards in that suit.

There is a simple way to expose this kind of psychic. South should have doubled one spade for penalties. East would have been unable to stand this, and would have "confessed" the psych by retreating to two hearts. Now North can bid two spades, and a contract of four spades would have resulted.

Note that this treatment is similar to the action to be taken when your partner's opening has been over-called by your right-hand opponent. If he made the bid you wanted to make, you double for penalties.

I would say that there is no sound basis for criticizing West's failure to raise spades. East's bid might have been made with a weakish hand lacking heart support. More important, though—North's double showed spades and South's notrump bid did as well. Looking at three spades in his own hand, it wasn't too difficult for West to decide that East might be trying a bluff bid.

Index

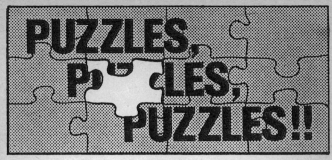